"*In the School of Prophets* throws fresh light on the integral relationship between prophecy and mysticism in Merton's life and writings. Mining a range of sources sometimes overlooked in Merton studies, Ephrem Arcement ably guides the reader beneath the surface of the many-faceted diamond that is Merton's paradoxical spirituality of solitude and social engagement, resistance and hope. Especially in Merton's engagement with poetic visionaries like Blake and Vallejo, Arcement gestures to Christian hope as seeking to cut through the 'great tangled knot of lies' in mass society even while recognizing the 'flowering of ordinary possibilities' hidden in everyday life. An aptly rich and multilayered study of Merton's Christ-haunted spirituality, still drawing us in, one hundred years after his birth."

> —Christopher Pramuk
> Associate Professor, Theology
> Xavier University
> Author of *At Play in Creation: Merton's Awakening
> to the Feminine Divine*

"Ephrem Arcement situates Merton's prophetic life and witness, most pronounced in the final decade of his life, within a much broader understanding of the prophetic vocation, integrating many seemingly diffuse elements from throughout Merton's life. *In the School of Prophets* is a thoughtful, challenging treatise that underscores Merton's stature as a true man of God, like the prophets of old, calling us forward and challenging us to labor for the fidelity to God to which Merton himself strived. This is a refreshing and vital approach to understanding Merton's prophetic vocation."

> —Dr. Paul M. Pearson
> Director and Archivist
> Thomas Merton Center
> Bellarmine University

CISTERCIAN STUDIES SERIES: NUMBER TWO HUNDRED SIXTY-FIVE

In the School of Prophets

The Formation of Thomas Merton's Prophetic Spirituality

Ephrem Arcement, OSB

Cistercian Publications
www.cistercianpublications.org

LITURGICAL PRESS
Collegeville, Minnesota
www.litpress.org

A Cistercian Publications title published by Liturgical Press

Cistercian Publications
Editorial Offices
161 Grosvenor Street
Athens, Ohio 54701
www.cistercianpublications.org

1	2	3	4	5	6	7	8	9

Library of Congress Cataloging-in-Publication Data

Arcement, Ephrem.
    In the school of prophets : the formation of Thomas Merton's prophetic spirituality / Ephrem Arcement, O.S.B.
        pages cm. — (Cistercian studies series ; number two hundred sixty-five)
    Includes bibliographical references.
    ISBN 978-0-87907-265-0 — ISBN 978-0-87907-497-5 (ebook)
    1. Merton, Thomas, 1915–1968.   2. Prophecy—Christianity.   I. Title.
BX4705.M542A73   2015
271'.12502—dc23   2014032012

See intro p. xxii

For my parents,
Warren and Nancy Arcement,
whose unfailing support has made this book
and so much more possible

Contents

Abbreviations

CS   Cistercian Studies Series

ed.   edition, editor, edited by

MW   Monastic Wisdom Series

n.   note

NRSV   New Revised Standard Version

ocso   Order of Cistercians of the Strict Observance

RB   Rule of Saint Benedict

repr.   reprinted

trans.   translation, translator, translated by

vol(s).   volume(s)

Acknowledgments

Various excerpts by Thomas Merton, from THE COLLECTED POEMS OF THOMAS MERTON, copyright © 1947 by New Directions Publishing Corporation. Reprinted by permission of New Directions Publishing Corp.

Pablo Antonio Cuadra, "Written on a Roadside Stone During the First Eruption," translated by Steven White. Used by permission of Steven White.

Mark Van Doren, "Prophet," in *The Selected Letters of Mark Van Doren*, ed. George Hendrick (Baton Rouge: Louisiana State University Press, 1987), 235. Used by permission of the Estate of Mark Van Doren.

The following permissions were in process at time of publication:

Thomas Merton, *A Search for Solitude: Pursuing the Monk's True Life*, ed. Lawrence S. Cunningham, The Journals of Thomas Merton, vol. 3 (New York: HarperCollins, 1996).

Thomas Merton, *Disputed Questions* (New York: Harcourt Brace Jovanovich, 1960).

Introduction

A Life in Formation

Perhaps one of the most defining aspects of the personality of Thomas Merton (1915–1968), the popular and unconventional Trappist monk of the Abbey of Our Lady of Gethsemani near Bardstown, Kentucky, was his refusal ever to view his life as a finished product. Rather, life for him meant growth. Monastic life, in particular, was a call to live life vowed to intense and unending growth. Openness to new ideas thus marked his spiritual disposition. Curiosity propelled him toward the discovery of that longed-for insight that would expand his ever-widening consciousness. His unrelenting desire for deeper knowledge and understanding would lead him down varied and sometimes controversial paths (controversial, at least, according to the expectations for a Trappist monk of his era). Aware of the hazards that accompany such pursuits, he trod along, nonetheless, toward the goal of an integrated, unified life.[1]

Because of a high esteem for new ideas, Merton approached life with childlike eagerness. The humility that is the foundation of the monk's spiritual quest is evident in the way he allowed himself to be influenced by others, even when aspects of their ideas or lives were disagreeable to him. He had the unusual ability to engage, discriminate, sift, discern, and apply other people's valuable ideas to his life without ever causing these people to feel devalued because of ideas that he ignored or left by the wayside. He was a

---

[1] Interpreting Merton's spiritual journey through the lens of "integration" is highlighted by two books edited by M. Basil Pennington: *Thomas Merton, My Brother: His Journey to Freedom, Compassion, and Final Integration* (Hyde Park, NY: New City Press, 1996); and *Toward an Integrated Humanity: Thomas Merton's Journey*, CS 103 (Kalamazoo, MI: Cistercian Publications, 1988).

consummate ecumenist. Any assessment of Merton's life or thought must, therefore, consider its dynamic and evolving nature. Fortunately, those interested in evaluating the formation of the various aspects of his life and thought have a life vividly laid bare in his voluminous journal writing and thousands of letters.[2]

The seven volumes of journals published between 1995 and 1998 offer a rare glimpse into the motivating influences on Merton's life and demonstrate the formation of many of his evolving ideas.[3] In those journals he chronicled nearly thirty years of his life almost uninterruptedly—beginning with his first entry on May 2, 1939, and concluding with his final entry on December 8, 1968, two days before his untimely death. Much of what he wrote in these journals was edited and published in his lifetime: *The Sign of Jonas* (1953), *The Secular Journal of Thomas Merton* (1959), and *Conjectures of a Guilty Bystander* (1966). *The Asian Journal of Thomas Merton* (1973), *Woods, Shore, Desert* (1983), *A Vow of Conversation* (1988), and *Thomas Merton in Alaska* (1988) were all published posthumously. With the publication of the entire seven-volume corpus, the arc of Merton's life is openly displayed and his life comes into clearer focus. The journals also give access to the many struggles, uncertainties, and frustrations as well as breakthroughs and triumphs of a man in pursuit of God and a meaningful existence.

Many commentators consider the journals Merton's greatest achievement as a writer. Merton's secretary, Br. Patrick Hart, writes, "There is no denying that Thomas Merton was an inveterate diarist. He clarified his ideas in writing especially by keeping a journal. Perhaps his best writing can be found in the journals, where he

---

[2] Although it is uncertain how many letters Merton actually wrote, William Shannon states, "Four thousand would be a conservative figure; probably, the number is much higher." See William H. Shannon, "Letters," in *The Thomas Merton Encyclopedia,* ed. William H. Shannon, et al. (Maryknoll, NY: Orbis Books, 2002), 255 (hereafter *Encyclopedia*).

[3] Merton stipulated in the Merton Legacy Trust, drawn up the year before his death, that the journals could be published whole or in part at the discretion of the Merton Legacy Trust but only after the official biography had been published and at least twenty-five years after his death.

was expressing what was deepest in his heart with no thought of censorship."[4] And Lawrence Cunningham suggests, "It was in the published journal, especially, that one finds the most fecund of his spiritual insights. It is those books that will most endure not because they are interesting or timely but because they reflect the experiences of a person who was deeply centered and whose whole life was an exercise in absorbing knowledge in order to become a caring and wise person."[5]

The other major source that reveals Merton's progressive maturation is the five volumes of selected letters published between 1985 and 1994: volume 1, *The Hidden Ground of Love;* volume 2, *The Road to Joy;* volume 3, *The School of Charity;* volume 4, *The Courage for Truth;* and volume 5, *Witness to Freedom.* Published independently from this series is *Thomas Merton and James Laughlin: Selected Letters,* the correspondence between Merton and his longtime publisher and friend. It was Evelyn Waugh, the editor of the British edition of *The Seven Storey Mountain,* entitled *Elected Silence,* who advised Merton early in his writing career "to put books aside and write serious letters and to make an art of it."[6] Merton took the latter part of this admonition to heart and subsequently produced a prodigious collection of correspondence ranging from such topics as spirituality and monasticism to poetry and literature to social and religious concerns, as well as a substantial collection to his family and friends. William Shannon insightfully comments, "Letters are important sources of knowledge about a person and also about the age in which that person lived. . . . In reading letters, one meets persons in their full humanness; they reveal secret desires and ambitions. Often they uncover fears, imperfections, faults, and concerns. Merton's letters (as well as his journals) were the only

---

[4] Patrick Hart, preface to *Run to the Mountain: The Story of a Vocation,* by Thomas Merton (New York: HarperCollins, 1995), xi–xii, here xii.

[5] Lawrence S. Cunningham, ed., *Thomas Merton: Spiritual Master* (New York: Paulist Press, 1992), 36.

[6] William H. Shannon, preface to *The Hidden Ground of Love: The Letters of Thomas Merton on Religious Experience and Social Concerns,* by Thomas Merton (New York: Farrar, Straus and Giroux, 1985), v–viii, here vi.

bit of his writing that did not have to be submitted to the censors; hence, he could be his own uninhibited self."[7]

John Henry Newman said, "The true life of a person is found in his letters."[8] The letters of Thomas Merton are, unfortunately, among the most underappreciated of his writings. It seems that they have been thus far overshadowed by his journals and spiritual books. Yet the letters reveal a side of Merton that is not found elsewhere. They reveal him as a man of deep, personal compassion and concern for a staggering variety of individuals. Here he writes with candor and vulnerability, yet with selfless interest and a genuine desire to connect with others on the most profound level. His letter writing demonstrates a true exercise in creative interchange.[9] In comparing Merton's journals and letters, Shannon notes, "there is an important difference between these two similar forms of writing. Merton's journals tend to be more introspective and self-occupied. In his journals, he is necessarily talking to himself (though he certainly saw the real possibility that these journals would be published), whereas in his letters he is talking to, and building a relationship with, another person."[10]

Merton's journals and letters can be likened to two eyes through which he viewed the world: the eye that viewed his inner world (journals) and the eye that viewed the world around him (letters). These sources of self-expression often served as platforms through which he made known his own distinctive vision—for the world, for the church, for monasticism, for himself. They testify to the ever-increasing burden that he would come to bear for making

[7] See Shannon, "Letters," 255.

[8] Newman to his sister, Mrs. John Mozley, May 18, 1863. Cited in Shannon, "Letters," 255.

[9] *Creative interchange* is a phrase used by the American philosopher of religion Henry Nelson Wieman to describe the process of integrating diverse perspectives that allow people to learn from each other, come to understand each other, be corrected by each other, form a community with each other, and live in peace with each other. See Henry Nelson Wieman, *The Source of Human Good* (Carbondale, IL: Southern Illinois University Press, 1946).

[10] See William Shannon, "Letters," 256.

right all that was wrong in each of these spheres of his life. As the popular monk that he was to become, he would be offered a unique opportunity to become an influential voice—a prophetic voice calling for sense and justice in a most senseless and unjust century.

A Prophetic Spirituality

Attention to the prophetic nature of Merton's spirituality in Merton studies has tended to focus mainly on his writings on peace and monastic renewal. These were the most obvious outlets for the exercise of his prophetic ministry and found their greatest expression there. What has received little consideration are the underlying impulses and the motivating and formative forces of this prophetic ministry, namely, its spirituality.

In a conference given to the novices under his care on April 21, 1963, on the meaning of monastic spirituality, Merton described his understanding of the term *spirituality*. Spirituality, for Merton, was a way of life, a way of doing things for the salvation of one's soul. It involved the human way to God with its motives and responses to the Holy Spirit. It also involved one's ideas—how one thought about one's response to God. It was the life of one's whole being, not just mind or will. Most important, spirituality sought to unify the self. Monastic spirituality, in particular, was an intense, focused, and disciplined way of life that was completely devoted to the unification of the self in and with God.[11]

Merton's use of the terms *prophet*, *prophecy*, and *prophetic* is much more prevalent and varied than his use of the term *spirituality*. A chronological study of Merton's writings reveals a marked increase in the use of these terms after his epiphany on the corner of Fourth and Walnut Streets in Louisville. In reflecting on this experience, he wrote, "In Louisville, at the corner of Fourth and Walnut, in the center of the shopping district, I was suddenly overwhelmed with the realization that I loved all those people, that they were mine and I theirs, that we could not be alien to one another even

[11] Thomas Merton, *The Meaning of Monastic Spirituality*, Credence Cassettes AA2085, audiocassette (Kansas City, MO, n.d.).

though we were total strangers. It was like waking from a dream of separateness, of spurious self-isolation in a special world, the world of renunciation and supposed holiness. The whole illusion of a separate holy existence is a dream."[12] The date was March 18, 1958. Merton was forty-three years old and had ten years left to his life.

This decisive moment for Merton is often referred to as his "return to the world" after spending over sixteen years cut off from it within his strict enclosure.[13] His final decade would be subsequently characterized by an intense sense of responsibility and compassion for the world, which he saw as reeling under the effects of godlessness and bent toward self-destruction. In his writings during this period, particularly his journals and letters, Merton assumed not the role of savior, one who saw himself as the answer to the world's problems, but as prophet: one who communicates the truth of what God has revealed, no matter what the cost, in order to help reconcile the world to God.

Yet it would be a mistake to burden the "Fourth and Walnut" experience with too much significance in regard to Merton's prophetic interests. A study of Merton's early writings, particularly before he entered Gethsemani, reveals a young man very interested in the idea of the prophetic. Merton first referred to prophecy at the age of twenty-three, writing of William Blake. In a letter to his good friend from Columbia University, Robert Lax, dated August 11, 1938, he wrote, "I have studied William Blake, I have measured him with a ruler, I have sneaked at him with pencils and T squares, I have spied on him from a distance with a small spyglass, I have held him up to mirrors, and will shortly endeavor to prove the prophetic books were all written with lemon juice and must be held in front of a slow fire to be read."[14] What Merton alludes to

[12] Thomas Merton, *Conjectures of a Guilty Bystander* (1966; New York: Image Books, 1989), 156. For a more thorough analysis of the significance of this event, see below, pp. xxi–xxiii.

[13] See Christine M. Bochen, "The 'Fourth and Walnut' Experience," in *Encyclopedia*, 158–60, here 160.

[14] Thomas Merton to Robert Lax, New York, August 11, 1938, in *The Road to Joy: The Letters of Thomas Merton to New and Old Friends*, ed. Robert E.

in this passage is his preparation of his master's thesis, "Nature and Art in William Blake: An Essay in Interpretation," which he would complete the following year. Merton's interest in Blake as prophet and in the prophetic nature of his poetry resurfaced in his final decade.[15]

Merton's social concerns appeared very early, especially in his journals. The first issue that seems to have attracted his attention is race. In his journal entry on Good Friday 1940, after quoting a verse on the anointing at Bethany from the Gospel of Matthew, he wrote, "The apostles and, specifically in one Gospel, Judas, complained that this ointment was *wasted* in being poured upon Christ instead of being sold and the money given to the poor. Let the people, the so-called Catholics who argue against the 'imprudence' of certain actions—like, for example, admitting a Negro child to parochial school for fear all the white parents take away their children—remember the 'prudence' of Judas and freeze with horror!" (*Run*, 155). Concern for the racial situation in America had such an effect on Merton in his early twenties that he nearly moved to Harlem to work with Catherine de Hueck Doherty's Friendship House instead of entering Gethsemani.[16] Criticism of the war and America's role in it soon followed: "And if we go into the war, it will be first of all to defend our investments, our business, our money. In certain terms it may be useful to defend all these things, an expedient to protect our business so that everybody may have jobs, but if anybody holds up American business as a shining example of justice, or American politics as a shining example of honesty and purity, that is really quite a joke!" (*Run*, 221).

After Merton's entry into Gethsemani at the end of 1941, by far the most substantive source for his early prophetic formation

Daggy (New York: Farrar, Straus and Giroux, 1989), 142. Merton's correspondence with Robert Lax is consistently marked by a playful, Joycean style.

[15] For an extended treatment of Blake's influence on Merton's prophetic spirituality, see chap. 1.

[16] Thomas Merton, *The Seven Storey Mountain* (New York: Harcourt Brace, 1948), 357–60.

as a monk was the biblical prophets. Three in particular appear frequently in his journals of this period, as well as in many of his early poems: Jonah, Elijah, and John the Baptist. Jonah first appears in a journal entry dated February 26, 1952. Reflecting on the meaning of Ash Wednesday, Merton wrote, "Receive, O monk, the holy truth concerning this thing called death. Know that there is in each man a deep will, potentially committed to freedom or captivity, ready to consent to life, born consenting to death, turned inside out, swallowed by its own self, prisoner of itself like Jonas in the whale."[17]

For Merton, the story of Jonah and the whale bore multiple layers of meaning. Fundamentally, it was the paradoxical, transformative experience everyone must undergo or perish. The whale was death, which brings forth life. Jonah is the sign of that life coming out of death—the sign of resurrection. Merton explains its significance in the prologue to his first collection of published journals, significantly titled *The Sign of Jonas*:

> The sign Jesus promised to the generation that did not understand Him was the "sign of Jonas the prophet"—that is, the sign of His own resurrection. The life of every monk, of every priest, of every Christian is signed with the sign of Jonas, because we all live by the power of Christ's resurrection. But I feel that my own life is especially sealed with this great sign, which baptism and monastic profession and priestly ordination have burned into the roots of my being, because like Jonas himself I find myself traveling toward my destiny in the belly of a paradox.[18]

In the prologue to *The Sign of Jonas* Merton for the first time likens the monk to a prophet: "A monk can always legitimately and significantly compare himself to a prophet, because the monks are the heirs of the prophets. The prophet is a man whose whole life is a living witness of the providential action of God in the world.

---

[17] Thomas Merton, *Entering the Silence: Becoming a Monk and Writer*, ed. Jonathan Montaldo (New York: HarperCollins, 1996), 469.

[18] Thomas Merton, *The Sign of Jonas* (New York: Harcourt Brace, 1953), 11.

Every prophet is a sign and a witness of Christ. Every monk, in whom Christ lives, and in whom all the prophecies are therefore fulfilled, is a witness and a sign of the Kingdom of God" (Sign 11).

The prophet Elijah is an important figure in the early development of Merton's understanding of the relationship between contemplation and action. Merton's lengthy poem "Elias—Variations on a Theme," from his 1957 collection *The Strange Islands,* envisions the prophet as "one who has discovered his oneness with all reality, who resonates with the needs and hopes of others because he has found these very needs and hopes in his own depths, who has been made aware that because the center of the self is not the self but God, to experience one's true center is to pass beyond the self without leaving the self."[19]

With a large number of references to John the Baptist, Merton signals his favorite prophet. This preference was true in both his early monastic years and in his final decade. The earliest tribute to the Baptist is the poem from Merton's 1946 collection *A Man in the Divided Sea*, entitled "St. John Baptist."[20] John the Baptist reappears in Merton's 1947 collection *Figures for an Apocalypse*, in both "St. John's Night" (171–72) and "Winter Afternoon" (185–86), and in his 1949 collection *The Tears for the Blind Lions* in "The Quickening of St. John the Baptist" (199–202). These early references envision the Baptist as fulfilling a role similar to that of Elijah, namely, as the symbolic figure who unites the contemplative and the prophetic roles within a single vocation.

Reading these early references to the biblical prophets leads to an understanding that Merton believed that when a person makes the decision to enter a monastery, that person in effect makes the decision to assume a prophetic mantle. For Merton the vocation to be a monk was the vocation to live a prophetic life, even before the monk spoke or wrote. The early Merton understood that the silent communication of a life wholly devoted to God in humility and obedience speaks with a power and authority that leads others to

---

[19] See Patrick O'Connell, "The Strange Islands," in *Encyclopedia*, 455.
[20] Thomas Merton, *The Collected Poems of Thomas Merton* (New York: New Directions, 1977), 122–26.

a confrontation with the divine. Yet Merton was also a writer—a writer who understood that his vocation to write was a vocation to make known the hidden truths of God. Thus in Merton this dual vocation of monk and writer would become a uniquely influential source for the exercise of his own prophetic spirituality and contribute significantly to his own personal integration.[21]

Nearly all of these early prophetic intimations reappeared with renewed interest and force after his epiphany in 1958. Still, as is abundantly evident from the citations above, the Louisville experience did not mark the beginning of Merton's interest in the prophetic. What significance, then, did it play in the formation of Merton's prophetic spirituality?

An Insight of Reconciliation

On a cold Saint John's Day in the final days of 1957, Merton found himself feeling overwhelmed by the stack of Christmas cards before him waiting to be opened. This moment, after spending six-

---

[21] A problem arises in defining the vocation of Thomas Merton. Should he be considered primarily a monk who was also a writer or primarily a writer who was also a monk? Or should the vocations be understood as more intertwined—a monk-writer or a writer-monk? It is important to note that Merton wrestled greatly over the reconciliation of these two vocations throughout his lifetime, especially during the first few years after entering Gethsemani. In his preface to *A Thomas Merton Reader*, he wrote, "If the monastic life is a life of hardship and sacrifice, I would say that for me most of the hardship has come in connection with writing. It is possible to doubt whether I have become a monk (a doubt I have to live with), but it is not possible to doubt that I am a writer, that I was born one and will most probably die as one. Disconcerting, disedifying as it is, this seems to be my lot and my vocation." See preface to *A Thomas Merton Reader*, ed. Thomas P. McDonnell (Garden City, NY: Image Books, 1974), 13–18, here 17. In spite of this self-deprecating assertion of his own monastic vocation, I would argue that Merton's vocation should be fundamentally understood as being a monk and contemplative whose primary mode of expression and creativity appeared in writing. In short, it was not simply his ability as a writer that made Merton so influential—it was his ability to communicate the hidden things of God.

teen years in the enclosure of his monastery, spurred his first overt reflection about a new way of conceiving a monk's relationship to the world: "But a monk *should* have something to do with the world he lives in and should love the people in that world. How much they give us and how little we give them. My responsibility to be in all reality a peacemaker in the world, an apostle, to bring people to truth, to make my whole life a true and effective witness to God's Truth."[22] He expanded on this new stance toward the world just two days later: "Until my 'contemplation' is liberated from the sterilizing artificial limitations under which it has so far existed (and nearly been stifled out of existence) I cannot be a 'man of God' because I cannot live in the Truth, which is the first essential for being a man of God. It is absolutely true that here in this monastery we are enabled to systematically evade our real and ultimate social responsibilities. In any time, social responsibility is the keystone of the Christian life" (*Search*, 151).

These passages highlight Merton's mood leading up to the Louisville experience and are necessary components for a correct interpretation of the event. The unrest within his soul about the way he saw monasticism as evading its social responsibility for a so-called higher vocation was already percolating when he visited Louisville two and a half months later.

Merton wrote two versions of his Louisville epiphany, the first the day after the event occurred and the second eight years afterward, for publication in *Conjectures of a Guilty Bystander*. The first version of the experience begins with the insight of his radical unity with all humankind—his waking from "the dream of separateness" —waking to the illusion of a "'special' vocation to be different" (*Search*, 182). In this version Merton is overwhelmed with joy at his fundamental sameness with the rest of the world: "Thank God! Thank God! I am only another member of the human race, like all the rest of them. I have the immense joy of being a man!" (*Search*, 182). In reflecting on the women walking on the streets, he describes

---

[22] Thomas Merton, *A Search for Solitude: Pursuing the Monk's True Life* (New York: HarperCollins, 1996), 149 (emphasis his).

how his vow of chastity has allowed him to recognize that the beauty of the "woman-ness that is in each of them is at once original and inexhaustibly fruitful bringing the image of God into the world. In this each one is Wisdom and Sophia and Our Lady" (*Search*, 182).

This insight led him to recount a dream he had had in late February in which he encountered "Proverb," a young Jewish girl who personified the revelation of "virginal solitude" (*Search*, 176). On the streets of Louisville he recognized her once again: "Dear Proverb, I have kept one promise and I have refrained from speaking of you until seeing you again. I know that when I saw you again it would be very different, in a different place, in a different form, in the most unexpected circumstances. I shall never forget our meeting yesterday. The touch of your hand makes me a different person. To be with you is rest and truth. Only with you are these things found, dear child sent to me by God!" (*Search*, 182). Thus Merton had a mystical intuition of the radical humanness of his monastic vocation in his encounter with "Proverb," the beauty of the hidden Wisdom of God revealed to him in the women walking along the streets of Louisville. Henceforth he conceived of monasticism as being grounded in the world and depending on this groundedness for its authentic existence.

The second account of the vision, which appears in *Conjectures of a Guilty Bystander*, interestingly leaves out any reference to "Proverb." Instead, the "virginal solitude" of "Proverb" becomes the "secret beauty" of all hearts (*Conjectures*, 158). This extended reworking also includes Merton's most significant reference to Louis Massignon's notion of the expression *le point vierge* (*Conjectures*, 158). Merton explains the phrase: "At the center of our being is a point of nothingness which is untouched by sin and by illusion, a point of pure truth, a point or spark which belongs entirely to God, which is never at our disposal, from which God disposes of our lives, which is inaccessible to the fantasies of our own mind or the brutalities of our own will. This little point of nothingness and of *absolute poverty* is the pure glory of God in us" (*Conjectures*, 158). Merton goes on to explain that this *le point vierge* "is in everybody, and if we could see it we would see these billions of points of light coming together in the face and blaze of a sun that would make all the darkness and cruelty of life vanish completely" (*Conjectures*, 158).

In these two reflections of his epiphany in Louisville, Merton articulates an experiential insight of reconciliation; it is a certain validation of the movement of his spirit toward the world that had begun in the previous months. The experience gave him a mystical knowledge of the depth of a reality of which he had previously only seen glimpses. Everything now was one: the monk and the rest of humanity, contemplation and action, God and humankind. Henceforth, Merton saw differently—he became a different kind of contemplative. His contemplative awareness expanded from a myopic vision of God (limited, as interpreted within the confines of Catholic tradition) to a universal vision of God where "the gate of heaven is everywhere" (*Conjectures*, 158). He also became a different kind of monk—a monk liberated from isolationism and for dialogue and encounter. The experience did not signal the gradual distancing of himself from monasticism or the church, although he admittedly became disillusioned by many of the institutional aspects of each. His engagement with the world was consistently grounded in his vocation to contemplation and solitude. Therein, he insisted, rested the monk's unique gift and prophetic word to the world.

Themes of Merton's Prophetic Spirituality

In the epiphany of March 18, 1958, Merton also reconciled himself with his past. Subsequent journal entries as well as subsequent letters (the number of which exponentially increases after this date) reveal how many of the interests and passions that had occupied his premonastic mind were suddenly regrafted onto the vine of his new identity. He began to revisit writers who had interested him in his young adulthood—rereading them, reinterpreting them, allowing them to inform his new consciousness as a monk for the world. He particularly returned to William Blake, and he experienced a renewal of his interest in poetry. A new voice emerged in *Original Child Bomb* (1962), *Emblems of a Season of Fury* (1963), and, especially, *Cables to the Ace* (1968) and *The Geography of Lograire*

(1968). He devoted a vast amount of energy in the years following the Louisville experience to analyzing and commenting on social issues, especially race and war—the two issues with which he had wrestled in his student days at Columbia. Merton was now becoming a whole man, integrating what was good in his past into his present life situation as a redefined monk.

Merton's prophetic interests were perhaps the most notable and significant aspect of this reintegration. It is as if before the redefining event in Louisville, Merton had only flirted with the prophetic, whereas now he accepted it as a divine mandate. Louisville released him to live prophetically without restraint. It also provided him with the content of his prophetic activity, namely, *the reconciliation of all things in Christ through the dismantling of the illusion of separateness.*

Because of his newfound openness to the world outside the strict walls of monasticism, this central theme of Merton's prophetic spirituality later found development and shape through his interaction with a number of thinkers with whom he came into contact for the first time. As the extensive and substantive correspondence and journal entries during his final decade revealed, writers like Boris Pasternak, Albert Camus, and William Faulkner, philosophers like Søren Kierkegaard and Gabriel Marcel, Latin American poets like Cesar Vallejo and Pablo Antonio Cuadra, social activists like Mohandas Gandhi and Martin Luther King, Jr., social theorists like Herbert Marcuse and Jacques Ellul, and religious thinkers like Abraham Heschel and Louis Massignon, each in his own way, helped to shape Merton's mature prophetic consciousness.

A number of themes arose from Merton's creative interchange with each of these thinkers, forming the basis of his prophetic spirituality; many of these have received little attention in Merton studies. The first theme, developed through his study of Pasternak, Camus, Faulkner, Blake, and the Latin American poets, was the special value and power of poetic imagery and literature to convey prophetic insights. According to Merton, these writers had assumed the prophetic mantle that many of the church's theologians of his day had chosen to ignore. Second, Ellul and Marcuse helped Merton see the problem of making prophetic communication relevant to modern, technologized humanity. Third, the existentialists Kierkegaard and Marcel showed Merton that prophecy is grounded in a radical commitment to authenticity of life (i.e., to the true self) and compels one publicly to expose illusory social and personal structures of consciousness. Fourth, Gandhi and Martin Luther King, Jr., taught Merton that the proper Christian endeavor for the transformation of such illusory social structures is the prophetic stance of active non-violence, while his own spiritual tradition taught him that illusory personal structures are to be transformed in the life of contemplation. Thus the relationship between contemplative and prophetic spirituality became a major theme of Merton's final years.

PART ONE

The Writer as Prophet

Chapter 1

Learning How to See
Thomas Merton and the Prophetic Vision of William Blake

Simply put: Thomas Merton is the William Blake of our time.[1]

—Michael Higgins

Background

Merton grew up with William Blake. From Merton's earliest childhood days, his father, Owen, read to his firstborn the obscure yet fascinating and highly imaginative poetry of England's misunderstood eighteenth- and nineteenth-century visionary. The earliest interest that Merton's writings express toward Blake goes back to Merton's early letter to his friend Robert Lax from his student days at Columbia University. Referring to his meticulous study of the prophetic books of Blake, Merton informed Lax about his intention to make Blake the subject of his master's thesis. Merton submitted this thesis, "Nature and Art in William Blake: An Essay in Interpretation," in February 1939. Patrick O'Connell has offered a concise synopsis of the thesis:

> Merton's master's thesis consists of a short preface and two chapters. The first chapter, "Background and Development," surveys Blake's intellectual and artistic background and influences, both as writer and painter/engraver, with emphasis on his hostility toward rationalism and empiricism and defense of imagination and inspiration. The

[1] Michael W. Higgins, *Heretic Blood: The Spiritual Geography of Thomas Merton* (Toronto: Stoddart Publishing Co., 1998), 4.

second chapter, "Blake's Ideas on the Place of Nature in Art," contrasts nature as seen by the senses with nature transfigured by the imagination, and looks to insights from Thomist and Indian theories of art, as represented by Maritain and Coomaraswamy, not as influences on Blake but as a framework for understanding the nature of authentic artistic creativity.[2]

The topic of prophecy or any description of Blake as a prophet is not found in Merton's thesis. His focus, rather, is wholly on nature and art. The poetry analyzed, however, is that of Blake's prophetic books, a series of obscure and mythic works that seek to express Blake's ideas about the soul's effort to liberate itself from rationalism and organized religion. These prophetic ideas can certainly be found throughout the course of Merton's own spiritual journey, particularly in his penchant for apophatic spirituality and his critique of an overly institutional monasticism.

Besides the master's thesis, Merton's other major early references to Blake appear in *The Seven Storey Mountain*. Reflecting back on his early years, Merton as a young monk reminisces about his particular attraction to one of the most instrumental sources for his own spiritual formation:

> Meanwhile there was one discovery of mine, one poet who was a poet indeed, and a Romantic poet, but vastly different from those contemporaries, with whom he had so little to do. I think my love for William Blake had something in it of God's grace. It is a love that has never died, and which has entered very deeply into the development of my life.
>
> Father had always liked Blake, and had tried to explain to me what was good about him when I was a child of ten. The funny thing about Blake is that although the *Songs of Innocence* look like children's poems, and almost seem to have been written for children, they are, to most children, incomprehensible. Or at least, they were so to

---

[2] See Patrick O'Connell, "The Literary Essays of Thomas Merton," in *The Thomas Merton Encyclopedia*, ed. William H. Shannon, et al. (Maryknoll, NY: Orbis Books, 2002), 260–63, at 262–63.

me. Perhaps if I had read them when I was four or five, it would have been different. But when I was ten, I knew too much. I knew that tigers did not burn in the forests of the night. That was very silly, I thought. Children are very literal-minded.[3]

In considering Blake's paradoxical nature, Merton continues: "How incapable I was of understanding anything like the ideals of a William Blake! How could I possibly realize that his rebellion, for all its strange heterodoxies, was fundamentally the rebellion of the saints. It was the rebellion of the lover of the living God, the rebellion of the one whose desire of God was so intense and irresistible that it condemned, with all its might, all the hypocrisy and petty sensuality and skepticism and materialism which cold and trivial minds set up as unpassable barriers between God and the souls of men" (*Seven Storey Mountain*, 87). Writing directly of Blake's influence on him, Merton states,

> The Providence of God was eventually to use Blake to awaken something of faith and love in my own soul—in spite of all the misleading notions, and all the almost infinite possibilities of error that underlie his weird and violent figures. I do not, therefore, want to seem to canonize him. But I have to acknowledge my own debt to him, and the truth which may appear curious to some, although it is really not so: that through Blake I would one day come, in a round-about way, to the only true Church, and to the One Living God, through His Son, Jesus Christ. (*Seven Storey Mountain*, 88)

Further along in *The Seven Storey Mountain*, when Merton is recounting his days at Columbia University preparing to write his master's thesis, he returns to Blake: "But oh, what a thing it was to live in contact with the genius and the holiness of William Blake that year, that summer, writing the thesis!" (*Seven Storey Mountain*, 189–90). Comparing Blake to the other eighteenth- and nineteenth-century

---

[3] Thomas Merton, *The Seven Storey Mountain* (New York: Harcourt Brace, 1948), 85–86.

Romantics, he writes, "Even Coleridge, in the rare moments when his imagination struck the pitch of true creativeness, was still only an artist, an imaginer, not a seer; a maker, but not a prophet" (*Seven Storey Mountain*, 190). Merton here offers an early assessment of his understanding of Blake as a prophet.

Although Blake is noted for his emphasis on imagination in the creative process, that is not what, according to Merton, makes him a prophet. There is a creative gift that exceeds the imagination—that goes beyond the mind's natural capacities. Blake was a prophet, Merton thought, because he was a *seer*: "He wrote better poetry when he was twelve than Shelley wrote in his whole life. And it was because at twelve he had already *seen*, I think, Elias, standing under a tree in the fields south of London" (*Seven Storey Mountain*, 190; emphasis added). In other words, Merton says that Blake was a prophet because he had the ability to see what others did not. This prophetic gift allowed Blake to know the solitude of Elijah even as a very young man. Elijah here also connotes Blake's uncompromising commitment to his own inspired vision of reality and the persecution that inevitably results from sharing it.

Merton concludes this section of his autobiography by telling of the tremendous effect his study of Blake had on him: "By the time the summer was over, I was to become conscious of the fact that the only way to live was to live in a world that was charged with the presence and reality of God" (*Seven Storey Mountain*, 191). For Merton, Blake was a Christian mystic, however heterodox, consumed with the vision of God. In a response to a letter from Mario Falsina, dated March 25, 1967, Merton answers a number of questions posed to him. One question concerns the reasons for his conversion: ". . . besides the grace of God. First of all the discovery of a metaphysical sense of Being, and an intuition of God as *ens a se*, pure actuality. Then the mystical ideas of William Blake."[4] It is precisely this sense of Blake as visionary mystic that awakened within Merton his own desire to be "charged with the presence and reality of God."

---

[4] Thomas Merton, *The Road to Joy: The Letters of Thomas Merton to New and Old Friends*, ed. Robert E. Daggy (New York: Farrar, Straus and Giroux, 1989), 348.

Blake Recapitulated

1959

After the publication of *The Seven Storey Mountain*, William Blake rarely appears in Merton's journals, letters, or books. It was not until 1959 that Merton, somewhat accidentally, revisited his favorite Romantic poet: "When I was in Louisville I picked up, on the wing, 'by chance' Blake's poems and realized again how much I love them, how much I am at home with him. Reading the prophetic books with immense enjoyment—feeling thoroughly at home in them now, though I don't follow all the cast of characters. It is a life-long study in itself. . . . Blake is *never* merely indifferent. Always if not inspired, at least very alive. Never dead. I love Blake."[5]

About a month later, on September 12, Merton wrote Czesław Miłosz, "I have been reading William Blake again. His reply to Caesar seems like psychosis, but it is valid and consistent and prophetic: and involves no *Ketman* except perhaps a very little of it, on the surface, with some of his 'friends' who had money but did not understand him. And this did not get into any of his writing."[6]

Ketman, as Christine Bochen explains, "is a term with an Arabic etymology, which in some Muslim circles means the practice of mental reservation whereby, in an unfriendly regime, one withholds the full statement of one's religious convictions. Miłosz adopts the term to name the ways in which people in Eastern Europe 'act' in ways that mask their views and values in order to survive in a society

[5] Thomas Merton, *A Search for Solitude: Pursuing the Monk's True Life*, ed. Lawrence S. Cunningham, The Journals of Thomas Merton, vol. 3 (New York: HarperCollins, 1996), 315–16.

[6] Czesław Miłosz, the Nobel Prize-winning author, was a regular correspondent of Merton. Miłosz's *The Captive Mind* (New York: Vintage Books, 1953), about the plight of Polish intellectuals under a repressive regime, garnered Merton's attention and initiated a correspondence that lasted throughout Merton's final decade. See Thomas Merton, *The Courage for Truth: The Letters of Thomas Merton to Writers*, ed. Christine M. Bochen (New York: Farrar, Straus and Giroux, 1993), 64.

dominated by 'the Party'" (*Courage*, 64). Merton's reference to *Caesar* in his letter is the archetypal symbol of the "unfriendly regime." Merton is saying that Blake's prophetic books, while difficult to unravel, are a "valid and consistent and prophetic" statement that fully bears his religious convictions—that holds no punches. Blake, according to Merton, was not one to mask his imaginative vision. He didn't care whether others might misunderstand him. He was utterly convinced that the poet must write out of his most authentic self—to convey what he saw with his imagination, however subversive, shocking, or obtuse. This was, for Merton, the foundational element of what made Blake's poetry prophetic.

1964

After this brief appearance of Blake in 1959, Merton did not mention Blake again until 1964, when he again accessed him as an interpretive lens through which to understand the spirituality of the Shakers. At the beginning of that summer, Merton found himself on one of his frequent visits to the hospital in Louisville. Writing to Ray Livingston on May 11, he mentions having recently read Blake: "I was in the hospital too, and got to read some Blake and some things about Blake in the U. of Louisville library on my way in and out. How few are the people who see."[7] Then, a couple of months later on July 20, to Mrs. Edward Deming (Faith) Andrews, the wife of the Shaker scholar and enthusiast who had asked Merton to write an introduction to their book *Religion in Wood: A Book of Shaker Furniture*, he writes, "In the preface I have been bold enough to bring in quite a lot about William Blake. I hope you will not think this too venturesome, but I thought it would be worthwhile to write a preface that was an essay in its own right, and I hope it will add to the book."[8]

---

[7] Thomas Merton, *Witness to Freedom: The Letters of Thomas Merton in Times of Crisis*, ed. William H. Shannon, Thomas Merton Letters, vol. 5 (New York: Harcourt Brace, 1995), 247. Ray Livingston was chair of the Department of English at Macalester College in St. Paul, Minnesota.

[8] Thomas Merton, *The Hidden Ground of Love: The Letters of Thomas Merton on Religious Experience and Social Concerns*, ed. William H. Shannon (New York: Farrar, Straus and Giroux, 1985), 40.

Merton opens his introduction with this passage from Blake's *Jerusalem*:

> Prepare the furniture, O Lambeth, in thy pitying looms!
>
> The curtains, woven tears and sighs, wrought into lovely
>   forms
>
> For comfort: there the secret furniture of Jerusalem's
>   chamber is wrought.
>
> Lambeth, the Bride, the Lamb's Wife loveth thee:
>
> Thou art one with her, and knowest not of self in thy
>   supreme joy.
>
> Go on, builders in hope, tho' Jerusalem wanders far
>   away
>
> Without the gate of Los, among the dark Satanic wheels.[9]

Merton used these lines to draw immediate comparisons between Blake and the Shakers. As he noted in the opening paragraph, the more each is understood, the more comparisons will be made. Though Blake probably knew very little about the Shakers, if anything at all, his creative impulses, according to Merton, bore profound similarities to theirs.

Merton began his identification of these similarities by first highlighting the "wild and hermetic theology" of each. Yet he cautioned that neither was as incoherent or eccentric as many had initially seemed to believe. Imagination, he said, was another common feature. Merton had already come to see that Blake's understanding of imagination was fundamental to his understanding of reality: it is the essence of life—its very nature. The Shakers too, in Merton's view, held the imagination fundamental to their understanding of reality. But the imagination did not work alone in the creative process. It was intertwined with and dependent on religious inspiration. Merton certainly recognized that connection: "It is no exaggeration to say that the simple and 'lovely forms' which emerged

---

[9] William Blake, *Jerusalem*, i. Quoted in Merton, "Introduction," in *Religion in Wood: A Book of Shaker Furniture*, by Edward Deming Andrews and Faith Andrews (Bloomington, IN: Indiana University Press, 1966), vii–xv, here vii.

from the fire of Shaker religious inspiration had something to do
with what Blake called 'the secret furniture of Jerusalem's chamber'"
("Introduction," *Religion in Wood*, viii). As Merton explained, the
craft of Blake's poetry and of the Shakers' woodwork were both
essentially spiritual. The outward expression of both found their
source in inner inspiration and reflected their inner world. In this
way, as he noted, their art revealed and communicated inner realities
of meaning: "Neither the Shakers nor Blake would be disturbed
at the thought that a work-a-day bench, cupboard, or table might
also and at the same time be furniture in and for heaven: did not
Blake protest mightily at the blindness of 'single vision' which saw
only the outward and material surface of reality, not its inner and
spiritual 'form' and the still more spiritual 'force' from which the
form proceeds? These, for Blake, were not different realities. They
are one" ("Introduction," *Religion in Wood*, viii).

In this way, too, their art was prophetic: "And the 'fourfold vision' of religious and creative 'imagination' (more akin to prophetic
vision than to phantasy) was needed if one were to be a 'whole
man,' capable of seeing reality in its totality, and thus dwelling and
expanding spiritually in 'the four regions of human majesty'" ("Introduction," *Religion in Wood*, viii). In order to expound his meaning
of "fourfold vision," Merton provided this poem from Blake:

> Now I a fourfold vision see
> And a fourfold vision is given me;
> 'Tis fourfold in my supreme delight
> And threefold in soft Beulah's night
> And twofold always. May God us keep
> From single vision and Newton's sleep![10]

John Beer, in his *William Blake: A Literary Life*, provides helpful
commentary on the fourth level of Blake's "fourfold vision":

> Single vision was the dead vision of contemporary math-
> ematical rationalism, whereas the vision by which he

---

[10] William Blake, Letter to Thomas Butts, November 22, 1802. Quoted
in Merton, "Introduction," in *Religion in Wood*, viii.

customarily worked was the twofold, which customarily
sought to find inner significance within the normal everyday, but which, as he is explaining, carried its own dangers
of fear of the future along with the delights of creativity.
Above the fear and vision granted to artists like himself
he envisaged two further realms: the "threefold" vision of
innocent pleasure given to those enjoying the pleasures
of marriage and domesticity (termed "Beulah" from his
reading of Isaiah and *The Pilgrim's Progress*) and the supreme "fourfold" of supreme vision—at once absolute
in its certainty and essentially unseizable for purposes of
immediate visual representation.[11]

It is this "fourfold vision" of Blake that Merton describes as
being "akin to prophetic vision." Unfortunately, Merton does not
specifically state what he means by "prophetic vision." He simply
describes it as being closely related to Blake's "fourfold vision."
From this comparison, however, it can be deduced that Merton's
idea of "prophetic vision" comprises religious and creative imagination, like Blake's "fourfold vision," but may also in some way
differ from it. The difference, however, need not be emphasized.
Merton's concern here is to highlight their similarities. What is
most significant about this comparison is that Merton sees Blake's
fourth fold of his "fourfold vision" as a type of mystical vision.
Perhaps Merton is saying that it is specifically this fourth fold that
provides the necessary components for truly "prophetic vision."

Shaker furniture, for Merton, was an expression of Shaker spirituality. In this way, the craftsmanship of the Shakers was like the poetry
and drawings of Blake. Their art sprang from an inner force—out of
the mystery of God within. Blake's "fourfold vision" was the key to
Merton's understanding of the spirituality of Shaker craftsmanship.
He described the work of the Shakers thus: "There were of course
rules to be obeyed and principles by which the work was guided: but
the work itself was free, spontaneous, itself responding to a new and
unique situation. Nothing was done by rote or by slavish imitation.

---

[11] John Beer, *William Blake: A Literary Life* (New York: Palgrave Macmillan,
2005), 126.

The workman also had a vocation: he had to respond to the call of God pointing out to him the opportunity to make a new chest of drawers like the ones that had been made before, only better. Not necessarily better in an ideal and absolute sense, but better adapted to the particular need for which it was required. Thus the craftsman began each new chair as if it were the first chair ever to be made in the world!" ("Introduction," *Religion in Wood*, x). So in Merton's judgment this direct dependence on the Spirit of God grounded the work of the Shakers in a form of mysticism that added mystery and luminosity to their particular form of craftsmanship.

Merton goes on to observe that Shaker vision is "peculiarly and authentically American" ("Introduction," *Religion in Wood*, xi). While he was often quite critical of America, here his description of the American spirit of the Shakers is quite positive. The Shakers, according to Merton, unquestionably "felt themselves called to be a force for social renewal in the world which surrounded them. They had the gift to express much that is best in the American spirit. They exemplified the simplicity, the practicality, the earnestness, and the hope that have been associated with the United States. They exemplified these qualities in a mode of humility and dedication which one seeks in vain today in the hubris and exasperation of our country with its enormous power!" ("Introduction," *Religion in Wood*, xi). The Shakers, along with Henry David Thoreau, Emily Dickinson, and William Faulkner, represented for Merton the American spirit in its purest and most prophetic form, before America finally succumbed to the consumerism and materialism of his day.

The prophetic task of recovering the lost spirit of simplicity, innocence, and hope that characterized the Shakers was primarily the work of the spiritual imagination, Merton thought, arguing that it was because this religious and creative imagination had become impotent, sterile, and dead that America had fallen into "an era of violence, chaos, destruction, madness, and slaughter" ("Introduction," *Religion in Wood*, xiii). As he wrote, "'Imagination,' for Blake, is the faculty by which man penetrates ultimate reality and religious mystery" ("Introduction," *Religion in Wood*, xiii). For both Blake and the Shakers, it was the task of the creative imagination and religious vision to be more than "merely static and contemplative" ("Introduction," *Religion in Wood*, xiv). They were to be "active and dynamic" ("Introduction," *Religion in Wood*, xiv) in expressing that vision in creative work—ultimately a work of redemption. Commenting on the dangers facing a world without this creative imagination and redemptive work, Blake offers a prophetic view of humankind's modern plight: "Art degraded, imagination denied, war governed the nations."[12]

The power of Shaker craftsmanship, according to Merton, lay in its chastity, simplicity, and honesty—and in the fact that "it is never conscious of itself, never seeks recognition, and is completely absorbed in the work to be done" ("Introduction," *Religion in Wood*, xiv). Such power, based on the Shakers' spirit of simple dependence on God, is, as Merton observes, "perhaps the last great expression of work in a purely human measure, a witness to the ancient, primitive, perfect totality of man before the final victory of machine technology" ("Introduction," *Religion in Wood*, xv). This observation led Merton to ask a series of probing and ominous questions: "is such a spirit, such work, possible to men whose lives are in full technological, sociological, and spiritual upheaval? Will such a spirit be possible in the future world that will emerge from the present technological revolution, that world whose outlines can barely be discerned? Is Shaker craftsmanship and its spirit necessarily bound up with a more primitive technology, or can it find a way to direct and inform machine production?" ("Introduction," *Religion in Wood*, xv).

Although Merton declines to answer any of these questions, by using Blake as a means of interpreting Shaker spirituality and craftsmanship, he means to say that there remains a hope that the future can be saved from total technological, sociological, and spiritual upheaval, but only by means of the recovery and exercise of the creative imagination and religious spirit that so characterized the prophetic vision of William Blake.

[12] William Blake, "Laocoön" (cited in Merton, "Introduction," *Religion in Wood*, xiv).

1968

While Merton took up Blake briefly in 1959 and a little more substantially in 1964, it was not until his final year, 1968, that he returned to Blake with full force. On March 9 of that year, Merton recorded in his journal, "Back to Blake—after thirty years. I remember the profound overturning of the roots that took place in my study of him. And the same—even much more profound, is required."[13] Merton articulated this "much more profound" overturning mainly in response to his grappling with Thomas J. J. Altizer's *The New Apocalypse: The Radical Christian Vision of William Blake*.[14] He primarily expressed his response in two essays, "The Death of God and the End of History"[15] and "Blake and the New Theology."[16]

Merton situated his essay "The Death of God and the End of History" in part four of *Faith and Violence*. Each of the four parts of the book deal with various themes of crisis that Merton saw as pressing issues for the church and for the world. Part four addresses the theme of belief and unbelief, with particular interest in the critique of the "death of God" movement on institutional religion and orthodox theology. Merton begins the essay by exploring the claims of the "death of God" advocates. They identified themselves as fervent Christian iconoclasts, who thought their ideas were vitally necessary for both Christianity and the world if Christianity was to maintain any relevance in the modern world. As Merton explained their position, "The kerygma of the 'death of God' is

[13] Thomas Merton, *The Other Side of the Mountain: The End of the Journey*, ed. Patrick Hart (New York: HarperCollins, 1998), 63.

[14] Thomas J. J. Altizer, *The New Apocalypse: The Radical Christian Vision of William Blake* (East Lansing, MI: Michigan State University Press, 1967).

[15] "The Death of God and the End of History" was initially printed in *Theoria to Theory*, 2, no. 1 (1967): 3–16, but was later published in *Faith and Violence: Christian Teaching and Christian Practice* (Notre Dame, IN: University of Notre Dame Press, 1968), 239–58.

[16] "Blake and the New Theology" first appeared in *The Sewanee Review* 76, no. 4 (1968): 673–82, but was later published in *The Literary Essays of Thomas Merton* (New York: New Directions, 1981), 3–11.

then, in fact, *not* a categorical affirmation that 'God does not exist' over against a dogma of his existence. Still less is it a declaration that he 'never existed.' It is rather a declaration that the question of God's existence has now become irrelevant. An announcement of 'good news': God as a problem no longer requires our attention" (*Faith and Violence*, 240). John A. T. Robinson, Dietrich Bonhoeffer, Rudolph Bultmann, and Thomas J. J. Altizer are among the radical theologians (some more radical than others) with whom Merton dealt in his essay "The Death of God."

Toward the end of the essay, Merton turns his attention to Altizer. According to Merton, Altizer, with his treatment of William Blake in *The New Apocalypse*, shed new light on the God-is-dead movement. What was unique about Altizer's approach, Merton said, was that his death-of-God kenoticism did not simply imply "passive submission to power politics" (*Faith and Violence*, 256). On the contrary, Altizer made Blake the model for the "prophetic radical Christian" (*Faith and Violence*, 257). Blake's power lay in the fact that he was a visionary who "chose to confront the awesome reality of history as the total epiphany of the sacred."[17] Merton noted that according to Mircea Eliade, it is the tendency of religion "to dissolve history or to evade it" (*Faith and Violence*, 257), and it is the prophetic tradition of the Old Testament and the ongoing development of later Judaic and Christian prophecy that embraces history without evading it. For Altizer, said Merton, it was Blake, the radical Christian prophet, who had the faith to come face to face with a "totally fallen history" and find in it "the redemptive epiphany of Christ."[18] Such faith is possible, he said, because it is at once both "acceptance and reversal" (*Faith and Violence*, 258). Merton explains the paradox:

> the reversal is not a rejection of history in favor of some-
> thing else that is totally outside history. The reversal comes
> from within history accepted, in its often shattering real-
> ity, as the focus of salvation and epiphany. It is not that

[17] Altizer, *The New Apocalypse*; quoted in Merton, *Faith and Violence*, 257.
[18] Altizer, *The New Apocalypse*; quoted in Merton, *Faith and Violence*, 257.

the world of Auschwitz, Vietnam and the Bomb has to be cursed and repudiated as the devil's own territory. That very world has to be accepted as the terrain of the triumph of love not in the condemnation of evil but in its forgiveness: and this is certainly not an easy truth when we confront the enormity of the evil! (*Faith and Violence*, 258)

Whereas "The Death of God and the End of History" only mentions *The New Apocalypse*, "Blake and the New Theology" is a review essay *in toto* of Altizer's book. Merton begins his essay by observing how many writers have dismissed Blake as being too esoteric and lost in his own subjective world of myth and symbol to say anything relevant or useful—"that he was a madman who wrote a few good poems and many bad long ones" ("Blake and the New Theology," 3). Perceptions were changing, however, and Blake was faring better with more contemporary readers: "They have shown themselves more and more inclined to recognize him as a prophet and apocalyptic visionary who had a very real insight into the world of his time and of ours" ("Blake and the New Theology," 3). This change of perception, according to Merton, was probably due to the atrocities of two world wars, the atomic bomb, and the chaos that had resulted throughout the world. Merton goes on to explain what he means by describing Blake as a prophet: "In this situation Blake can be read as a 'prophet' not of course in the sense of one who exactly predicts future events, but in the more traditional sense of one who 'utters' and 'announces' news about man's own deepest trouble—news that emerges from the very ground of that trouble in man himself. And of course the intensity of Blake's prophetic fervor was increased by the anger with which he viewed the blind complacencies of rationalism, of Enlightenment deism, and of the established Churches" ("Blake and the New Theology," 3).

Merton saw Blake in light of his reading of the Hebrew prophets, whose function was to highlight the sin of Israel's disobedience and idolatry in order to influence their reconciliation with God. Fervor and anger were characteristic of both and denoted the passionate, uncompromising nature of the prophetic vocation of each. For Merton, Blake's prophecies were against "the blind complacencies" that had suffocated the spontaneity of imagination and the creative impulse. Blake's prophetic task was to use his intuitive capabilities to recover spiritual vitality. A certain amount of righteous indignation was warranted—even necessary. As Michael Higgins observes, "Merton and Blake both possessed the spiritual qualities of the biblical prophet and rebel: the capacity for righteous anger mingled with insight" (*Heretic Blood*, 69).

At this point Merton begins his analysis of Altizer's *The New Apocalypse*. The first few paragraphs of the analysis of the book demonstrate just how well Blake's thought corresponded to the tenets of radical theology. As Merton stated, "Radical theology could hardly find a better and more persuasive prophet" ("Blake and the New Theology," 5). Merton was in agreement with Altizer in much of his treatment of Blake. He affirmed Altizer's reading of Blake as neither an orthodox Christian mystic nor a purely heterodox anti-Christian seer. Altizer considered Blake to be fundamentally a revolutionary seer. Blake's unique prophetic spirit could only be understood, Altizer said, by realizing Blake to have "passed through an interior reversal and transformation of the Western Christian tradition" (*New Apocalypse*, xvi).

With Altizer, Merton acknowledged Blake's virulent views of the church's having perverted Christian truth for its own power and prestige. Instead of becoming "the lover of man who empties himself to become identified with Man" ("Blake and the New Theology," 5), he had said, the church had become "a scepter whom man sets up against himself, investing him with the trappings of power which are not 'the things of God' but really 'the things that are Caesar's'" ("Blake and the New Theology," 5). Again, Merton agreed with Altizer in seeing Blake as a visionary whose vision was "a total integration of mysticism and prophecy, a return to apocalyptic faith which arises from an intuitive protest against Christianity's estrangement from its own eschatological ground" ("Blake and the New Theology," 6). He also agreed with Altizer's judgment "that Blake saw official Christendom as a *narrowing* of vision, a foreclosure of experience and of future expansion, a locking up and securing of the doors of perception. He substituted for it a Christianity of openness, of total vision, a faith which dialectically

embraces both extremes, not seeking to establish order in life by
shutting off a little corner of chaos and subjecting it to laws and
to police, but moving freely between dialectical poles in a wild
chaos, integrating sacred vision, in and through the experience of
fallenness, as the only locus of creativity and redemption" ("Blake
and the New Theology," 6).

But Merton criticized Altizer for his utilization of Hegel's dialectical method in interpreting Blake. Merton saw this employment
of Hegel as superficial and forced. One obvious difference between
Blake and Hegel, he pointed out, arose in their understanding of
the nature of *coincidentia oppositorum*: "what for Hegel would be
'coincidence' . . . is for Blake something totally different, the fourfold creative and prophetic vision in which opposites do not merely
come together and fuse in synthesis, but are restored to a higher
unity, an alchemical wedding of loving and fiery elements made all
the more ardent by separation" ("Blake and the New Theology," 6).

Thus Merton was not so sure that Altizer had "found the right
key" ("Blake and the New Theology," 6) for interpreting Blake.
Merton did, however, see in Blake a dialectical method in a more
restricted sense: "But in any case there is a ground of dialectic in
Blake which, though not Hegelian, is nevertheless fully concerned
with man's predicament in the world and deals with history not
with a simple 'yes' or a simple 'no' but with a 'total acceptance, if
ultimate reversal, of the full reality of a fallen history'" ("Blake and
the New Theology," 6). Blake's "fourfold creative and prophetic
vision," Merton pointed out, served as the conduit through which
humankind is redeemed and thrust into a "higher unity." This restoration of contraries is not simply the work of the intellect, but for
Blake, "it was, and had to be, a mystical and prophetic experience
involving the whole man" ("Blake and the New Theology," 7). This
soteriological evolution transcends historical process.

At this point in his analysis of Altizer, Merton becomes critical
of the new theology's total negation of the transcendence of God in
favor of his immanence in history alone. This total *kenosis* of the so-
called static God into the dynamic God, or, put philosophically, the
act of Being into the *activity of becoming* is critiqued by Merton, who
saw process philosophy and theology as "considerably less alive

and dynamic" ("Blake and the New Theology," 9) than scholasticism. Altizer's depiction of life stuck on the historical plain without the capacity for transcendence was, for Merton, a misreading of Blake: "The revelation of God as life-giving Spirit is surely a revelation of him as *not* solitary and remote but as completely 'given,' 'poured out' in the world and man, and so, if you will, kenotic. But Altizer completely ignores all this and hence has to try to reach this same end by the fuzzy romanticism of a Godhead-process, immanent within history" ("Blake and the New Theology," 10).

This critique set aside, Merton did find Altizer's reading of Blake commendable, particularly in Altizer's treatment of Blake's eschatological vision, which Merton believed to be "the most important thing about this book" ("Blake and the New Theology," 10):

> He has certainly not toned down the apocalyptic and prophetic character of Blake's vision, but has sought to do it full justice. In so doing, he has also frankly faced the central importance of that most odious and unpopular of Christian doctrines: the fall. Without the fall not only is Christianity itself emptied of meaning, but Blake too becomes incomprehensible. Eschatology is the vision of a totally new and final reality, a cosmic reversal that brings ultimate meaning and salvation to the fallen world. That reality is, in effect, the total integration of God and Man in Christ—that is to say, in concrete and communal Mankind united not by politics but by mercy. ("Blake and the New Theology," 6)

Prophetic Anti-poetry?

According to Michael Higgins,[19] Blake's influence on Merton is expressed most fully in Merton's so called anti-poetry, which

---

[19] No writer has done more to demonstrate Blake's influence on Merton. Besides his book *Heretic Blood*, Higgins has also published a number of essays: "A Study of the Influence of William Blake on Thomas Merton," *The American Benedictine Review* 25, no. 3 (1974): 377–88; "Monasticism as Rebellion: Blakean Roots of Merton's Thought," *The American Benedictine Review* 39 (1988): 177–88; and "Merton and the Real Poets: Paradise Re-Bugged,"

Higgins describes as "a poetry replete with irony and protest, a method of coping with the contemporary disarray of language and meaning, a latter-day Blakean strategy" (*Heretic Blood*, 57). This notion of anti-poetry, which Merton espoused in the final year of his life, was provided to him by the Chilean poet Nicanor Parra. Merton himself describes the anti-poet as one who "'suggests' a tertiary meaning which is *not* 'creative' and 'original' but a deliberate ironic feedback of cliché, a further referential meaning, alluding, by its tone, banality, etc., to a *customary and abused context*, that of an impoverished and routine sensibility, and of the 'mass-mind,' the stereotyped creation of quantitative preordained response by 'mass-culture.'"[20]

Merton's two final books of poetry, *Cables to the Ace or, Familiar Liturgies of Misunderstanding* and *The Geography of Lograire*, are his contribution to this genre of anti-poetry. Higgins describes these works as Merton's "two great Blakean 'myth-dreams,'" which "reflect Merton's conviction that the tyranny of mind and power in Western culture suppresses the genuine spirituality and life-affirming imagination, the meaning-generating capacity of words and silence, so integral to other cultures: aboriginal; oriental; extinct" (*Heretic Blood*, 56–57). Higgins's description of Merton's anti-poetry is reminiscent of Blake's understanding of the prophetic function in the spiritual life. Anti-poetry's prophetic role is to parody the nonsense and confusion of modernity's suppressed imagination and spirit. In so doing, its mimicry exposes the irrational and illogical thought patterns that, Merton thought, characterized much of the twentieth century in the Western world. Words have become empty and meaningless—only noise. Anti-poetry's metaphorical "gibberish" ultimately seeks to reveal the great need for silence and true communication.

Higgins offers this important insight into understanding *Cables to the Ace*: "In *Cables* form *is* content; it does not contain or trans-

---

Merton Annual v. 3. Studies in Culture, Spirituality and Social Concerns, ed. E. E. Daggy and Robert Daggy (New York: AMS Press, 1991), 175–86.

[20] Thomas Merton, *The Asian Journal of Thomas Merton* (New York: New Directions, 1968), 286.

mit a message, it simply *is* a message. The title of the poem itself suggests the identification of the means of transmission with the content transmitted, for a cable is both the electrical apparatus by which the message is channeled and the message or cablegram itself. The medium is the message" (*Heretic Blood*, 182). Higgins sees Merton's *Cables* as a culminating fulfillment of the Blakean imperative of reconstituting, by means of vision and imagination, humankind's wholeness and spiritual unity:

> In Blake's poetry the vision is worked out in his prophetic books, with the Apocalypse, Jerusalem, and the final re-integration through Jesus or the Spiritual Imagination. In *Cables* Merton resolved to "assist once again at the marriage of heaven and hell" (Cable 1); he continues the Blakean dream: "These words were once heard, uttered by a lonely, disembodied voice, seemingly in a cloud" (Cable 9). (*Heretic Blood*, 180–81)

Further, Higgins's Blakean reading of *Cables* leads him to interpret the poet's prophetic job as a recovering of Paradise:

> Although the poet is nurtured "by the fancies / Of female benefactors," these benefactors are in fact emanations from the one female, Sophia/Virgin/Urthona, the love of whom is paradise. To see paradise, to know wisdom, one must love and wait for the *point vierge*, "that moment of awe and inexpressible innocence." The "unspeakable secret," this "ace of freedoms," is the poet's discovery, the full perfection of which means death. In a powerfully Jungian and prophetic conclusion to Cable 74 Merton speaks of the mandala, the ancient symbol in integration and fulfillment, in connection with the "distant country" of his approaching death:

> > Better to study the germinating waters of my wood
> > And know this fever: or die in a distant country
> > Having become a pure cone
> > Or turn to my eastern abstinence
> > With that old inscrutable love cry
> > And describe a perfect circle

Before the poet's annihilation by Wisdom, an experience which he describes as "a perfect circle," "having become a pure cone," he assists in the recovery of paradise through poetry—the language of his vision, the sacrament of his "discovery"—freeing Imagination from the shackles of Urizenic perception. Authentic paradisal poetry explores new possibilities through a daring revitalization of idea, word, and sound and, in his anti-poetic epics, Merton attempts to give "the world another chance." (Higgins, "Merton and the Real Poets," 181)

"Urizenic perception" represents, for Merton, perception that is inhibited by empiricism and doubt because it is blind to imagination, passion, and spiritual realities. Thus such perception is only superficial, prohibited from truly seeing. Even more, such perception leads to dangerous consequences: "The tyranny of Urizen consists in trying to govern by abstract codes based on mathematical reasoning and materialism, and it brings about a vicious circle of oppressions and wars."[21] On the other hand, Blake and Merton, for Higgins, are poets who seek to recover Paradise through prophetic perception. Such poetry, for Merton, is the only truly "valid poetry":

All really valid poetry (poetry that is fully alive and asserts its reality by its power to generate imaginative life) is a kind of recovery of paradise. Not that the poet comes up with a report that he, an unusual man, has found his own way back into Eden: but the living line and the generative association, the new sound, the music, the structure, are somehow grounded in a renewal of vision and hearing so that he who reads and understands recognizes that here is a new start, a new creation. Here the world gets another chance. Here man, here the reader discovers himself getting another start in life, in hope, in imagination, and why? Hard to say, but probably because the language itself is get-

[21] Thomas Merton, "Nature and Art in William Blake: An Essay in Interpretation," M.A. Thesis, Columbia University, February 1939; in Merton, *Literary Essays*, 385–451, here 428.

ting another chance, through the innocence, the teaching, the good faith, the honest senses of the workman poet.[22]

With *The Geography of Lograire*, left unfinished at the time of his death, Merton continues his anti-poetic myth-dream by means of a literary journey to the four corners of the earth. The four quadrants—north, south, east, and west—represent facets of Merton's own spiritual quest, recounting personal experiences and historical incidents mixed together with past legends and primitive beliefs. Higgins sees Merton's final poetic work as a fitting culmination for one of the twentieth century's greatest spiritual explorers. Yet he also sees *Geography* as a starting point of future exploration: "This final testament to his poetic powers was merely the beginning of an effort to expand the range of his poetic genius by 'imploding' his vision through fragmenting his language, torturing meanings, desecrating all Reason's Laws, and exorcizing the demon within that bid him serve the Master, Thought and all his minions, Words" ("A Study," 385).

Higgins's insightful reading of *Geography* continues: "Merton, in quest for the God within, followed his imaginative pulse that chartered new regions of the spirit through a panoply of discordant images and shattered metaphors, dared oblivion and thirsted for a widening of vision, that brought him not death but life. The tyranny of language was to be undone by Word" ("A Study," 386–87). As Merton himself writes, "A poet spends his life in repeated projects, over and over again attempting to build or to dream the world in which he lives."[23]

In this brief excerpt, Merton once again emphasizes the role imagination plays in the life of the poet. He defines the poet as one who "dream(s)," or the one who lives and creates from his or her own imagination. The task of the poet is to "build" and create a better world. It is to see what only he or she can see and

[22] Merton, "Louis Zukofsky—The Paradise Ear," in *Literary Essays*, 128–33, here 128.
[23] Thomas Merton, *The Collected Poems of Thomas Merton* (New York: New Directions, 1977), 457.

write that vision into existence. *The Geography of Lograire* is about
a geography of imagination described cryptically in mythic form,
mostly employing the tragic experiences of the past in order to
hold out the possibility of a future of eschatological hope. It is a
geography of spiritual longing for a place of rest after a lifetime of
intense soul searching.

How effective, though, has Merton's anti-poetry been in building up the world in which he longed to live? Not everyone is as
enthusiastic as Higgins in evaluating Merton's experimentation in
"myth-dreams." The most significant criticism of such an approach
can be found in Dennis McInerny's *Thomas Merton: The Man and
His Work*:

> One could say . . . that in my critique of *Cables to the Ace*
> and *The Geography of Lograire* I simply miss the point, that if
> these two works are fragmented and disjointed it is because
> they were deliberately intended to be such in order to mir-
> ror and pass judgment upon the fragmented and disjointed
> nature of our age. The message, in other words, is as much
> in the form as in the content. To stand in judgment of a
> chaotic age, as a poet and prophet, one must speak chaot-
> ically. All I can say in response to this is that I am perfectly
> aware of the point; it is just that I do not agree with it. One
> does not intimidate or dispel linguistic chaos by yet more
> linguistic chaos. I stand with E. B. Strunk who claimed
> that the only way to cope adequately with confusion was
> unconfusedly. To write about confusion confusedly only
> compounds the confusion, and that was what Merton was
> doing by his anti-poetry.[24]

Higgins himself cautions of the insufficiency of anti-poetry:
"Antipoetry has its purposes, but it also has its very clear limitation" (*Heretic Blood*, 263). These criticisms highlight the ambiguous
nature of anti-poetry. While it seeks to imagine and create a better
world through its mimicry and intended confusion, it ultimately

---

[24] Dennis Q. McInerny, *Thomas Merton: The Man and His Work*, CS 27
(Washington, DC: Consortium Press, 1974), 43–44.

fails to accomplish its goal because it forfeits one of the primary tasks of the poetic/prophetic imagination, to communicate symbolically, yet concretely, a reality of possibility that is not yet but that is somehow attainable.[25] Perhaps one way of understanding the prophetic nature of anti-poetry is by distinguishing between *negative* and *positive* modes of prophecy.[26] A *negative* mode of prophecy is purely iconoclastic—it seeks to reveal and destroy what is contrary to the will of God. A *positive* mode of prophecy seeks to express the will of God in the context of a situation that has forsaken that will. Anti-poetry, with its assault on language itself as a way of revealing the confusion and inner contradictions of a given age, would be a purely *negative* mode of prophecy. It reveals and seeks to destroy without offering a positive and meaningful alternative.

Concluding Remarks

Merton's revisitation of Blake at the different periods of his life reveals some notable particularities about Blake's impact on the formation of Merton's prophetic spirituality. First, Blake's prophetic spirituality was an *expression of his mysticism.* For Merton, identifying Blake as a prophet meant primarily identifying Blake as a *seer*—a visionary. This is the main theme of Merton's treatment of Blake in *The Seven Storey Mountain.* Second, the letter to Czesław Miłosz in 1959 shows that Merton considered Blake a prophet because Blake boldly asserted his own imaginative vision in the face of ridicule and misunderstanding. He had decided that his creative

[25] Walter Brueggemann, *The Prophetic Imagination* (Philadelphia: Fortress Press, 1978), 49–50, offers three tasks of the prophetic imagination: (1) "To *offer symbols* that are adequate to the horror and massiveness of the experience which evokes numbness and requires denial," (2) "To *bring to public expression those very fears and terrors* that have been denied so long and suppressed so deeply that we do not know they are there," (3) "To *speak metaphorically but concretely about the real deathliness that hovers over us and gnaws within us,* and to speak neither in rage nor in cheap grace, but with the candor born of anguish and passion."

[26] Brueggemann speaks about the two tasks of prophecy: dismantling and energizing (*The Prophetic Imagination,* 109).

spiritual intuitions held too much significance to be made more palatable for the sake of the status quo. Third, through his treatment of the Shakers in his introduction to *Religion in Wood*, Merton gave concrete application to his appreciation and understanding of Blake's prophetic vision and imagination. Shaker spirituality, for Merton, embodied the prophetic spirit of William Blake. The Shakers were those whose vision penetrated into ultimate reality and religious mystery and who lived in the creative vitality of a pure and simple imaginative spirit. The spirit of the Shakers was prophetic because they sought to recover through their imagination the lost innocence, simplicity, and hope that had become threatened by the technological advances of modernity.

Fourth, Merton developed his interest in Blake's ideas about the prophetic imagination by grappling with Thomas J. J. Altizer's *The New Apocalypse*. While Merton was not keen on Altizer's interpretive approach to Blake, he saw great strength in Altizer's book for demonstrating Blake's relevant value as a true prophet and apocalyptic visionary. Merton argued that this book showed Blake as a prophet because he was one who "'utters' and 'announces' news about man's own deepest trouble—which is man himself" ("Blake and the New Theology," 3). Out of this "trouble," Merton believed, the prophetic imagination envisions and creates a hopeful future of greater peace and justice. This eschatological hope becomes all the more real in light of the extent of humankind's fallenness.

Commentators, especially Higgins, considered Merton's Blakean poetic experimentation in anti-poetry prophetic because of its implicit critique of the way "one-dimensional man"[27] had for-

---

[27] Herbert Marcuse's *One-Dimensional Man* (Boston: Beacon Press, 1964), which Merton read in 1968, describes the consciousness that results from a technological, mass-production society. Merton, writing in his journal on November 7, 1968, says, "Marcuse has shown how mass culture tends to be anticulture—to stifle creative work by the sheer volume of what is 'produced,' or reproduced. In which case, poetry, for example, must start with an awareness of its contradiction and *use* it—as antipoetry—which freely draws on the material of superabundant nonsense at its disposal. One no longer has to parody, it is enough to quote—and feed back quotations

feited metaphysical realities for a purely pragmatic consciousness. Its muddled mimicry while trying to parody such a consciousness ultimately lost much of its prophetic power because it faltered in being faithful to one of the basic tenets of the poetic/prophetic imagination, which is to be concrete enough to move people toward higher consciousness.[28]

The significance of William Blake's influence on Merton is revealed in both its perduring value, from childhood until death, and in the immense personal affection that Merton consistently showed toward someone who may be described as a kindred spirit, even when not always being in full agreement with him. Merton saw in Blake an imaginative mind and prophetic spirit that lived in a certain immediacy of spiritual realities. Even as a student at Columbia University, Merton held Blake to be a Christian mystic, in spite of all his heterodox ideas. As he recounted many years later, it was this Blake, the mystic, who would influence him to embrace Roman Catholicism. The irony of this action was surely not far from Merton's own mind. He was certainly aware that Blake was an intense critic of organized religion.

This fact demonstrates something significant about Merton's ability to learn from others yet think for himself, even as an impressionable college student. Merton never wholeheartedly swallowed the ideas or worldview of a particular thinker. Rather, he studied them with an open mind, integrated what rang true, and dismissed what didn't. This ability to study discriminatingly was certainly the

---

into the mass consumption of pseudoculture" (Merton, *Other Side*, 262). For further treatment of Marcuse and anti-poetry, see David D. Cooper, "From Prophecy to Parody: Thomas Merton's *Cables to the Ace*," *The Merton Annual*, vol. 1 (New York: AMS Press, 1988), 215–33.

[28] It is apparent that Merton understood Blake's prophetic books as nonetheless truly prophetic. He believed that it was the task of the reader to do the hard work of comprehending and interpreting the poetry. The prophetic nature of the poetry would then become obvious. It is my opinion that this view is true insofar as Blake's prophetic books carry comprehensible meaning. With anti-poetry, however, which may be meaningfully meaningless, such words, in so far as they are meaningless, lose their positive prophetic significance.

case with Blake, who Merton felt was misunderstood by a culture that had forsaken the intuitive for the scientific. In a sense, Merton believed Blake had lived in the wrong century (something that can also be said of Merton!). Yet, as Merton saw it, this feeling of being a fish out of water, of going against the grain, gave Blake the psychological impetus to develop his prophetic spirituality. In Merton's reading, the vitality of Blake's imaginative spirit refused to be smothered by Enlightenment rationalism. Rather, Blake chose to live from his authentic self and become a "prophet against empire."[29] It was this prophetic restlessness and need for authentic self-expression that Merton appreciated most about Blake and with which he most identified.

---

[29] This description of Blake was used by David V. Erdman, *Blake: Prophet Against Empire: A Poet's Interpretation of the History of His Own Times* (Princeton, NJ: Princeton University Press, 1969).

Chapter 2

Finding Prophetic Inspiration in Latin America

They are strong, sometimes angry, full of clear intuitions, free from the involvement, the desperation and self-frustration of some of the voices here, so many of the voices here.[1]

—Thomas Merton

Merton's fascination with Spanish can be traced back to a journal entry of December 14, 1939, where he exuberantly listed "some splendid words in Spanish."[2] The inspiration for this list was a book of poetry he had been reading by the Spanish writer Federico Garcia Lorca. Three days later he offered another such list, afterward stating, in typical Mertonian hyperbole, "Lorca is easily the best religious poet of this century" (*Run*, 106). Soon thereafter, he also began to read the poetry of Saint John of the Cross, poetry that would play a significant role in his early formation as a monk. It was at this time that Merton began to hear the call of Latin America.

In April 1940, Merton took what would be his only trip to a Latin American country. After some deliberation about whether he had enough money to travel to Mexico or only to Cuba, Merton decided on Cuba. The Cuban trip offered him an experience of

---

[1] Merton to Alejandro Vignati, November 1, 1964, in Thomas Merton, *The Courage for Truth: The Letters of Thomas Merton to Writers*, ed. Christine M. Bochen (New York: Farrar, Straus and Giroux, 1993), 234.

[2] Thomas Merton, *Run to the Mountain: The Story of a Vocation*, ed. Patrick Hart, The Journals of Thomas Merton, vol. 1 (New York: HarperCollins, 1995), 104.

Catholicism that, he said, was "warm and natural, as well as . . . supernatural."[3] It also gave him a profound religious experience that etched itself deeply into his consciousness. As he recounted both in his journal and later in *The Seven Storey Mountain*, he experienced an epiphany that rivaled his experience in downtown Louisville, as well as a later experience at Polonnaruwa shortly before his death. The event took place in the Church of San Francisco in Havana:

> Before any head was raised again the clear cry of the brother in the brown robe cut through the silence with the word *"Yo Creo . . . "* "I believe" which immediately all the children took up after him with such loud and strong and clear voices, and such unanimity and such meaning and such fervor that something went off inside me like a thunderclap and without seeing anything or apprehending anything extraordinary through any of my senses (my eyes were open on only precisely what was there, the church), I knew with the most absolute and unquestionable certainty that before me, between me and the altar, somewhere in the center of the church, up in the air (or any other place because in no place), but directly before my eyes, or directly present to some apprehension or other of mine which was above that of the senses, was at the same time God in all His essence, all His power, God in the flesh and God in Himself and God surrounded by the radiant faces of the thousands million uncountable numbers of saints contemplating His Glory and Praising His Holy Name. And so the unshakeable certainty, the clear and immediate knowledge that heaven was right in front of me, struck me like a thunderbolt and went through me like a flash of lightning and seemed to lift me clean up off the earth. (*Run*, 217–18)

Also significant was Merton's visit to Our Lady of Cobre, which gave him the inspiration to write what he described as "the first

---

[3] Michael Mott, *The Seven Mountains of Thomas Merton* (Boston: Houghton Mifflin, 1984), 150.

real poem I had ever written."[4] Included in his *Thirty Poems*, "Song for Our Lady of Cobre" reads:

> The white girls lift their heads like trees,
> The black girls go
> Reflected like flamingos in the street,
>
> The white girls sing as shrill as water,
> The black girls talk as quiet as clay.
>
> The white girls open their arms like clouds,
> The black girls close their eyes like wings:
> Angels bow down like bells,
> Angels look up like toys,
>
> Because the heavenly stars
> Stand in a ring:
> And all the pieces of the mosaic, earth,
> Get up and fly away like birds.[5]

According to Merton correspondent Stefan Baciu of the University of Hawaii, this poem "became a symbolic expression of rapport in his dialogue with Latin Americans."[6] Also included in *Thirty Poems* is "In Memory of the Spanish Poet Federico Garcia Lorca." These two early poems, along with the Cuban experience as a whole, proved to be seeds from which Merton's empathy for and attraction to the spirit of the Latin American poets would blossom.

Only a bit later, in the early 1950s, Merton became interested in Portuguese-speaking Latin Americans. Both Alceu Amoroso Lima and Benedictine Sister Emmanuel de Souza e Silva assisted in introducing Merton's writings into Brazil (Lima with introductions

---

[4] Thomas Merton, *The Seven Storey Mountain* (New York: Harcourt Brace, 1948), 283.

[5] Thomas Merton, *The Collected Poems of Thomas Merton* (New York: New Directions, 1977), 29–30.

[6] Robert E. Daggy, "'A Man of the Whole Hemisphere': Thomas Merton and Latin America," *The American Benedictine Review* 42, no. 2 (1991): 122–39, at 127–28.

and Silva with translations). In *Conjectures of a Guilty Bystander* Merton expressed an intense attraction to Portuguese and Brazil:

> The Brazilian poets: a whole new world. To begin with, Portuguese is a wonderful language for poetry, a language of admiration, of innocence, of joy, full of human warmth and therefore of humor: the humor that is inseparable from love, that laughs at the uniqueness of each individual being not because it is comical or contemptible but because it is unique. Uniqueness, the innocent self, is always surprising, and surprise is humorous as well as wonderful, on this human level.[7]

Merton most eloquently expressed his fondness for the whole of Latin America, however, in the preface he wrote in 1958 to the Argentine edition of his *Complete Works*:

> It seems that I have heard the voice of all the hemisphere in the silence of my monastery, a voice that speaks from the depths of my being with a clarity at once magnificent and terrible: as if I had in my heart the vast and solitary pampas, the brilliant hoarfrost of the Bolivian plateau, the thin air of the terraced valleys of the Incas, the splendor and suavity of Quito, the cold plains of Bogota, and the mysterious jungles of the Amazon. It seems that entire cities with great opulence and terrible indigence side by side live inside me. It seems that the ancient civilizations of Mexico, older even than Egypt, gather in unspeakable silence in my heart. It seems that I hear in the even more profound silence of Peru the forgotten syllables of ancient wisdom which contains in its secrets an image of truth that no man has recognized, an image, symbolic and prophetic, like that of Jesus Christ. It seems that the unending beauty of the New World with its limitless possibilities moves within me like a giant sleeper in whose presence I am unable to remain indifferent. In reality, it seems at times that this presence inside me speaks with the voice of God Himself; and I struggle vainly to grasp and to understand

[7] Thomas Merton, *Conjectures of a Guilty Bystander* (1966; New York: Image Books, 1989), 13.

some word, some syllable of the destiny of the New World—
the destiny that is still hidden in the mystery of Providence.[8]

In this passage, Merton articulates one of the most significant
discoveries he made in his engagement with the writers of Latin
America: that their primitive cultures were filled with "symbolic
and prophetic" images and realities that were under threat of extinction by the Westernization of modern societies. His dialogue
with the Nicaraguan poet Ernesto Cardenal, who entered the novitiate at Gethsemani in 1957, gave Merton insight into the cultural
and religious situation of the various Latin American countries. The
relationship of the two men continued through correspondence
after Cardenal's 1959 departure because of health reasons, until
Merton's death in 1968.

Merton's correspondence with Cardenal is marked by expressions of frustration at and critique of conditions in the church, along
with the role the United States was playing in the demise of many of
the cultural values of Latin America. Much of their correspondence
on these subjects takes on a particular prophetic tone:

> My concept of the Church, my faith in the Church, has been
> and is being tested and purified: I hope it is being puri-
> fied. . . . I do not complain, I do not criticize but I observe
> with a kind of numb silence the inaction, the passivity, the
> apparent indifference and incomprehension with which
> most Catholics, clergy and laity, at least in this country,
> watch the development and pressure that builds up to a
> nuclear war. It is as if they had all become lotus-eaters. As
> if they were under a spell. . . . I resist this bad dream with
> all my force, and at least I can struggle and cry out, with
> others who have the same awareness.[9]

---

[8] Thomas Merton, *Honorable Reader: Reflections on My Works*, ed. Robert E.
Daggy (New York: Crossroad, 1989), 40.

[9] Merton to Cardenal, December 24, 1961, in *Courage*, 129–30. This is
one example among many of Merton's critique of nuclear proliferation
and the church's failure to speak out against it and other matters he saw as
endangering the world. Nuclear proliferation lies at the heart of Merton's

Latin American poets were a frequent topic of discussion in Merton's correspondence with Cardenal. The letters to Cardenal begin to reveal Merton's admiration for what he considered to be Latin America's "prophetic quality": "First of all the poem about Bartolomé de Las Casas is most moving, and so is the article about the mystical tree which seems to me to have a deeply prophetic quality. . . . *Ventana* is very alive and appeals to me more than most other 'little magazines.' Again it has a prophetic quality in it, and a simplicity that is lacking in the more frustrated or the more pretentious publications."[10] This particular "prophetic quality" was further elucidated in Merton's thought as he delved more deeply into his study of the poets throughout America's Southern Hemisphere.

One aspect that clearly emerges in Merton's correspondence with Cardenal, though, is the contrast that Merton saw between the two hemispheres: "I say the future belongs to South America: and I believe it. It will belong to North America too, but only on one condition: that the United States becomes able to learn from South and Latin America and listen to the voice that has so long been ignored (a voice which even ignores itself and which must awaken to its own significance), which is a voice of the Andes and of the Amazon (not a voice of the cities, which alone is heard, and is comparatively raucous and false)."[11]

Merton saw a more authentic form of life, particularly in religious and monastic life, in Latin America: "it is here that one finds, I think, some of the most authentic and honest spiritual life in the world of our time. In the monasteries there is still simplicity and joy among some of the monks but the structure is so false

---

writings on peace and non-violence and is one of the areas where Merton most powerfully assumes the prophetic mantle. This was the case until 1962, when Merton's religious superiors no longer allowed him to publish on the theme. He was vindicated, however, by Pope John XXIII's *Pacem in Terris*, which appeared the following year, although he was still forbidden to publish on the subject.

[10] Merton to Cardenal, November 17, 1962, in *Courage*, 137.

[11] Merton to Cardenal, March 10, 1964, in *Courage*, 144.

and artificial that one has a hard time keeping serious about it, and it is often very discouraging" (*Courage*, 145).[12] These remarks reveal that a preliminary component of Merton's understanding of the "prophetic quality" of Latin America was tied up with his recognition of the simplicity and authenticity of the Latin American way of life, especially religious life. Thus, simplicity and authenticity were for him constituent aspects of the prophetic in the Latin American people.

By 1965, Merton began to find reason to hope for the spiritual renewal of the church, largely as a result of the work of the Second Vatican Council. Writing to Cardenal on the day of Cardenal's ordination to the priesthood, Merton had reason to be optimistic: "it is certainly happy that a new spirit of understanding and originality is breathing in the Church, and even some of the most conservative elements are forced to recognize it and adjust to it. I am sure that the coming years will be very creative and that prophetic initiatives may be very evident."[13] The context of this comment reveals not only Merton's confidence in the council but also—even more poignantly—his confidence in his friend Cardenal, in whom Merton saw an embodiment of those who would fulfill the role of carrying out the church's "prophetic initiatives."

Cardenal symbolized for Merton the simple, authentic contemplative-poet who was giving voice to the true spirit of Latin America. Cardenal more than anyone else helped Merton recognize that voice and understand it. That voice's prophetic quality would lure him to discover for himself the spirit of Latin America, mediated mainly through the writings of her vibrant poets, such as Pablo Antonio Cuadra, José Coronel Urtecho, and Alfonso Cortés in Nicaragua, Jorge Carrera Andrade in Ecuador, Nicanor Parra in Chile, Octavio Paz in Mexico, Susana Soca in Uruguay, and Carlos

---

[12] Merton's desire for an authentic form of monasticism, which is the central theme of his writings on monastic renewal, was largely inspired by the witness of monastic life in South America. He made several efforts to transfer his stability to continue his monastic life in South America, but none proved fruitful.

[13] Merton to Cardenal, August 15, 1965, in *Courage*, 151.

Drummond de Andrade and Fernando Pessoa in Brazil. Merton carried on a lively correspondence with many of these, as well as publishing translations of their work. He was also exposed to former Latin American poets with whom he found great affinity: Rubén Darío from Nicaragua, César Vallejo from Peru, and Pablo Neruda from Chile.

Two important correspondents who helped Merton gain exposure throughout Spanish-speaking Latin America were Argentinians: Victoria Ocampo and Miguel Grinberg. Out of this extensive cast, three poets in whom Merton found particular prophetic inspiration emerge and warrant analysis: the Nicaraguans Pablo Antonio Cuadra and Alfonso Cortés, and the Peruvian César Vallejo. What surfaces through Merton's writings on these poets can be considered his elucidations of that peculiarly "prophetic quality" of the Latin American voice.

Listening to Awakening Voices: The Prophetic Ear of Pablo Antonio Cuadra

A cousin of Ernesto Cardenal, Pablo Antonio Cuadra (1912–2002) shared many poetic aspirations with his beloved relative. Both took great interest in the Indian cultures of Central and South America and felt that Western civilization had all but completely muffled their pure and authentic voices. Merton and Cuadra explored this topic in their correspondence and sought to discover a solution to this problem. The remedy that resulted from their assessment of the situation revealed their profound faith in the power of poetry to awaken minds and hearts to wisdom. Both Merton and Cuadra heard the wisdom of the ancient civilizations of Latin America and, with their powerful pens, devoted themselves to giving it a voice.

Precisely such so-called indigenous wisdom attracted Merton to Cuadra's poetry. Merton's esteem for Cuadra's poetry shines in Merton's introductory essay to his translations of Spanish poetry that first appeared in *Emblems of a Season of Fury* in 1963: "He has therefore joined the ranks of those who have created what is undoubtedly the finest and most authentically 'American' poetry of Latin America."[14] Cuadra's authenticity, for Merton, lay in the manner in which he was able to capture the "Indian past" of Central America and make it live "with an unconquerable and flourishing energy through the unmatched prestige of the ancient plastic arts, architecture, folklore, and music, as well as in the texts of ancient Indian poems and dramas" ("Pablo Antonio Cuadra," 321). The pre-Colombian Chorotega pottery served as the inspiration for Cuadra's award-winning book, *El Jaguar y la luna*. In the original Spanish versions, Cuadra offered drawings taken from stylized Nahoa themes. Such poetry, with its combination of poem and picture, made *El Jaguar y la luna* "singularly effective" for Merton ("Pablo Antonio Cuadra," 322). Cuadra's book received the prestigious Rubén Darío prize for Central American verse in 1959. Darío's own poetry inspired Merton to write, "All true poetic genius tends to generate prophetic insight. The poet cannot help but listen to awakening voices that are not yet audible to the rest of men."[15] The truth of this statement he would certainly have applied to Cuadra, whose prophetic ear, Merton said, heard what the "rest of men" could not or would not and gave expression to it in penetrating imagery.

Cuadra's *El Jaguar y la luna* opens with "Cup with a Jaguar for the Drinking of Health." It effectively expresses the indelible stamp that the Ibero-American Indian past left on Cuadra's creative sensibilities. Małgorzata Poks's insightful study on Merton's relationship with the Latin American poets demonstrates this relationship:

> The poem's controlling metaphor is that of a ceramics artist at work, but the original Artist is absent from view, save in the imprint he has left on the clay of creation. The jaguar, worshipped as a god by Cuadra's ancestors, stamped the created world "with his hostile but harmonious mark," his

---

[14] Thomas Merton, "Pablo Antonio Cuadra," in *The Literary Essays of Thomas Merton*, ed. Patrick Hart (New York: New Directions, 1981), 321–22, here 321.

[15] Thomas Merton, "Rubén Darío," in *The Literary Essays of Thomas Merton*, ed. Patrick Hart (New York: New Directions, 1981), 305–6, here 305.

art providing the exemplar for the art of man. What the prototypical Artist achieved so gracefully and effortlessly, his human counterpart must attempt to "copy" in the blood of self-annihilation. Once we follow the implications of this image, it becomes clear that the artist is none other than the jaguar priest sacrificing himself on the altar of his god by "copying" the divine self-communicating act.[16]

Merton's translation of Cuadra's poem reads:

> He has stamped the clay with his hostile
> But harmonious mark
> And I with clay and blood
> Upon this amphora
> Copy his claw!
>
> A ball of rage
> Clenched over the earth
> For the wine of the drunken accident
> Hailed by your death. (*Collected Poems*, 950)

What Cuadra offers in this poem is a view of artistic life as participation in the creative action of God. By the stamp (the image) of the Artist upon the clay of human lives, and in proportion to humans' act of copying (or faithfulness to) that stamp, they participate in the revelation of divine life ("Hailed by your death").

Such a revelation, though, bears a paradoxical twist symbolized in the use of *wine*. Wine is a source of joy as well as drunken stupor, of celebration as well as violence, of life as well as death. This vessel is simultaneously the symbol of harmony (through faithful participation in one's true self) and disharmony (through the disruption of the divinely established order of reality). And as Poks suggests, "the 'toast' prophesies a violent ('drunken') and victorious 'accident' that the dictator will be forced to 'hail' by

---

[16] Małgorzata Poks, *Thomas Merton and Latin America: A Consonance of Voices* (Saarbrücken, Germany: Lambert Academic Publishing, 2011), 153. For a full treatment of Merton's reading of *El Jaguar y la luna*, see 153–74 of Poks's book.

his death" (*Thomas Merton and Latin America*, 154). Poks also reads this poem as "the artist's manifesto, a pledge to the ethics of rebellion" (*Thomas Merton and Latin America*, 154). By this statement, she implies that creative, prophetic life is only so to the extent that it remains true to itself and to its participation in the divine, creative impulse. Such faithfulness, while offering some a clear path to follow, will inevitably infuriate others.

In the face of such anger, the prophet/artist presents his or her own rage in rebellion at whatever cost. In so doing, he or she reestablishes the harmony in the world that had been destroyed by unfaithfulness to the stamped image on the human identity. In this short poem, then, Cuadra, by masterfully utilizing ancient Indian-pottery motifs and wedding them to poetic imagery, takes the reader from the journey of the discovery of identity, the struggle of remaining faithful to that identity, and the paradoxical restoration of all things in the sacrificial death of one's self. What emerges is a vision of the poet as a prophetic hearer who is able to communicate the inaudible creative impulses of an ancient civilization both to encourage and critique the present world and thereby to transform it.

Although Merton did not translate Cuadra's poem "Written on a Roadside Stone During the First Eruption," he greatly admired it, saying, "It is a magnificent poem, and an admirable example of the current political situation with its Indian themes! I really like that prophetic fusion of the past and the present, giving the poem an eternal character, a very religious and solemn aspect!"[17] The subject of the poem is Acahualinca—the famous site of the earliest fossilized footprints (presumably from the eruption of a nearby volcano) in the Western Hemisphere as well as the site of contemporary poverty, squalor, and oppression. Cuadra here boldly states his deep compassion for the oppressed poor of his native Nicaragua, represented here by "Acahualinca," in imagery that is at the same time an excoriating indictment of those political oppressors—the Somoza regime—whose dictatorial policies helped to perpetuate the exploitation and abuse of Nicaragua's most vulnerable. Stephen White offers this translation:

[17] Merton to Cuadra, October 13, 1958, in *Courage*, 180.

We will cry over the footprints of those who fled from
Acahualinca.

Our exodus began here.

They heard the cavernous voice of the monster.
From the high trees they watched the dirty beheaded giant,
the rugged back, only the rugged breast vomiting anger.

We will abandon our country and our kin
because a sterile god has dominated our land.
Our people watched the mindless giant,
they heard the roar of the faceless force.

We will not live under the blind power's domination!
We will break our grinding stones,
        our earthen jugs
        the plates we cook on,
to lighten the load of the exiled!

Here, our footprints remained
        upon the ash.[18]

Cuadra's emphasis on his all-but-forgotten native ancestry,
represented here by the "footprints of those who fled from Acahualinca," and his ability to fuse that ancestry with the other
all-but-forgotten poor and oppressed of his day are what Merton
considered a "prophetic fusion of past and present." What resulted
in the poem was an enduring prophetic denunciation of oppressive
regimes of all times, regardless of circumstance or motivation.
Merton described this "eternal character" of Cuadra's poem as a
"very religious and solemn aspect" precisely because of the way it
bestows value on the vulnerable and oppressed, criticizes the op-
pressor, and uses imagery in a universally applicable way. Merton
employed this technique in many of his own prophetic writings on
peace and non-violence, most notably his poetic essay "A Letter to
Pablo Antonio Cuadra Concerning Giants."

[18] The translation by Stephen White is located at http://www.dariana
.com/Panorama/PAC_poemas-ingles-2.htm.

Written in early September 1961 at the height of Merton's writing on issues of justice and peace and shortly before the censors of his order forbade Merton to write any longer on the subject,[19] "A Letter to Pablo Antonio Cuadra Concerning Giants" draws from the prophet Ezekiel's figures of Gog and Magog (symbolizing the United States and Russia) to demonstrate the destructive course on which the two world powers had embarked. The so-called letter holds up Latin America—the "Third World"—as the hope for global renewal should Gog and Magog annihilate each other. Merton explained himself to Cuadra in a letter dated September 16, 1961:

> The piece is really an article, . . . and the giants in question are of course the big power blocs that are beginning to enter the final stages of the death struggle in which they will tear each other to pieces. Though the moment of supreme crisis may come quite suddenly and probably will, I do not think it is immediately near. But I think it is inevitable, unless there is some very remarkable intervention of Providence. Since I trust such intervention may take place, I see no reason for becoming desperate or even excited. However the sober facts seem to point to a nuclear war in the near future. Since there is at least a serious possibility of this, I felt that my position called for some kind of a statement of where I stand, morally, as a Christian writer.[20]

Merton addressed the letter to Pablo Antonio Cuadra for two reasons: first, since Cuadra was the editor of the newspaper *El Pez y La Serpiente*, Merton knew that his letter would probably receive a broad readership, and, second, he knew Cuadra would understand and appreciate its message, since he was writing in a similar vein on political issues in Nicaragua. Writing to Dona Luisa Coomaraswamy, Merton referred in passing to the reason that he

[19] "A Letter to Pablo Antonio Cuadra Concerning Giants" was first published in *Blackfriars* in February 1962 and later published in *Emblems of a Season of Fury* (New York: New Directions, 1963).
[20] Merton to Cuadra, September 16, 1961, in *Courage*, 189.

sent the letter to Cuadra: "This question of standing by while they prepare manipulations that could easily lead to the destruction of the human race is not my idea of honesty. Hence I feel that something must be said and I am starting in Latin America, where it may still be listened to."[21]

Like Cuadra, Merton was moved to use his influence and poetic abilities to bring to consciousness what seemed clear and logical to him. Yet he wrote his letter with such force that, upon considering its implications, he surprised even himself at its "bitter and unjust" tone. What resulted from his self-reflection, as he expressed it in his journal, was a revealing glimpse into the uncertainty and precariousness he saw in his own motivations. It also provides a further glimpse into his ability to question and critique himself: "This is the point. This weakness and petulancy, rooted in egoism, and which I have in common with other intellectuals in this country. Even after years in the monastery I have not toughened up and got the kind of fibre that is bred only by humility and self-forgetfulness. Or rather, though I had begun to get it, this writing job and my awareness of myself as a personage with definite opinions and with voice, has kept me sensitive and afraid on a level on which most monks long ago became indifferent."[22]

What Merton laments here is his own lack of ability to speak his conscience with wisdom and humility—without egoistic concern. Yet he knew that he had to speak. He struggled to acquire the ability to speak the truth *in love*, free from bitterness and hatred: "I am always too vehement. Bitterness can do no good at a time like this. There is too much senseless bitterness, too much hatred justified by a 'just cause,' too much hatred in the service of truth, even in the service of God. This is the great lie which the West seems unable to

[21] Merton to Dona Luisa Coomaraswamy, September 24, 1961, in Merton, *The Hidden Ground of Love: The Letters of Thomas Merton on Religious Experience and Social Concerns*, ed. William H. Shannon (New York: Farrar, Straus and Giroux, 1985), 132.

[22] Thomas Merton, *Turning Toward the World: The Pivotal Years*, ed. Victor A. Kramer, The Journals of Thomas Merton, vol. 4 (New York: Harper-Collins, 1996), 162.

see and now the East is learning to be far more blind and fanatical in their attachment to this lie than we have been" (*Turning*, 163). Merton is here articulating the desire of the monk, the desire for a pure heart from which to live and speak. He recognizes the dangers of prophetic utterance from a heart full of hate—one that demands justice yet is without mercy. He sees such a prophet as only an accomplice in the bitterness and hatred that he or she outwardly condemns. His answer to such a predicament? "So we continue to live and try to seek truth. Each must do so with courage and indefatigable patience, constantly discerning it from the obsessive fictions of the establishment everywhere."[23]

Prophetic Madness for a Mad World: The Original Intuition of Alfonso Cortés

In May 1962 Merton began translating poems of Alfonso Cortés (1893–1969),[24] the Nicaraguan poet who was known as "El Poeta Loco." Merton's compassion and admiration for the eccentric and disturbed poet are evident. In his introduction to his translations of Cortés, Merton recalls the incident in which "Cortes went mad one February night . . . in the house of the one Nicaraguan poet who has enjoyed a world-wide reputation: Rubén Darío."[25] Merton went on to explain how "Ernesto Cardenal, as a child, going to the school of the Christian Brothers in León, used to look in the door of Darío's house and see Cortes inside, chained to a beam" ("Alfonso Cortes," 311). Cortés remained in Darío's house for a number of years before being transferred to a hospital. Writing to Cardenal a few days after translating the Cortés poems, Merton commented on this newly discovered Nicaraguan poet: "I think he is a most absorbing and wonderful figure, in some sense prophetic."[26] To Cortés himself, Merton wrote, "You are as a matter of fact a poet

[23] Merton to Cuadra, August 1, 1963, in *Courage*, 191.
[24] Eleven poems originally appeared in *Emblems of a Season of Fury*.
[25] Thomas Merton, "Alfonso Cortes," in *Literary Essays*, 311–12, here 311.
[26] Merton to Cardenal, May 22, 1962, in *Courage*, 132.

to whom God has given a very original intuition, even in a prophetic sense."[27] The meaning of this "original intuition" and "prophetic sense" is revealed in four main sources: the introduction to
Merton's translations of Cortés's poetry, Cortés's poems themselves, Merton's correspondence with Cardenal, and Merton's own
poem "To Alfonso Cortes."

   In his introduction to his translations of the Cortés poems,
Merton states, "Cortes has written some of the most profound
'metaphysical' poetry that exists. He is obsessed with the nature
of reality, flashing with obscure intuitions of the inexpressible"
("Alfonso Cortes," 311). The poems that Merton admired most,
those written in Cortés's more lucid moments, were those that he
described as not only metaphysical but also "surrealistic, with a
deep, oneiric, and existentialist character of its own" ("Alfonso
Cortes," 311). Merton goes into greater detail about Cortés's sur-
realism in a letter to Cardenal:

> The thing that strikes me most about his poems . . . is
> his extraordinary ontological sense, his grasp of objective
> being. He is much more than a surrealist. Indeed he is the
> only true surrealist, for instead of going like them to the
> heart of a subjectivity which is at the same time all real
> and all unreal, he plunges to the heart of a transobjective
> subjectivity which is the purely real, and he expresses it in
> images as original and as eloquent as those of Blake. He
> is one of the most arresting poets of the twentieth century,
> and in my opinion certainly one of the very greatest. He
> really has something to say.[28]

   In Merton's view, this metaphysical plunge into one's own
"transobjective subjectivity" is a plunge into a dimension of reality
that is beyond space and time. It is glimpsing into the *point vierge*
where life bursts forth with incomprehensible energy. What Cortés
did with his poetry, Merton noted, was to reveal how "to live in
the full, bewildering, and timeless dimension of a life so shattering

---

[27] Merton to Cortés, April 20, 1965, in *Courage*, 177.
[28] Merton to Cardenal, May 22, 1962, in *Courage*, 132–33.

in its reality that it seems to be madness" ("Alfonso Cortes," 312). Cortés, the surrealist poet in search for ultimate reality (sur-reality), must, therefore, brace himself for this treacherous journey:

> Room of the guilty one
> Evil place of bad luck
> No presentiment of this
> Was possible,
> Now double your deathly terror,
> Lend thy attraction to my works,
> That my soul, thrust out of land and home,
> May not dread the king's torment.[29]

For Cortés, this journey was the journey of "Dirty Souls" in search of silence and stillness—of "vast essences which keep / Secrets of dreams in the enormous heart."[30] Cortés's concern for distance, space, and time and their place in the soul's journey toward the ultimately real are the main themes of both "Dirty Souls" and "Great Prayer." In these poems distance is seen as that which both separates and unites—a type of alluring quality that draws together precisely because it is apart:

> Between, above and under skies,
> The distance of which I tell you,
> Is the idea giving fragrance
> To subtle relationships, slab
> Stones,
>
> Silence,
> Stillness belonging to the soul of things![31]

---

[29] "Aegeus in Prison," in Merton, *Collected Poems*, 943. Poks explains that "The meditation on the king of Athens' sinister seclusion, an emblem of 'mad Alfonso's' own predicament, is meant as a preparation for the unforeseeable difficulties the poet will have to brave in the future in his poetic and spiritual adventure" (*Thomas Merton and Latin America*, 92).

[30] "Dirty Souls," in Merton, *Collected Poems*, 944.

[31] "Dirty Souls," in Merton, *Collected Poems*, 944.

In order to bask in this "idea giving fragrance," the soul must do two
things: pray and dream. These two functions of the soul resolve the
obstacle of distance and transcend the barriers of space and time:

> Time is hunger, space is cold
> Pray, pray, for prayer alone can quiet
> The anxieties of void.
> Dream is a solitary rock
> Where the soul's hawk nests:
> Dream, dream, during
> Ordinary life.[32]

The existential alienation of "the anxieties of void" that "prayer
alone" resolves is the soul's discovery of the truth. Hidden within
the "soul of things," the discovery of truth was for Cortés no simple
task in light of humankind's existential state:

> Fate is dead. God is in man
> What man is in God. Art caves in
> Upon itself. Truth is a name
> Reason a dilemma: all is a tomb.[33]

Poks contrasts Cortés's fateful proclamation in his opening
stanza to the "ravings" of the Nietzschean madman, saying they
have "nothing in common," yet she considers Cortés's judgment
to be "just as final and just as prophetic" (*Thomas Merton and Latin
America*, 105). For her they are both "proclaiming the same event"
(*Thomas Merton and Latin America*, 105). In her analysis of this opening stanza from "The Truth," she explains that the fatalistic idol of
life experienced as a void proves ultimately to be "a convenient
fiction with which to gloss over our failure to confront existential
freedom" (*Thomas Merton and Latin America*, 105). This stultify-
ing fear, she says, thus prevents humankind from traversing the
rough and scary terrains and "tombs" of its false reality in order to
find the truly real in the God within. According to Poks, Cortés's

---

[32] "Great Prayer," in Merton, *Collected Poems*, 944–45.
[33] "The Truth," in Merton, *Collected Poems*, 948.

"The Truth" presents "a declaration of liberation from slavery more authentic and profound than Nietzsche did" (*Thomas Merton and Latin America*, 105). The rest of the poem reads:

> The only law that centers you in virtue
> Prophet, wise man, artist, proletarian,
> Is mystery: if a womb is with child
> If a tree with fruit: if the sun is every day.
>
> No good more actual than the present now
> No good future better than
> Your good guess today,
> Work is more useful than the dawn;
> Stronger than destiny is pain.
>
> Ideals? For what, if they are dreams?
> Memories? What do they matter to what lies ahead?
> Future is half the past: an end
> Is what is every minute made real.[34]

"The Truth" is addressed to the "prophet, wise man, artist, proletarian," because these are the distinctive individuals who are able to grasp, through their marginalized perspective, the "mystery" in life's everyday experiences. It is a mystery longing to be known in "the present now." The truth is encountered not in "ideals" or "memories" but in "what is every minute made real." Reality is entered into in the simple ordinariness of "work" and in the pregnant possibilities of "pain." With "The Truth," Cortés becomes the spiritual director, guiding his readers by hand through the dark and dangerous pathways of unreality into the life-giving world of the present moment, bursting forth from within and all around.

Merton makes his affection and compassion for Cortés explicit in his own poem from *Emblems of a Season of Fury*, "To Alfonso Cortes." In it Merton addresses the mad poet as a "mad saint" whose personal eccentricities have caused onlookers to see only "droll" characteristics, leaving them in confusing dismay:

---

[34] "The Truth," in Merton, *Collected Poems*, 948.

> You stand before the dark
> Wet night of leaves
> In glasses and a witty hat
> With a tropical guitar,
> And the white crumpled
> Clothes of sugar countries.
> So droll, to be the mad
> Saint of a hot republic![35]

Noting the ironic perspective of these opening lines, Poks asks this insightful question: "Is it the point of view of the onlooker, who sees a personage in a 'witty hat' and appreciates the curious irony of fate that gives metaphysical insight to a deranged mind while denying it to the sane; or is it the opinion of Cortés, who, like a court jester, subverts the sham of official 'seriousness' with his wit and prophetic madness, and in his madness inexplicably, perhaps even unnoticeably, manages to outwit the wiser men and women?" (*Thomas Merton and Latin America*, 85). Indeed it is both. And Cortés offers no defense to his comical characterization but only an assured and optimistic smile:

> You smile in a mist of years
> Where your country has placed you
> To think about the paper
> You hold in your hand:
> For critical services
> At some unrecorded time
> The Nation awards you
> This empty room. ("To Alfonso Cortes," 356)

Merton here describes what he perceives as the unjust reaction that Nicaragua had to one of her most original visionaries. For his prophetic madness, Cortés is awarded "This empty room"—a permanent hospital cell. Yet to such a gesture Cortés offers no retali-

---

[35] All quotations from "To Alfonso Cortes" come from Merton, *Collected Poems*, 355–56.

atory response. His docility in the face of ill treatment and ridicule is Merton's way of relating him to the docile Jesus of Nazareth, who was likewise ridiculed and deemed a madman (John 10:20), thereby vindicating Cortés. The poem concludes:

> Have you noted in cryptograms
> Upon the tiny white leaf
> Some fortunate index,
> Some sign of the age?
>
> Or do you announce
> A central tumult
> Out of reach of their patrols?
>
> No, you stand still
> And you begin to smile
> As you read rainbows
> On the empty paper. ("To Alfonso Cortes," 356)

It was ultimately not a prophetic declaration of "Some fortunate index, / Some sign of the age," or the announcement of "A central tumult" that characterized Cortés's prophetic madness. Rather, it was the more authentic and truly saner prophetic response revealed in a simple smile and in the reading of "rainbows on the empty paper." Poks makes the connection between Cortés's smile here and Merton's illuminating experience before the smiling Buddhas at Polonnaruwa, where Merton experienced the world in which "all problems are resolved and everything is clear, simply because what matters is clear."[36] The prophetic message that Cortés's smile communicates, being much more potent than condemning and retaliating denunciation, is a message of prophetic hope—a hope arising from a penetrating intuition into spiritual realities.

---

[36] Thomas Merton, *The Other Side of the Mountain: The End of the Journey,* ed. Patrick Hart, The Journals of Thomas Merton, vol. 7 (New York: Harper Collins, 1998), 323. Quoted in Poks, *Thomas Merton and Latin America,* 87.

César Vallejo: "Prophet of Our Time and Our Hemisphere"[37]

Merton was first introduced to the Peruvian poet César Vallejo (1892–1938) by Pablo Antonio Cuadra sometime in 1958. Four years later, in 1962, Merton wrote the novelist Henry Miller telling of his work on translating some of Vallejo's poems: "As for translations, I am translating bits of César Vallejo, who is to me a most significant and meaningful voice, and moves me most deeply, probably because of his Indian resonances. He is the greatest of all the great South American poets we have had in this century, I think."[38]

Four of these translations appeared the following year in *Emblems of a Season of Fury*: "Anger," "Black Stone on Top of a White Stone," "Estais Muertos," and "Peace, the Wasp." Merton's affection and admiration for Vallejo continued in the upcoming years. To Margaret Randall, in a letter of January 1963, Merton described Vallejo as "the poet of our century who seems to have the most to say."[39]

Later that year, Merton began a lasting correspondence with Clayton Eshleman, who was also working on translations of Vallejo's poetry. Merton's initial letter to Eshleman contained his first thorough consideration of Vallejo's significance. Because Vallejo was not easily accessible, Merton took special joy in learning of Eshleman's interest in Vallejo and quipped, "I think all the poets in America could translate Vallejo and not begin to get him."[40]

The reason for Merton's high esteem for Vallejo appeared in his statement that Vallejo "is the most universal, Catholic in that sense (the only real sense), poet of this time, the most Catholic and universal of all modern poets, the only poet since (Who? Dante?) who is anything like Dante."[41] Expounding on Vallejo's universal, Catholic, identity, Merton explains, "So what I mean is that Vallejo

[37] Merton to Von Balthasar, August 7, 1964, in *The School of Charity: The Letters of Thomas Merton on Religious Renewal and Spiritual Direction*, ed. Patrick Hart (New York: Farrar, Straus and Giroux, 1990), 227.

[38] Merton to Miller, August 7, 1962, in *Courage*, 276.

[39] Merton to Randall, January 15, 1963, in *Courage*, 215.

[40] Merton to Eshleman, June 1963, in *Courage*, 254.

[41] Merton to Eshleman, June 1963, in *Courage*, 254.

is totally human, as opposed to our zombie poets and our little girl poets and our incontinents. I have never really thought out all that must begin to be said about Vallejo, but he is tremendous and extraordinary, a huge phenomenon."[42] In contrast to the poets of North America, with whom Merton had little affinity and, here, spoke pejoratively, he described Vallejo as the consummate humanist precisely because he was alive—an awakened voice with something meaningful to say—and not like a "dead body moved by evil spirits,"[43] speaking excessive and thoughtless pleasantries.

In the same letter to Eshleman, Merton drew a comparison between Vallejo and the popular Chilean poet Pablo Neruda, saying that Vallejo was "so much more magnificent . . . precisely because he is in every way poorer. No matter what they do with Vallejo, they can never get him into anybody's establishment (Neruda walked in very easy without giving the slightest trouble.)."[44] Herein lies Vallejo's significance in Merton's mind, and the importance of his and Eshleman's translations. Vallejo's uniqueness is found, in a way similar to Cortés's, in his commitment to his own vision of reality amidst the many illusions of mass society. Thus not only was this work of translation a worthy project in and of itself, but it was also a project "of very great and urgent importance for the human race."[45] Vallejo's unusual ability to remain centered in the truly real led Merton to describe him as "a great eschatological poet, with a profound sense of the end (and yet of the new beginnings that he does not talk about). All the others are running around setting off firecrackers and saying it is a national holiday or emergency or something. Or just lolling around in a tub of silly words."[46]

Here Merton reveals his own proclivity for an eschatological vision of reality. Not everyone would see in Vallejo's poetry a

---

[42] Merton to Eshleman, June 1963, in *Courage*, 254–55.

[43] Merton to Sr. M. Emmanuel, in *Hidden Ground*, 200. This is a definition of *zombie* that Merton gives to Sr. M. Emmanuel, after which he explains his use of the term in his writings: "The expression 'zombie' in my books refers to the alienated, stupid, bourgeois or other mass-man."

[44] Merton to Eshleman, in *Courage*, 255.

[45] Merton to Eshleman, in *Courage*, 255.

[46] Merton to Eshleman, in *Courage*, 255.

vision of life fulfilled. Vallejo's penchant for originality and total commitment to meaningful communication was, for Merton, the great soteriological endeavor that would triumph over the meaninglessness and impotent communication of mass society. Vallejo substantiated for Merton that the poetic word can save.

Merton again expressed his love for Vallejo in a letter to the Cuban poet Cintio Vitier, further developing his views on Vallejo's prophetic and eschatological significance: "I think that an understanding and love of Vallejo, this Inca and Prophet, is the key to the deep realization of the problems and predicaments of the two Americas today."[47] Merton's letter to Vitier again highlighted both his esteem for the poetry of Latin America and his criticism of the poetry of the United States. The hope for true poetic creativity, in Merton's estimation, belonged to the poets of the Southern Hemisphere, "all gathered around Vallejo as around its deepest center and as a kind of source of life."[48] Latin American poetry, he said, "tends to be more personal and more prophetic than that of the U.S. while at the same time speaking for 'the people' more than the individualist and sometimes hermetic subjectivism of the U.S. poets."[49]

Shortly after sending this letter to Vitier in May of 1964, Merton expressed similar sentiments to Hans Urs von Balthasar: "Vallejo is certainly, in a very obscure way, a prophet of our time and our hemisphere. A witness of our misery and confusion. He is the Incas' version of Baudelaire, and so simple."[50] What Baudelaire did for nineteenth-century Paris in exposing individual and societal moral complexities along with the vices that accompanied a decadent culture, Merton thought, Vallejo did for his own people. Implicit within this comparison with Baudelaire may also be found a reference to the prophetic use of symbols. Baudelaire is known for his use of sound and symbol to create atmosphere and add layered meaning to images used in his poetry. Merton saw Peruvian poetry as possessing similar characteristics. As he had already noted in his preface

---

[47] Merton to Vitier, May 26, 1964, in *Courage*, 239.
[48] Merton to Vitier, May 26, 1964, in *Courage*, 239.
[49] Merton to Vitier, May 26, 1964, in *Courage*, 239.
[50] Merton to von Balthasar, Aug. 7, 1964, in *School*, 227.

to the Argentine edition of his *Complete Works*, he wrote, "It seems that I hear in the even more profound silence of Peru the forgotten syllables of ancient wisdom which has never died and which contains in its secrets an image of truth that no man has recognized, an image, symbolic and prophetic, like that of Jesus Christ."[51]

It was poets like Vallejo, Merton thought, who had begun giving voice to these "forgotten syllables of ancient wisdom." These symbolic and prophetic sounds caught his attention, and he noted them in the poems he translated. Vallejo's use of the theme of death in "Black Stone on Top of a White Stone" and "Estais Muertos" serves as an example to illustrate Merton's insights into the symbolic and prophetic nature of Vallejo's poetry.

The opening stanza of "Black Stone on Top of a White Stone" expresses the poem's starkness and sobriety. Yet it also contains a sense of peaceful resignation:

> I shall die in Paris, in a rainstorm,
> On a day I already remember.
> I shall die in Paris—it does not bother me—
> Doubtless on a Thursday, like today, in autumn.[52]

This is Vallejo's own embrace of his personal mortality. He is confronted with the reality of his own existence and is somehow able to be at complete peace with it. In these lines, Poks notes, "The poet's voice is calm and prophetic; the vision of suffering and unbearable loneliness accepted with, one might almost say, *sancta indifferentia*" (*Thomas Merton and Latin America*, 209). Vallejo's resignation toward death continues in the final two stanzas:

> It shall be a Thursday, because today, Thursday
> As I put down these lines, I have set my shoulders
> To the evil. Never like today have I turned
> And headed my whole journey to the ways where I am
>   alone.

[51] Thomas Merton, "Preface to the Argentine Edition of *The Complete Works of Thomas Merton*," in Merton, *Honorable Reader*, 40.

[52] All quotations from Vallejo's "Black Stone on Top of White Stone" come from Merton, *Collected Poems*, 1000.

> César Vallejo is dead. They struck him,
> All of them, though he did nothing to them.
> They hit him hard with a stick and hard also
> With the end of a rope. Witnesses are: the Thursdays,
> The shoulder bones, the loneliness, the rain and the
>   roads . . .

Merton's reference to Vallejo's being "in every way poorer" than Neruda is substantiated in these lines. Vallejo, standing proxy for all humankind, has no option but death. This existential awareness is an opportunity for identification with Christ's own humble obedience and submission to the Father's will. Like Christ's, such submission need not be an occasion of despair. Rather, Vallejo's resignation and faith are evident in his subtle use of time. Vallejo steps outside of time, having "already remembered" the fateful moment of his death. Poks observes, "This prophetic memory of the future is but a distillation of a lifetime of Passion Thursdays already endured, a summary experience refined to a point of white heat by the particular Thursday when the poem is being written" (*Thomas Merton in Latin America*, 210). She also sees Vallejo's use of time as a way of transcending the linear and historical plane and argues that in so doing, he makes himself "out to be a quintessential monk" (*Thomas Merton in Latin America*, 210). It is the life of the monk whose mystical identification in Christ, in a peculiar way, embodies Paul's verse from Colossians: "For you have died, and your life is hidden with Christ in God" (Col 3:3). It is precisely the monk's living death that is a sign of eschatological hope: "When Christ your life appears, then you too will appear with him in glory" (Col 3:4).

"Estais Muertos" continues the theme of humankind's existential stance before death. Vallejo again deals with his subject matter of factly:

> You people are dead.
> What a strange manner of being dead. Anyone might say
>   that
> you were not.
> But, in truth, you are dead.

You float like nothing behind that membrane which, suspended from zenith to nadir, comes and goes from dusk
to dusk, trembling in front of the sonorous box of a wound
which to you is painless. Well, I assure you that life is in
the mirror and that you are the original: death.[53]

Here Vallejo assumes the voice of the prophet, boldly declaring
what no one wants to hear: the news that the life being lived may
have no metaphysical basis in reality. The prophet warns against
false hope, which would assuage the reality of the human condition, that of nothingness, and insists emphatically on the need to
come face to face with "the original." It is only at such a point that
authentic living begins:

While the wave goes and while the wave comes, with what
impunity one can be dead! Only when the waters swell and
break on the shores in front of them, and when the waves
pile one on top of the other, then you transfigure yourselves
and, imagining you are about to die, you discover the sixth
string which does not belong to you.[54]

The discovery of "the sixth string" is the discovery of humankind's only hope—divine grace. It is the discovery of the Other,
which is so deep within that it can only be grasped through the
pulverizing pressures of our annihilation. For Poks, it is a type of
"sixth sense" that is able to perceive these inner depths as well as
an echo of the "sixth day of creation," which awakens humankind
to its original image (*Thomas Merton and Latin America*, 213). Yet the
extent of death's hold on life is brought out in the following stanza:

You are dead, never having at any time before this been
alive. Anyone might think that since you do not exist now,
you might have existed at some other time. But in truth
you are the cadavers of a life that never was. Pathetic fate,
never to have been anything at any time, but only dead! To

---

[53] All quotations from "Estais Muertos" come from Merton, *Collected Poems*, 1000–1001.

[54] The final stanzas of this poem were printed as prose.

be a dry leaf without ever at any time having been a green one. Orphaned beyond all other orphans!

Human life left to itself knows no experience of authentic living. There is, therefore, no past experience on which to draw to guide one out of the tomb of life as those who are living know it. Past notions of peace and joy and happiness are only fabrications of life—illusions that keep humankind fastened to the grave. The prophet speaks one more emphatic mortal cry:

> Yet for all that the dead are not, and cannot be, cadavers of a life they have not lived. They have forever died of life.
>
> You are dead.

The final word is spoken and the casket lid is sealed. What about "the sixth string?" Does hope in the end die in despair? Not necessarily. According to Poks, "This hope . . . while not denied, must remain suspended, like the figurative membrane, between the dusk of *arché* and that of *télos*, while 'aliveness' itself remains in the grave, reduced to the state of ontological silence" (*Thomas Merton and Latin America*, 214). This is the state of humankind before God: lifelessness. The only possible way out of the tomb is through divine intervention. Vallejo, the prophet, echoing the great Pauline themes of faith, grace, and human corruption, proclaims the despised message of true liberation.

Concluding Remarks

Thomas Merton's love and affection for Latin America and her poets is a recurring theme in the writings of his final decade. This theme is particularly evident in his prolific correspondence with many of the creative writers from the Southern Hemisphere. These letters reveal the struggles he had in identifying himself with the poetic community of the United States, saying time and time again how much more he felt in sympathy with the spirit and creative impulses of Central and South America than with those of North America.

The relationship with Ernesto Cardenal exposed Merton to these creative impulses, which he would come to say bore a particular "prophetic quality." This prophetic quality, which he first saw in Cardenal himself, revealed itself in simple and authentic living, in a life more impressed by the deep and forgotten sounds of wisdom of America's ancient civilizations than by the "raucous and false" noises of Westernization and technological advance. For the same reasons he also considered Cardenal's cousin, Pablo Antonio Cuadra, to be a prophetic writer. Cuadra saw value in those threatened sounds of wisdom and gave voice to them in his poetry. *El Jaguar y la luna* and "Written on a Roadside Stone During the First Eruption" are both examples of Cuadra's ability to wed past and present in a prophetic fusion that critiques current injustices while offering a remedy to humankind's waywardness, found precisely in the lessons of America's ancestors that Cuadra espoused. Merton follows suit in his "Letter to Pablo Antonio Cuadra Concerning Giants," offering a blistering critique of the arrogance and greed of the unbridled nationalism of his day. This poetic essay is a fine example of Merton's prophetic writings on peace and non-violence.

Merton's correspondence with "El Poeta Loco," Alfonso Cortés, reveals how Merton saw in Cortés's madness a peculiar prophetic revelation that shines when one touches the really real. Knowing this "original intuition" or "transobjective subjectivity," Merton held, is knowing "the Truth" and requires great stamina and self-assurance in the face of ridicule, since this Truth appears as madness to those living in the falsities of a fabricated existence. This spiritual journey, he explained, is traversed in the vessel of faith and imagination whose compass is the really real, revealing itself in the present moment.

The really real is also the central theme of the poetry of César Vallejo. Vallejo, to whom Merton referred as "Inca and Prophet," earned Merton's highest affection and admiration. Vallejo, in Merton's estimation, had solved the problems of the Americas, because he more than any other poet wrote in a way that exposed the deep vapidity and confusion of modern America. By his sophisticated use of symbolic and prophetic imagery, Vallejo pierced through the crusted obfuscations of America's delusional tendencies. His poetry, Merton further said, pointed toward an eschatological existence that is only accessible by coming face to face with the reality of one's illusory existence.

From this examination of what Merton describes as the prophetic elements in Latin American poetry, as well as through an analysis of some of the poems of Pablo Antonio Cuadra, Alfonso Cortés, and César Vallejo, to all of whom Merton repeatedly refers as prophetic, three major themes arise. First, Merton understood poetry as having a unique "prophetic quality" because its symbolic language and imagery can reveal the hidden wisdom of the past and use it both to critique and to offer perspective to contemporary situations. A type of listening—an attentive ear—is therefore required to grasp this hidden wisdom. Second, the attentive ear of the Latin American poets was developed through their intentional, simple, and authentic living. Thus, Merton concluded that the prophetic spirit was characterized by a singularity of focus on the most real, a focus that provides the capacity to see through superficial and dehumanizing tendencies and allows the freedom to write from a place of radical truth. Third, the "prophetic quality" of poetry is soteriological and eschatological in nature in that it bears within itself the capacity to heal, save, and reveal a saner and more just existence for humankind. James Joyce's *A Portrait of the Artist as a Young Man*, which had a significant influence on Merton, says it this way: *Contrahit orator, variant in carmine vates.*[55] These three prophetic qualities of poetry can be read as explications of Merton's definition of a poem: "any piece of writing or spoken utterance which, in symbolic and rhythmic language, seeks to communicate a deep and direct experience of life in some aspect or other. A poem however cannot be confined to mere teaching, nor is it necessarily 'inspirational' or even serious. It must however in some way or other strive to be more memorable and more challenging than mere prose."[56]

---

[55] James Joyce, *A Portrait of the Artist as a Young Man* (1916; New York: Washington Square Press, 1998), 168. The translation provided by the edition reads, "The orator summarizes, the poet or prophet transforms." The influence of *A Portrait of the Artist as a Young Man* on Merton's conversion is chronicled in *The Seven Storey Mountain*, 211–12.

[56] Merton to Jan Boggs, Feb. 9, 1966, in Merton, *The Road to Joy: The Letters of Thomas Merton to New and Old Friends*, ed. Robert E. Daggy (New York: Farrar, Straus and Giroux, 1989), 338.

Chapter 3

The Prophetic Spirituality
of "Message to Poets"

The poets have much to say and do: they have the same mission as the prophets in the technical world. They have to be the conscious-ness of the revolutionary man because they have the keys of the subconscious and of the great secrets of real life.[1]

—Thomas Merton

Background

The occasion for Merton's "Message to Poets" was a gathering of the new emerging Latin American poets, along with a few young North Americans, in Mexico City in February 1964. The gathering came about out of a shared vision and love for poetry and the need for solidarity and mutual encouragement among these young, highly visionary people seeking inspiration in poetic expression. It crystalized spontaneously through the initiative of mostly poor poets from throughout the hemisphere. Merton reported that one attendee, for instance, "sold her piano to make the trip from Peru."[2] Miguel Grinberg, one of Merton's Latin American correspondents, invited Merton to attend, presumably for the purpose of addressing

[1] Merton to Ludovico Silva, April 27, 1967, in Thomas Merton, *The Courage for Truth: The Letters of Thomas Merton to Writers*, ed. Christine M. Bochen (New York: Farrar, Straus and Giroux, 1993), 230.

[2] Thomas Merton, "Message to Poets," in *The Literary Essays of Thomas Merton*, ed. Patrick Hart (New York: New Directions, 1981), 371–74. A "Message to Poets" was originally published in excerpts in *The Americas*, April 16, 1964, but was subsequently published in full in *Raids on the Unspeakable* (New York: New Directions, 1966), 371–74, here 371.

the group and offering them affirmation and encouragement in their creative endeavors. Because Merton was not allowed to attend, he wrote a "Message to Poets." This opportunity allowed Merton to express his heartfelt solidarity with the poetic impulses he saw budding in these young Latin American writers. At the heart of his "Message" is the necessity that the poet acquire a prophetic spirit, which he felt was required for a poet to speak anything meaningful to the modern world.

Merton's "Message" should be read as prophetic literature employing both words of warning and words of exhortation. In opposition to the "calculating" and "magical" use of language arising from a "collective" life that relies on "arbitrary values without life and meaning" is the life of "innocence," where life is experienced in immediacy yielding creative insights that help the human person penetrate through the "illusory measurements men build" and embrace a more authentic existence. As Patrick O'Connell summarizes, "He calls on the poets . . . to prophesy, by which he means to bring out the hidden meaning beneath the surface of everyday life. He calls for words that seek not to persuade but to point toward the silence beyond words. He encourages the poets to accept their marginality, the insecurity and abjection of a 'dervish' existence, and concludes by urging them to strip away all secondhand ideas for the sake of the immediacy of an experience of the 'water of life.'"[3]

Merton's twofold goal in this essay was to establish his solidarity with the poetic community of Latin America and to introduce his view of the phenomenological dynamism of poetic creativity. He accomplished this goal in his opening sentences: "We who are poets know that the reason for a poem is not discovered until the poem itself exists. The reason for a living act is realized only in the act itself. This meeting is a spontaneous explosion of hopes" ("Message," 371). Poetry happens, he wrote, as an effect of living. It is an unfolding of life itself in poetic expression. In this sense, it

---

[3] Patrick F. O'Connell, "Theory of Poetry," in *The Thomas Merton Encyclopedia*, ed. William H. Shannon, et al. (Maryknoll, NY: Orbis Books, 2002), 360–63, here 362–63.

can be deduced that, for Merton, poetry writes itself. Living spontaneously is thus a prerequisite for writing meaningful poetry. Such spontaneity, he said, was the cause of the "spontaneous explosion of hopes" that had assembled this poetic community. Merton's description of the gathering as "a venture in prophetic poverty" refers to the spiritual impulse at work in drawing a group of like-minded artists with meager monetary resources together to explore the possibilities of their common vocation. Such an impulse is prophetic because it reveals "a living expression of the belief that there are now in our world new people, new poets who are not in tutelage to established political systems or cultural structures—whether communist or capitalist—but who dare to hope in their own vision of reality and of the future" ("Message," 371).

Merton thus saw the prophetic spirit of the poet as one guided by countercultural principles and motivations. Poets, he said, find their source of life in something other than the status quo, and these poets had heard an original message and were fired with the need to make it known. The fire of this spiritual impulse, Merton argued, was their common bond. He referred to that impulse as the "Spirit of Life," which he said had gathered these poets together because of having something to say to them—something they could not hear in their own isolation. Merton's idea of prophetic activity here was thus communal in orientation, with the voice of the "Spirit" discerned in the midst of the gathered community open to the spontaneity of this creative "Spirit."

The body of Merton's "Message" is an exposition of the contrasting voices he introduces in the first paragraph, namely, the voice of the "Spirit of Life" with the voice of what he will call "collective life."[4] By pitting one against the other, he brings the prophetic voice of the "Spirit of Life" into clearer focus.

---

[4] Merton's use of the term *collective* is extensive. It first appears in his journal entry of May 6, 1949. This phrase from D. S. Savage highlights the intimate relationship Merton saw between poetry and prophecy fifteen years before he wrote his "Message to Poets": "It seems inherently probable that in his isolation from the mass society (reference to reaction against the Whitman-Vachel Lindsay tradition in verse) the American poet, forced

In contrast to the solidarity of the poets brought together by living in the spontaneity of the "Spirit of Life," Merton argued, "collective life" gathers together through planned, tactical convictions or matters of policy, "since these are affairs of prejudice, cunning, and design" ("Message," 371). The life of the poet, on the other hand, is characterized by "innocence." Such "innocence" is a result of living in fidelity to "*life* rather than to artificial systems" ("Message," 372). Merton likens living innocently to the sunlight, seasons, and rain: "It is something that cannot be organized, it can only happen. It can only be 'received.' It is a gift to which we must remain open" ("Message," 372). The poet must always stand guard against the seeds of doubt "collective life" seeks to sow, since it is through such doubt that "innocence" is lost. How does the poet stand guard against such seeds of doubt? Through faith, since "all innocence is a matter of belief" ("Message," 372). By keeping steadfastly open to life "in the spirit," the poet assures himself or herself

---

back into his interior life, will be led to discover the reality of the individual and the relevance of the metaphysical-religious perspectives which open up when the individual existence, and not the collective being of society, is taken as the central point of reference for the adventure of human experience. *And he may as poet, prophet and seer open a way for the eventual transformation of the quality of American life from within.* Such a transformation will depend upon the reversal of the current of modern life: that is to say upon the subordination of civilization to culture, and of culture to the inner life and destiny of man in relation to the metaphysical absolute. It will be a religious transformation." See *Entering the Silence: Becoming a Monk and a Writer,* ed. Jonathan Montaldo, The Journals of Thomas Merton, vol. 2 (New York: Harper Collins, 1996), 309. Merton continued to use the term *collective* throughout his journals in order to contrast the consciousness of the status quo with a contemplative consciousness. He often uses the term *collective* in association with descriptions of "personality" (*Entering the Silence,* 381), "corruption" (*A Search for Solitude,* 197–98), "judgments" (*A Search for Solitude,* 341), "immorality" (*A Search for Solitude,* 341), "sin" (*A Search for Solitude,* 341), "illusions" (*Turning toward the World,* 86, 299), "obsession" (*Turning toward the World,* 117), "authority" (*Turning toward the World,* 343), "will" (*Dancing in the Water of Life,* 92), "power" (*Dancing in the Water of Life,* 92), "might" (*Dancing in the Water of Life,* 92), and "myths" (*Dancing in the Water of Life,* 225).

of staying in tune with the Spirit's voice despite the cacophony of distracting noises sounding from "collective" society.

Merton also argued that collective life contributed to the formation of "illusory measurements" built by a world with "arbitrary values without life and meaning, full of sterile agitation" ("Message," 372). It becomes the task of the poet in the face of such "illusory measurements" and "metaphysical doubt" to "denounce," "remain united against," "refuse," and "reject" all that is contrary to the pure voice of the Spirit. The poet must never treat the "collective" mind as a validly contrary alternative—it is pure illusion and must be exposed as such, since it has no metaphysical basis in reality.

In context, Merton compared the poet to a monk. Remaining outside the categories of the "collective" mind is the monk's common vocation and prophetic task. Such opposition will not be understood by the collective mind. Collective consciousness only understands itself—only what "they themselves have decreed" ("Message," 373). Such self-understanding is not because people are simply ignorant and lazy slaves to their own limited perspective, but because "they are crafty ones who weave words about life and then make life conform to what they themselves have declared" ("Message," 373). Such "word-magic" can be interpreted as a type of false prophecy, an impure form of language coming from an impure spirit, deliberately unintelligible, which appeals to the vulnerable will. The poet's responsibility in the face of such false prophecy is not "derision" but true prophecy. It is in contrast to this idea of "word-magic" or false prophecy that Merton shares his thoughts on his meaning of true prophecy.

It is clear that Merton was aware of the various meanings attached to the word *prophecy*, as well as of its various functions.[5] On more than one occasion in his writings he dismissed the facile understanding of prophecy as prediction. Rather, the function of prophecy in his "Message to Poets" is more in line with the biblical

[5] See tapes from his novitiate conferences, *Life and Prophecy* (TM9) and *The Prophets* (A4520 and A4521). *The Prophets* was given in July of 1962. The date of *Life and Prophecy* is unknown. Both were published by Credence.

tradition of the Hebrew prophets, a tradition in which he had himself been immersed for many years before 1964. Like the Hebrew prophets, Merton's prophet is one inspired not to predict but "to seize upon reality in its moment of highest expectation and tension toward the new" ("Message," 373). "Reality" here, for Merton, is alive, dynamic, and filled with spiritual vitality. It seeks to reveal itself in an ever-evolving thrust toward the future. It is the bearer of eschatological hope. It is in the voice of the prophet that "reality" finds its resolve from built-up tension. The prophet here becomes the pregnant mother giving birth to a "new" reality. The prophet's task, therefore, is to "seize" on this moment of birth. To "seize" implies the active participation of the prophet in the birthing process. Merton saw the prophet not simply as the passive conduit through which the Spirit speaks. Rather, he or she conveys something more organic. It can be inferred that the prophet is like one who sings in harmony with the melody of God's new song resounding from within his or her own inner, creative resources.

Merton goes on to point out that this tension is a matter of discovery, not "in hypnotic elation but in the light of everyday existence" ("Message," 373). He also here dismisses the notion of prophecy as the ecstatic utterance of those caught up in a spiritual frenzy.[6] Merton's "prophet," rather, has both feet firmly planted on the ground of "reality." This process of "discovery," which is the responsibility of the prophet, is the contemplative dimension of the prophetic process. The poet must develop a contemplative awareness through which he or she sees the unfolding of reality as it reveals itself in the pregnant moments of everyday life. Those caught up in "hypnotic elation," he said, are too prone to be thwarted by the illusory impulses of humanity's fallen nature to be able to see reality in its pure form—to hear its unalloyed message. The "innocence" of the poet protects him or her from imposing a personal version of reality on the Reality of the unfolding "Spirit of Life."

---

[6] See *Life and Prophecy*. Here Merton contrasts the classical prophets with the *nabi*, those prophets who prophesied through ecstatic frenzies, referring to Jeremiah's critical lament over such prophets in Jeremiah 23.

Merton understood a poem as the culmination of the "Spirit's" prophetic thrust—it is the prophecy. It is not prediction, because "it is itself the fulfillment of all the momentous predictions hidden in everyday life" ("Message," 373). It is, rather, "the flowering of ordinary possibilities" ("Message," 373). Prophecy, for Merton, is thus the natural climax of those in tune with reality. With poetry, "it is the fruit of ordinary and natural choice" ("Message," 373).[7] It is these fruits born through the obedience of poets to the Spirit of Life that will "calm the resentments and the rage of man" ("Message," 373).

Merton expands his emphasis on the spirituality of the poet as one living in the ordinary immediacy of everyday life as he writes about the non-persuasive nature of poetry. Writing poetry is an apophatic endeavor, he said. It points "beyond all objects into the silence where nothing can be said" ("Message," 374). Poetry, he implies, arises out of silence and moves back into silence. Its function, if it can be said to have one, is to move the reader into silence, not the silence of a lifeless void but the fecund silence of the Spirit of Life. This poetry leading into silence is prophetic because it is a cure to "all victims of absurdity who lie dying of a contrived joy" ("Message," 374). It exposes falsity, illusion, and superficiality. Merton reveals his affinity for Sufism with an analogy: "Let us then recognize ourselves for who we are: dervishes mad with secret therapeutic love which cannot be bought or sold, and which the politician fears more than violent revolution, for violence changes nothing. But love changes everything" ("Message," 374).

Merton also explains the poet as the voice of healing love that heals the contrivances and distortions of the "politician" through authentic and humble expressions of truth. Paradoxically, such "innocent" expressions "are stronger than the bomb" ("Message," 374). Although a poet's life is often characterized, like the dervish's, by "insecurity and abjection," the "nobility" and prophetic power

---

[7] Although Merton at times used the terms *prophecy* and *poetry* interchangeably, he never explicitly equated them. He seemed to believe that poetry was very compatible with prophetic expression but not to hold that all poetry is prophetic in nature.

of its marginalized existence is found in the embrace of his or her own integrity.

By discussing the apophatic, non-persuasive nature of poetry just after the prophetic nature of poetry, an approach that would normally be considered persuasive, Merton seems to contradict himself. Does he? The answer to the question depends on whether Merton actually considered the prophetic nature of poetry to be intentionally persuasive or not. In other words, did Merton believe that the poet writes poetry to effect change in people, or is such an effect a natural one of his or her fidelity to living open to the Spirit of Life as a poet? Although he did not state the answer to this question within his "Message to Poets," he seems to favor the latter view both in allusions within his "Message" and in other works.

What is certain, however, is Merton's assertion that the vocation of both the poet and the prophet is rooted in contemplative living. Poetry and prophecy are, thus, as was stated before, "the flowering of ordinary possibilities" and "the fruit of ordinary and natural choice" ("Message," 373).[8] The comment that immediately follows, "This is its innocence and dignity," reveals something particular about Merton's approach to both poetry and prophecy. One could argue that it is precisely in their non-coercive humility and "innocence" that the words of the prophetic poet become persuasive.

The metaphorical antithesis between Plato and Heraclitus that concludes the essay reveals Merton's deep affinity for the philosopher of vitality and change, as well as his skepticism about technological innovators who pride themselves with the thought that their ideas "run the world" but really lead only to "banalities and abstractions" ("Message," 373). His solution to the ideas of these "technological Platos" was living in the immediacy of Heraclitus's vital ever-moving river of life. Heraclitus thus became for Merton the symbolic figure whose approach to life most completely characterized the poet's (as well as the prophet's) proper consciousness and subjective orientation. In Heraclitus, he said, was immediacy,

---

[8] The non-persuasive nature of Merton's idea of prophecy also corresponds with his approach to ecumenical dialogue at this time in his life.

innocence, openness, humility, vitality, creativity, possibility, hope, spirit. As Merton put it, "He was one of those rare spirits whose prophetic insight enabled them to see far beyond the limited horizons of their society."[9] While most people ridiculed Heraclitus, he was one who "preferred loneliness to the warm security of their collective illusion" ("Herikleitos," 266).

Merton summed up his view of the contemplative, poetic, prophetic vocation of Heraclitus in his 1960 essay, "Herakleitos the Obscure":

> The aristocratic contempt of Herakleitos for the conventional verbalizing of his fellow citizens was something other than a pose, or a mad reflex of wounded sensibility. It was a prophetic manifestation of intransigent honesty. He refused to hold his peace and spoke out with angry concern for truth. He who had seen "the One" was no longer permitted to doubt, to hedge, to compromise, and to flatter. To treat his intuition as one among many opinions would have been inexcusable. False humility was an infidelity to his deepest self and a betrayal of the fundamental insights of his life. It would have been above all a betrayal of those whom he could not effectively contact except by the shock of paradox. Herakleitos took the same stand as Isaias, who was commanded by God to "blind the eyes of this people" by speaking to them in words that were too simple, too direct, too uncompromising to be acceptable. It is not given to men of compromise to understand parables, for as Herakleitos remarked: "When the things that are right in front of them are pointed out to them, they do not pay attention, though they think they do."
>
> This is the tragedy which most concerns Herakleitos—and which should concern us even more than it did him: the fact that the majority of men think they see, and do not. They believe they listen, but they do not hear. They are

---

[9] Thomas Merton, "Herakleitos the Obscure," in *A Thomas Merton Reader*, ed. Thomas P. McDonnell (Garden City, NY: Image Books, 1974), 258–71, here 258.

"absent when present" because in the act of seeing and hearing they substitute the clichés of familiar prejudice for the new and unexpected truth that is being offered to them. They complacently imagine they are receiving a new light, but in the very moment of apprehension they renew their obsession with the old darkness, which is so familiar that it, and it alone, appears to them to be light.[10]

In invoking Heraclitus as the exemplary symbol of the contemplative, prophetic poet, Merton, as this passage shows, touches on a number of common themes that appear in many of his works on the prophetic nature of poetry. These two paragraphs from "Herakleitos the Obscure" reveal seven aspects of Merton's views about poetry. First, the prophetic poet bears contempt for "conventional verbalizing." The "prophetic manifestation of intransigent honesty," which he said was the poet's justifiable response in the face of such "conventional verbalizing," demonstrates his insistence on the poet's deep devotion to linguistic honesty and meaningfulness. The prophetic poet always speaks the truth; indeed, he or she even speaks with "angry concern for truth." Second, the prophetic poet has a contemplative awareness of "the One." He or she "sees," "intuits," and has "insight." Merton frequently uses such words to describe the contemplative gaze required of the prophetic poet. It is the single way in which the prophet and poet hear what God is revealing. Third, the prophetic poet has an uncompromising commitment to the revelation of God. The intuition received from God is not simply "one among many opinions." There is no room for "false humility," since a denial of God's message would entail a denial of one's "deepest self and a betrayal of the fundamental insights of his life." Fourth, the prophetic poet uses paradox to shock the hearer into the awareness of a new reality. This parabolic technique plays on the expectation of the hearer, as the poet uses symbol, story, and imagination to expand the hearer's consciousness from the constrictions of limited perspective.

---

[10] Merton, "Herakleitos," 264–65. "Herakleitos the Obscure" first appeared in *Jubilee* in September of 1960.

This idea leads to the fifth point: Merton often uses examples from the Hebrew prophets to support his ideas about the nature of prophetic poetry. Here his reference to Isaiah serves to illustrate his previous points and leads to the sixth point, namely, that the "majority of men," the "collective life" of his "Message," are given to illusion: "they think they see, and do not." More than that, their illusion becomes delusion as they seek to justify themselves in the face of "the new and unexpected truth that is being offered to them." And this position, finally, leads to the seventh point, the conscious (and at times unconscious) motivations that the "majority of men" use to justify remaining in their own delusions. They are enslaved to the "familiar" and prefer their enslavement above change and liberation.

In summary, the prerequisite of Heraclitean-influenced prophetic poetry is for the poet to develop a contemplative awareness of God. The function of such a poet is to speak the truth unflinchingly, to liberate from illusion, to expand the hearer's consciousness, to make life more authentic and meaningful.

Chapter 4

Prophetic Fiction
Thomas Merton's Reading of Boris Pasternak, Albert Camus, and William Faulkner

*Individual human life became the life story of God and its contents
filled the vast expanses of the universe.*[1]

—Boris Pasternak

Thomas Merton's literary interests can be traced back to his
childhood days as a student in France and afterward at Oakham
School in Rutland, England. Already, at the Lycée Ingres in Montau-
ban, Merton had tried his hand at writing novels. Later, at Ripley
Court Preparatory School in Oakham in 1931 at the age of sixteen,
he became the editor of the school magazine, *The Oakhamian*. In
his student days at Columbia University, he affiliated himself with
the literary group on campus and served as the art editor of *The
Jester of Columbia*, where he published numerous cartoons, poems,
and editorials. During this time, he also published numerous book
reviews in the *New York Times Book Review* and the *New York Herald
Tribune Book Review*. His two earliest reviews appeared in May of
1938, one on *The World's Body* by John Crowe Ransom and the other
on *Laughter in the Dark* by Vladimir Nabokov.

Merton's early novels, *The Labyrinth*, *The Man in the Sycamore
Tree*, and *The Straits of Dover* (whose title eventually became *The
Night Before the Battle*), all of which were written in the summers of
1939 and 1940, were all burned before he left New York for Gethsemani. He spared one novel: *Journal of My Escape from the Nazis*. It

---

[1] Boris Pasternak, *Doctor Zhivago* (London: Pantheon Books, 1958), 413.

was eventually published a year after his death under the title of *My Argument with the Gestapo*. Merton would never again attempt to write fiction. That fact does not mean, however, that his interests in the genre completely disappeared with his profession of vows as a Trappist. Like many of his early interests, it lay dormant for a number of years during his early monastic formation, but in time it found new and reinvigorated expression.

It is no coincidence that the reemergence of Merton's literary interests coincided with his experience on the corner of Fourth and Walnut in downtown Louisville. Exactly two months after the experience he recorded in his journal his discovery of Boris Pasternak: "Above all, this year has marked my discovery of Pasternak. . . . This is a great writer with a wonderful imagination and all he says is delightful—one of the great writers of our time and no one pays much attention. . . . He is so good I don't see very well how the Reds can avoid killing him. Coming down the chapel steps and praying for his soul, a great one, a man who is spiritual in everything he thinks and says!!"[2] Pasternak and the "Pasternak Affair" (the controversy surrounding his being awarded the 1958 Nobel Prize for literature) occupied much of Merton's attention between the middle of 1958 until Pasternak's death in May of 1960. Merton's shared correspondence with Pasternak over the course of these two years, along with the essays he wrote about Pasternak, reveal his deep affection for the one he called "a prophet of a new age."[3]

Just a few years after Pasternak's death, Merton shifted his literary interests to two other novelists whose writing he considered highly prophetic: Albert Camus and William Faulkner.[4] In these two writers in particular, Merton saw the monastic function

---

[2] *A Search for Solitude: Pursuing the Monk's True Life*, ed. Lawrence S. Cunningham, The Journals of Thomas Merton, vol. 3 (New York: Harper-Collins, 1996), 203.

[3] Merton to Cuadra, December 4, 1958, in *The Courage for Truth: The Letters of Thomas Merton to Writers*, ed. Christine M. Bochen (New York: Farrar, Straus and Giroux, 1993), 182.

[4] While Camus and Faulkner wrote primarily fiction, Pasternak was also a prolific writer of poetry.

of prophetic witness being exercised most powerfully. As Patrick Hart recognizes, "This vision led Merton in the mid-sixties to shift his attention from formally religious writings to literary models."[5] After a visit from Jacques Maritain in the fall of 1966, Merton wrote to his publisher, James Laughlin, expressing a new approach he and Maritain felt was best in dealing with the theological and philosophical problems of the day: "Jacques Maritain and I both agreed that we thought perhaps the most living way to approach theological and philosophical problems now (that theology and philosophy are in such chaos) would be in the form of creative writing and literary criticism. I am pleased with the idea and it seems to make sense."[6]

Merton went on to write numerous essays in literary criticism, treating poets and novelists alike. Besides his essays on William Blake and Louis Zukofsky, Merton also discussed such writers as James Joyce ("News of the Joyce Industry" and "A Footnote from *Ulysses*: Peace and Revolution"), Edwin Muir ("The True Legendary Sound: The Poetry and Criticism of Edwin Muir"), Simone Weil ("The Answer of Minerva: Pacifism and Resistance in Simone Weil"), Roland Barthes ("Roland Barthes—Writing as Temperature"), J. F. Powers ("J. F. Powers—*Morte D'Urban*: Two Celebrations"), William Styron ("William Styron—Who Is Nat Turner?"), Flannery O'Connor ("Flannery O'Connor—A Prose Elegy"), Rolf Hochhuth ("The Trial of Pope Pius XII: Rolf Hochhuth's *The Deputy*"), and William Melvin Kelley ("William Melvin Kelley—The Legend of Tucker Caliban"), all of which were eventually published in 1981 in his collection *The Literary Essays of Thomas Merton*.[7] Most prominently featured in this thick volume, however, are essays on

---

[5] Patrick Hart, introduction to *The Literary Essays of Thomas Merton*, ed. Patrick Hart (New York: New Directions, 1981), xi–xvi, here xv.

[6] Thomas Merton to James Laughlin, October 8, 1966, in *Thomas Merton and James Laughlin: Selected Letters*, ed. David D. Cooper (New York: W. W. Norton, 1997), 301.

[7] Also featured in *Literary Essays* are a number of essays on related literary questions, including "Poetry, Symbolism and Typology," "Poetry and Contemplation: A Reappraisal," "Theology of Creativity," "Answers on Art and Freedom," and "Why Alienation Is for Everybody."

the three novelists Boris Pasternak, Albert Camus, and William Faulkner. In these essays, Merton explored the prominent themes of their work, especially highlighting their prophetic content. In fact, among all the people Merton describes as prophetic, these three novelists receive the highest approbation.

Boris Pasternak: "Prophet of a New Age"

In Boris Pasternak (1890–1960), Thomas Merton found a kindred spirit. Both were poets, both were novelists, both were lovers of nature, both wrote with prophetic conviction exposing the dehumanizing injustices of their day, and both were caught in situations that forced them to make deep personal sacrifices for a greater good. These similarities led Merton to write in his initial letter to Pasternak, "It is as if we met on a deeper level of life on which individuals are not separate beings."[8] In his journal, Merton expressed this affinity from another angle: "I am in closer contact with Pasternak than I am with people in Louisville or Bardstown or even in my own monastery—and have more in common with him" (*Search*, 225). Like the Latin American poets Merton was discovering at this time, Pasternak bestowed immense inspiration on Merton, by both his courageous living and his prophetic writing. When Merton wrote to Pablo Antonio Cuadra at the end of 1958, saying, "We can and should be prophets of its ['united, free America'] advent—just as Pasternak in Russia is a prophet of a new age,"[9] Merton was giving voice to his spirit's longing to help bring true unity and freedom to a fragmented and nationally segregated America. Pasternak's Russia faced a somewhat different predicament. Marxism threatened to control and constrain a nation, and Pasternak was the prophet who stood up to expose its dehumanizing effects. This bold witness of Pasternak won Merton's esteem and sparked a brief but lively correspondence lasting from 1958 until 1960.[10]

[8] Merton to Pasternak, August 22, 1958, in *Courage*, 87–88.
[9] Merton to Cuadra, December 4, 1958, in *Courage*, 182.
[10] A collection of the correspondence between Merton and Pasternak (three letters each) was published in *Six Letters: Boris Pasternak and Thomas*

In Merton's first letter to Pasternak, Merton expressed his deep affinity and love for Russian spirituality and her artists. He also expressed his desire to learn Russian "in order to try to get into Russian literature in the original"[11]—a desire that proved futile. Merton concluded his letter by expressing his admiration for Pasternak's courageous and important work as a writer:

> My dear Pasternak, it is a joy to write to you and to thank you for your fine poetry and your great prose. A voice like yours is of great importance for all mankind in our day. . . . The Russian leaders do not perhaps realize to the full how important and how great you are for Russia and for the world. Whatever may lie ahead for the world, I believe that men like yourself and I hope myself also may have the chance to enter upon a dialogue that will really lead to peace and to a fruitful age for man and his world. Such peace and fruitfulness are spiritual realities to which you already have access, though others do not. (*Courage*, 88)

Merton's prophetic eye for the authentically spiritual is evident in his admiration for Pasternak. Although Pasternak was not conventionally Christian, Merton saw in him "a chosen and Christian soul."[12] To Helen Wolff, Pasternak's publisher at Pantheon Books, Merton wrote, "I do believe he is very fundamentally Christian in the broad and prophetic sense that is vital today."[13] In a separate letter, also to Wolff, he would write of Pasternak's writing of resurrection and a new creation: "Pasternak could approach this mystery with the confidence of the poet who is at home with symbols. His love gave the symbols great power and his vocation in the end was prophetic in a sense that has been granted to few religious men in our time."[14] After viewing pictures of Pasternak's

---

Merton, foreword by Naomi Burton Stone, introduction by Lydia Pasternak Slater (Lexington, KY: The King Library Press, 1973).

[11] Merton to Pasternak, Aug. 22, 1958, in *Courage*, 88.

[12] Merton to Maritain, June 30, 1960, in *Courage*, 32.

[13] Merton to Wolff, June 22, 1959, in *Courage*, 98.

[14] Merton to Wolff, June 9, 1960, in *Courage*, 101.

funeral sometime in the summer of 1960, Merton again expressed to Wolff his deep appreciation for Pasternak's prophetic witness: "Really the pictures of the funeral floored me. They were tremendous, and a very moving witness to the love of the Russian people for the poet and prophet that has been given them—the only one in an age so dry of prophetic inspiration, and so full of the accents of false prophecy. . . . He is a great and eloquent witness of the resurrection and of immortality."[15]

Shortly after sending off his initial letter to Pasternak, Merton obtained a copy of *Doctor Zhivago*.[16] In order to understand why he saw Pasternak as "a prophet of a new age" and "a great and eloquent witness of the resurrection and of immortality," one must understand the import of Pasternak's novel for him. Merton offered his analysis of *Doctor Zhivago* and the significance of its achievement in two essays published in 1959: "Boris Pasternak and the People with Watch Chains," in the July issue of *Jubilee*, and "The Pasternak Affair in Perspective," in the November issue of *Thought*. Both of these essays, along with a brief introduction, "In Memoriam," appeared in his 1960 collection of essays, *Disputed Questions*, under the title "The Pasternak Affair."

The inclusion of "The Pasternak Affair" in *Disputed Questions*, indeed as its leading essay, supports Merton's intentions as set forth in his preface: "I think there is one theme, one question above all, which runs through the whole book. It is a philosophical question: the relation of the *person* to the *social organization*."[17] Applied to Pasternak, the form of this central theme takes shape as Merton discusses the struggle "of one outstanding and gifted person isolated in

---

[15] Merton to Wolff, July 23, 1960, in *Courage*, 102.

[16] In Pasternak's first two short letters to Merton, he expressed his disdain for his early writings, saying, "except the 'Dr. Zh' which you should read, all the rest of my verses and writings are devoid of any sense of importance" (Merton and Pasternak, *Six Letters*, 8). Herein is found another similarity between Pasternak and Merton, who also expressed much disdain for his early writings.

[17] Thomas Merton, *Disputed Questions* (New York: Harcourt Brace Jovanovich, 1960), viii.

the presence of a huge antagonistic totalitarian machine which turns against him the full force of its disapproval and stops short only of his physical destruction" (*Disputed Questions*, viii–ix).

Merton cast Pasternak's struggle against the "huge antagonistic totalitarian machine" in terms of false and true humanism. The false humanism of the Russian "totalitarian machine" was based, in Merton's view, on "a culture where man has first been completely alienated from himself by economic individualism, and then precipitated into the morass of mass-technological society which is there to receive us in an avalanche of faceless 'numbers'" (*Disputed Questions*, xi). In contradistinction, true humanism, he said, is the discovery of our true identity as being made in the image of God. It is entered through the door of our own solitude where we learn how to live with ourselves. Yet the life of true humanism carries with it implicit responsibility: "This discovery makes it impossible for us to evade the obligation of loving everyone else who bears in himself the same image" (*Disputed Questions*, xi). Merton saw in Pasternak the prophet of this true form of humanism and, in "The Pasternak Affair," expounded his thesis.

In Part 1, "In Memoriam," Merton, writing shortly after Pasternak's peaceful death at a writer's colony near Moscow in May of 1960, introduced the main events of Pasternak's life, including the political intrigue that surrounded his being awarded the Nobel Prize for Literature in 1958.[18] The award garnered worldwide attention, including the attention of many young Russian writers who saw in Pasternak "a prophetic figure, a man whose ascendency was primarily spiritual" (*Disputed Questions*, 4). His impact on the world for Merton was not so much grounded in what he wrote as in his witness as a genuinely spiritual man. As Merton asserted, "He became a kind of 'sign' of that honesty, integrity, sincerity which

---

[18] Merton made it a point to emphasize that Pasternak was awarded the Nobel Prize not for his novel *Doctor Zhivago* alone but also for his work in poetry, other prose works, and translations. Many Russians, understandably, did not see it that way. The category in which the award was given was "Literature," and Pasternak had written one novel, *Doctor Zhivago*, which had first been published (in Italian translation) in 1957.

we tend to associate with the free and creative personality. . . . In one word, Pasternak emerged as a genuine human being stranded in a mad world" (*Disputed Questions*, 5).

Yet it should be noted that Pasternak angered the Russian authorities and proved dangerous to their Marxist ideologies not simply because of his particular form of spiritual integrity but precisely because he chose to express himself and his panoramic vision of life in his novel. This conflict between personal conviction and communicative expression highlights a distinction Merton had a tendency to overlook in his descriptions of Pasternak's prophetic spirituality. Being so concerned with prophecy as a way of life grounded in authenticity and personal conviction, he at times diminished the particular value of prophecy as communication. Pasternak was prophetic not only because he possessed an authentic spirituality and genuine, personal convictions but also because while knowing the possible consequences, he chose to communicate his convictions anyway.

This is not to say that Merton failed to see the prophetic value of communication. Indeed, his other works prove otherwise. In the case of Pasternak, however, he seemed so enamored with the courageous and heroic way of life exemplified by his Russian friend that the prophetic power of *Doctor Zhivago* seemed almost secondary to him, as was not true of his evaluation of either Camus or Faulkner. This difference attests to the immense affection that Merton had for Pasternak primarily as a person and not primarily as a writer. Nevertheless, Merton did consider *Doctor Zhivago* a great work of prophetic fiction, as the remainder of "The Pasternak Affair" demonstrates.

In Part 2 of the work, "The People with Watch Chains," Merton discussed what made Pasternak's novel a truly great book: "it is in some way about everybody and everybody is involved in it" (*Disputed Questions*, 8). Its central (and not too obscure) theme, he said, was the triumph of life in all its pain, ambivalence, and mystery over "the illusory, frozen-faced *imago* of Life upon which Communism constructs its spiritless fantasies of the future" (*Disputed Questions*, 7–8). It is a story about a protagonist, not incidentally a poet, whose frustrated and confused life in the face of violence and oppression yields the creative and life-transforming impulses of the human spirit. It is about the ability of life to defy confinement and control, about the spiritual fecundity and creativity of the soul that, through its heroic suffering and endurance, dismantles all that seeks to destroy it. Ultimately, Merton said that it is about "the mystery of history as passion and resurrection" (*Disputed Questions*, 8).

Such life, for Merton, was revolutionary, though not in the sense of a rebel and non-conformist, who simply "wants to substitute his own authority for the authority of somebody else" (*Disputed Questions*, 11). Rather, it was revolutionary in the same way that the life of Gandhi was revolutionary. Merton noted that the protests of Pasternak and Gandhi were ultimately the same: "the protest of life itself, of humanity itself, of love, speaking not with theories and programs but simply affirming itself and asking to be judged on its own merits" (*Disputed Questions*, 11). He explained that this protest of love was essentially Christian in the sense that it was an "intense awareness of all cosmic and human reality as 'life in Christ' and the consequent plunge into love as the only dynamic and creative force which really honors this 'Life' by creating itself anew in Life's—Christ's—image" (*Disputed Questions*, 12). This vision of cosmic Christianity led Merton to identify Pasternak as "a prophet of the original, cosmic revelation: one who sees symbols and figures of the inward, spiritual world, working themselves out in the mystery of the universe around him and above all in the history of men. Not so much in the formal, and illusory, history of states and empires that is written down in books, but in the living, transcendental mysterious history of individual human beings and in the indescribable interweaving of their destinies" (*Disputed Questions*, 17–18).

This cosmic spirituality finds expression in Pasternak's protagonist in three primary vocations: as artist, symbolist, and prophet. As Merton commented, "It is as artist, symbolist and prophet that *Zhivago* stands most radically in opposition to Soviet society" (*Disputed Questions*, 18). For Merton, the relationship of each of these three vocations to the others is interdependent. In Merton's conceptualization, prophecy in *Doctor Zhivago* is a type of final cause of a particular type of spiritual impulse. Through the use of words in their symbolic form, the artist constructs prophetic communication.

This prophetic communication, in order to be most powerful and transformative, must flow from a life fully committed to its primal, spiritual impulse.

In Merton's view, fulfillment of this necessity is exactly what makes *Zhivago* and, by implication, Pasternak so prophetic. Merton perceived that it was against the "pseudo-scientific array of propaganda clichés" (*Disputed Questions*, 20) that the "Doctor Life" stood in diagnosing the sickness of Soviet society. His belief in intuition, a great sin according to the Marxists, allowed him to grasp the full meaning and implication of the situation as a whole. In *Zhivago*, the intuitive faculty was most alive and active in the poetic vocation, which is at once dynamic and contemplative. As Merton noted, "dynamic" and "contemplative" are "two terms which can only be synthesized in the heat of a prophetic ardor" (*Disputed Questions*, 20). He described the unfolding process of *Zhivago*'s prophetic communication in this way: "When in the moment of inspiration the poet's creative intelligence is married with the inborn wisdom of human language (the Word of God and Human Nature—Divinity and Sophia) then in the very flow of new and individual intuitions, the poet utters the voice of that wonderful and mysterious world of God-man-hood—it is the transfigured, spiritualized and divinized cosmos that speaks through him, and through him utters its praise of the Creator" (*Disputed Questions*, 20–21).

Ultimately, Merton understood prophecy as praise, that eschatological acclamation that moves all things in a definite direction. And in which direction does it move? Its movement is toward freedom. Not a political or social freedom, but a freedom found in a "new dimension of the future which we cannot yet estimate because it is not yet with us" (*Disputed Questions*, 24). Biblically understood, Merton thought that this prophetic utterance of praise was an utterance of *faith* that "calls into existence the things that do not exist" (Rom 4:17).

In the final section of "The Pasternak Affair," Merton focused on the spiritual implications surrounding the publication of *Doctor Zhivago*. He insightfully summarized the significance of Pasternak's spirituality as seen both through *Doctor Zhivago* and in his own quiet witness:

Pasternak stands first of all for the great spiritual values that are under attack in our materialistic world. He stands for the freedom and nobility of the individual person, for man the image of God, for man in whom God dwells. For Pasternak, the person is and must always remain prior to the collectivity. He stands for courageous, independent loyalty to his own conscience, and for the refusal to compromise with slogans and rationalizations imposed by compulsion. Pasternak is fighting for man's true freedom, his true creativity, against the false and empty humanism of the Marxists—for whom man does not yet truly exist. Over against the technological jargon and the empty scientism of modern man, Pasternak set creative symbolism, the power of imagination and of intuition, the glory of liturgy and the fire of contemplation. But he does so in new words, in a new way. He speaks for all that is sanest and most permanently vital in religious and cultural tradition, but with the voice of a man of our own time. (*Disputed Questions*, 31)

What was most striking about Pasternak's witness, for Merton, was the fact that even after surviving the worst of Stalin's purges, Pasternak, through his literary protest, still castigated Stalinism, and not while living as an exile but while living in the heart of Russia. Therein rested Pasternak's symbolic greatness and prophetic power.

That life is love is the great theme of *Doctor Zhivago*. This is precisely the salve that heals humankind's many illnesses. Pasternak had the insight that love is the ultimate expression of spirituality and freedom. He imbued his leading protagonist with this motivation, and it can be seen in the characterization of nearly every relationship throughout the novel. *Doctor Zhivago*, in a sense, can be read as an exploration of the various aspects of love. As Merton notes, "Every degree of true and false love makes its appearance in the book" (*Disputed Questions*, 49).

Merton saw this particular aspect of Pasternak's spirituality as highly influenced by Vladimir Soloviev's *The Meaning of Love*,[19]

---

[19] Vladimir Soloviev, *The Meaning of Love* (London: Centenary, 1945).

which explains the vocation of the human person as "to regenerate the world by the spiritualization of human love raised to the sophianic level of perfect conscious participation in the mystery of the divine wisdom of which the earthly sacrament is love" (*Disputed Questions*, 49). Pasternak's spirituality of love confirmed him to Merton as a Christian witness to the Gospel. For Merton, this component of spiritual life validated Pasternak's own belief in "Christ as the center of history" (cited in *Disputed Questions*, 62).[20] For him this spirituality of love also validated Pasternak's unfailing commitment to the supreme value of Christian humanistic thought, the value of *personalism*.

Merton was not alone in his evaluation of the fundamental Christian vision of Boris Pasternak. Neither was he alone in his assessment of Pasternak's prophetic spirituality. One critic, Nicola Chiaromonte, has remarked, "The final point of Pasternak's vision is the message of Christ, and what Christ means to him is absolute faith in man's innerness and freedom."[21] George Panichas held a similar opinion: "Pasternak's message to modern man is without doubt the result of his own search for truth, his devotion to the freedom of the artist, his unwavering belief in the greatness of man. His message and meaning must be understood in the light of their Christian humility and simplicity. . . . Pasternak's concept of love is complete precisely because it must be seen in the unity that is found in Christ."[22]

Pasternak underscored this Christian humanism early in *Doctor Zhivago* when he had Nikolai Nikolaevich, a former priest, say, "Gregariousness is always the refuge of mediocrities, whether they swear by Soloviev or Kant or Marx. Only individuals seek the truth, and they shun those whose sole concern is not the few indeed. I

---

[20] Merton, though placing this phrase in quotation marks, does not provide the reference in his text.

[21] Nicola Chiaromonte, "Pasternak's Message," *Partisan Review* 25 (1958): 127–34, here 133.

[22] George Panichas, "Pasternak's Protest and Affirmation," in *The Reverent Discipline: Essays in Literary Criticism and Culture* (Knoxville, TN: University of Tennessee Press, 1974), 284.

think one should be loyal to immortality, which is another word for life, a stronger word for it. One must be true to immortality—true to Christ!"[23] The triumph of the artist, symbolist, and prophet—all descriptions of both Pasternak and *Zhivago*—over the forces of evil is Pasternak's total affirmation of the supreme value of the goodness of life. Embedded within this affirmation of life, however, is an unmistakable protest. Panichas notes that "[Zhivago's] life symbolizes the immemorial protest against the dehumanization of man; his death immortalizes the struggle of man to free himself from those things and systems that would destroy the human soul. In this protest and in this affirmation Boris Pasternak built a monument to the divinity of all men" (*The Reverent Discipline*, 291). Merton would certainly be in enthusiastic agreement with Panichas's perceptive assertion.

In concluding "The Pasternak Affair," Merton offered his own prophetic observation about the significance of *Doctor Zhivago*:

> If we stop to think about what it says, we will realize that if Pasternak is ever fully studied, he is just as likely to be regarded as a dangerous writer in the West as he is in the East. He is saying that political and social structures as we understand them are things of the past, and that the crisis through which we are now passing is nothing but the full and inescapable manifestation of their falsity. For twenty centuries we have called ourselves Christians, without even beginning to understand one tenth of the Gospel. We have been taking Caesar for God and God for Caesar. Now that "charity is growing cold" and we stand facing the smoky dawn of an apocalyptic era, Pasternak reminds us that there is only one source of truth, but that it is not sufficient to know the source is there—we must go and drink from it, as he has done.
>
> Do we have the courage to do so? For obviously, if we consider what Pasternak is saying, doing and undergoing, to read the Gospel with eyes wide open may be a perilous thing! (*Disputed Questions*, 67)

---

[23] Pasternak, *Doctor Zhivago*, 9; cited in Merton, *Disputed Questions*, 65.

Found among Merton's unpublished manuscripts following his death was an essay entitled "Pasternak's Letters to Georgian Friends." Written in early 1968 at the request of Helen Wolff, this essay offers a further insight into Merton's understanding of Pasternak's prophetic spirituality.[24] Written with the same affection that characterized "The Pasternak Affair," the body of the essay focuses on Pasternak's devoted relationship to a number of Georgian poets and comments on his work of translating Georgian texts. Most significantly, however, the essay focuses on the nature of Pasternak's commitment to his art, which Merton described as a type of "ascesis of generosity" ("Pasternak's Letters to Georgian Friends," 88). This total commitment to the artistic endeavor, Merton noted, reflected an expression of Pasternak's poet friend, Tabidze. The expression *gadavarda*, which means "to throw oneself headlong," or as Merton put it, "to dive right into the life-stream without after-thought and without care," was, as Merton saw it, fully incorporated into Pasternak's life view ("Pasternak's Letters to Georgian Friends," 91).

Not simply a thrust into rivers of romantic ecstasy, *gadavarda* is a much more sober reality. It is the absolute surrender of the fully devoted artist to the demands of his or her craft. Through his or her ascetic discipline, the artist's particular work comes to life. Although an enriching experience, Merton wrote, "it is the terrible enrichment of poverty and nakedness, solitude and abandon" ("Pasternak's Letters to Georgian Friends," 91), or as Pasternak wrote, "Everywhere in the world one has to pay for the right to live on one's own naked spiritual reserves" (cited in "Pasternak's Letters to Georgian Friends," 91). Merton's reflection on *gadavarda* underscored his insistence on interpreting prophecy in terms of a spirituality and not in terms of a passing charismatic gift. The power and substantive value of prophecy he declared to be found in the total investment of one's life in hearing and communicating the Word of God. This investment requires great asceticism and

---

[24] "Ascesis of Sacrifice: Pasternak's Letters to Georgian Friends" was not published until 1978, in the first issue of *The New Lazarus Review*. It was reprinted in *The Literary Essays of Thomas Merton*, ed. Patrick Hart (New York: New Directions, 1981), 84–91.

growth in wisdom through insight and intuition, all of which necessitate the superior worth of the human person over any collective organization.

Merton's astute and compassionate reading of Boris Pasternak, the man and his writings, exemplified that particular prophetic insight that he valued so greatly in his beloved Russian friend. Merton was able to understand and appreciate the depth of Pasternak's prophetic witness because he possessed so many of the same prophetic sensibilities. Like Pasternak, Merton had the gift of seeing through the ephemeral and superficial and, with a discerning eye, identify what was sick in the human condition. Each entered fully into his own history and broke through the cultural and social conditions that threatened to deny the very soul of life. Indeed, as William Shannon asserts, "breaking through cultural restraints and seeing what could be is the role of the prophet."[25]

Albert Camus and the Prophetic Revolt

In 1957, the year before Pasternak was awarded the Nobel Prize for Literature, the prestigious award was given to Albert Camus (1913–1960). He was forty-four. In his banquet speech, he reflected on the baleful human situation in the first half of the twentieth century:

> These men, who were born at the beginning of the First World War, who were twenty when Hitler came to power and the first revolutionary trials were beginning, who were then confronted as a completion of their education with the Spanish Civil War, the Second World War, the world of concentration camps, a Europe of torture and prisons—these men must today rear their sons and create their works in a world threatened by nuclear destruction. Nobody, I think, can ask them to be optimists. And I even think that we should understand—without ceasing to fight

---

[25] William Shannon, *"Something of a Rebel": Thomas Merton, His Life and Works: An Introduction* (Cincinnati, OH: St. Anthony Messenger Press, 1997), 53.

it—the error of those who in an excess of despair have
asserted their right to dishonour and have rushed into the
nihilism of the era. But the fact remains that most of us, in
my country and in Europe, have refused this nihilism and
have engaged upon a quest for legitimacy. *They have had*
to forge for themselves an art of living in times of catastrophe
in order to be born a second time and to fight openly against the
instinct of death at work in our history.[26]

At about the time Camus received his Nobel Prize, this prolific
writer (besides novels, he also wrote numerous plays and essays)
caught Merton's attention, mainly through the recommendation of
Czesław Miłosz. As was often the case when Merton discovered
a new prophetic voice, he developed a certain fixation on Camus.
Merton quickly became enamored with this Algerian visionary
and artist who was speedily constructing an ethic that was at once
original and timely. Also, as was often the case, in the heat of en-
thrallment Merton began preparing a book. The book on Camus
never panned out, but seven penetrating literary essays resulted,
probing the work of one whom Merton considered both a "human"
and a "humble prophet."[27]

---

[26] "Albert Camus—Banquet Speech" (emphasis added), Nobelprize
.org, http://www.nobelprize.org/nobel_prizes/literature/laureates/1957
/camus-speech.html.

[27] Thomas Merton, *Conjectures of a Guilty Bystander* (1966; New York:
Image Books, 1989), 182. The seven essays on Camus, most of which were
published in the last three years of Merton's life in various literary journals,
were published collectively in *Literary Essays*. They are "The Plague of Camus:
A Commentary and Introduction" (written in June 1967 and first published
by The Seabury Press in 1968; *Literary Essays*, 181–217); "Camus: Journals
of the Plague Years" (completed in April 1967 and first published in *The
Sewanee Review*, Autumn 1967; *Literary Essays*, 218–31); "Terror and the Absurd: Violence and Nonviolence in Albert Camus" (written in August 1966
and first published in the February 1969 issue of *Motive* in an abbreviated
form; *Literary Essays*, 232–51); "Prophetic Ambiguities: Milton and Camus"
(written in October 1966 and first published in edited form in the *Saturday
Review*, April 15, 1967; *Literary Essays*, 252–60); "Camus and the Church" (first
appearing in *The Catholic Worker*, December 1966; *Literary Essays*, 261–74);

In his moving acceptance speech for his Nobel Prize, Camus interpreted his own life first and foremost as an artist. He described the work of the artist as a ministry of reconciliation: "The artist forges himself to the others, midway between the beauty he cannot do without and the community he cannot tear himself away from" ("Albert Camus—Banquet Speech"). Camus's program for the "art of living," the underlying theme in all of his writings, ought to be understood as an overflow of this compassionate impulse. It was his desire to bridge the gap between his own authentic experiences as an artist and the "absurdity" he found in the world around him. His instruments of reconciliation were his penetrating and revealing myths. With them he drew his readers along the labyrinthine pathways of his main ideas: absurdity, revolt, love. Although he was not a poet, his parabolic prose bears the marks of a poetic thinker. It carried with it a certain moral weight that was unmistakable and was characterized, especially in Merton's estimation, by a definite prophetic thrust.

Merton began his essay "Prophetic Ambiguities: Milton and Camus" with this observation: "Poets and poetic thinkers—men who construct myths in which they embody their own struggle to cope with the fundamental questions of life—are generally 'prophetic' in the sense that they anticipate in their solitude the struggles and the general consciousness of later generations."[28] Camus's *The Myth of Sisyphus* is just such a mythic work. In it and in *L'Étranger*, published the same year, 1942, Camus introduced his signature (if sometimes misunderstood) theory of the absurd. By the absurd, Camus generally meant "the absence of correspondence or congruity between the mind's need for coherence and the incoherence of the world which the mind experiences."[29]

"Three Saviors in Camus: Lucidity and the Absurd" (written in September 1966 and first published in *Thought*, Spring 1968; *Literary Essays*, 275–91); and "The Stranger: Poverty of an Antihero" (written in March of 1968 and first published in the Fall 1968 issue of *Unicorn*; *Literary Essays*, 292–301).

[28] "Prophetic Ambiguities: Milton and Camus," in *Literary Essays*, 252–60, here 252.

[29] John Cruickshank, *Albert Camus and the Literature of Revolt* (New York: Oxford University Press, 1960), 41.

Merton himself explained the absurd as "the gap between the actual shape of life and intelligent truth. Absurdity is compounded by the ambiguous and false explanations, interpretations, conventions, justifications, legalizations, evasions which infect our struggling civilization with the 'plague' and which often bring us most dangerously close to perfect nihilism when they offer a security based on a seemingly rational use of absolute power."[30]

Merton was quick, however, to debunk (on more than one occasion) a popular misinterpretation of Camus's doctrine of the absurd: that Camus taught it in order to promote it. On the contrary, Camus was not an advocate of the absurd. Rather, the absurd was an expression of Camus's insight into the current social situation, particularly in Europe. In actuality, Camus was a humanist who forged his own way through the fog of life and provided his own remedies to the nihilism surrounding him, remedies, he believed, of which neither left nor right was capable. This stance, Merton suggested, left Camus "in the very uncomfortable position of rejecting all the facile and doctrinaire generalizations of the mass movements and finding his own way in solitude" ("Camus and the Church," 257). In *The Myth of Sisyphus*, according to Camus scholar Robert de Luppé, the proper response to the absurd is learned: "to live in the present and not in the future."[31] As de Luppé goes on to explain, "The present is the continual struggle to sustain this vital consciousness. There is no question of comfort or of despair: the question is one of confrontation" (*Albert Camus*, 26).

L'Étranger, most often translated as *The Stranger*, is also at times translated as *The Outsider*.[32] Its protagonist, Meursault, who represents "the alienated man"[33] who insists on living authentically in his alienated state without self-justification—and is condemned for this very reason—can certainly be read as a characterization of

---

[30] Merton, "Camus and the Church," in *Literary Essays*, 261–74, here 268.

[31] Robert de Luppé, *Albert Camus*, trans. John Cumming and J. Hargreaves (New York: Funk & Wagnalls, 1968), 26.

[32] Robert de Luppé utilizes such a translation in *Albert Camus*.

[33] Merton, "The Stranger: Poverty of an Antihero," in *Literary Essays*, 292–301, here 292.

Camus's own philosophical reading of the culture in which he lived. Mentioning Camus's own explanation, Merton notes that "the Stranger 'is a man poor and naked' who 'refuses every mask' who 'refuses to lie . . . by saying more than he feels' but who is 'in love with the sun that casts no shadows' and is animated 'by a profound passion . . . for the absolute and for truth.'"[34] Such an existential commitment to "the absolute and for truth" does not need to be justified, Merton avers, because "it cannot be justified by being fitted into the context of something else that is less basic, less authentic, less real, but more easily reduced to rational formulas" ("The Stranger," 298). Merton pointed to the depth of Camus's thought in a passage that suggests much about the understanding Merton had of the relationship among solitude, authenticity, prophetic insight, and prophetic communication; it confirms the discussion above about his response to Pasternak, Blake, and the Latin American poets: "The authenticity and love toward which Camus tended were, then, beyond formulas of justification and explanation. They were also in some sense beyond the apprehension of an interior spiritual insight, beyond any *trémoussement prophétique* ['prophetic flutter']" ("The Stranger," 298).

What often arises out of authentic solitude, however, Merton thought, are the spiritual insights and "prophetic flutters" that give rise to prophetic communication. Such communication is the logical outcome of a life committed to the authentically real and grounded in spiritual vitality. This prophetic phenomenon he saw as revealing itself in the life of Meursault, who even though "living in apparent happiness in spite of unconscious alienation, becomes conscious of his actual condition, and becomes able to articulate his protest and resistance against what has caused it" ("The Stranger," 300).

In 1947, five years after the publication of *The Stranger*, Camus published his second novel, *The Plague*. In it Merton saw Camus develop his philosophical vision far beyond the scope of the absurd and explore the avenues of ethical response to the shortcomings of nihilism. As a "modern myth about the destiny of man" (Merton,

---

[34] From the American student edition of *The Stranger*, cited in "The Stranger," 298.

"The Plague," 181), *The Plague* was a manifestation of tyranny, evil, and death—the face of the absurd that must be resisted at all costs. Passive resignation or acquiescence means defeat.

The heroes of *The Plague*, Rieux and Tarrou, represent certain types of figures whom Merton called "saints without God" ("The Plague," 186), whose tireless and courageous work at saving the plagued town of Oran form the proper response to the "absurd" situation. On the other hand, the moralizing of Père Paneloux, the local Jesuit, is logically unsustainable and practically ineffective. Paneloux eventually apologizes for his uncharitable and judgmental sermonizing and follows Rieux and Tarrou in laying down their lives as members of a sanitary squad. The serum concocted against the plague eventually works but not before claiming the lives of both Paneloux and Tarrou. Camus's message is clear: the one who relentlessly and self-sacrificially fights against whatever destroys life is the true witness to human love and truth, not the one who simply condemns it from a pulpit.

The noble fight against the evil of the plague—the evil being, in subjective terms, a deficiency in the human spirit that curtails the inner freedom of the human person and nullifies the ability to fashion a course of action for the future—forms the basis of Camus's prophetic revolt. Merton sees two major components to Camus's strategic plan in combating this "absurd" evil in oneself and in the world. The first and foundational step involves the ability clearly to perceive one's existential situation. This is the moment of *lucidity*. As Merton explains, "The existential and poetic logic of Camus starts from an intuitive preference for lucidity as a fundamental human value, through which man discovers his own meaning and *chooses* to mean what he in fact is."[35] This lucid moment moves the human person away from the alienated state of indifference and grounds him or her in the reality of the existential and social circumstance, which is the absurd.

Yet Camus's *lucidity* is not merely recognition of the fact. It is a radical commitment to remain centered in one's own personal

[35] Merton, "Camus: Journals of the Plague Years," in *Literary Essays*, 218–31, here 224.

integrity in the face of the societal falsities and evils that threaten to redefine it. Embedded within the lucid moment of spiritual insight and commitment, though, is the power of human solidarity and compassion that begins to manifest itself in *trémoussement prophétique*, communicating some expression of revolt. For Camus, the very value of life is found precisely in this rebellion against evil. Merton points out that what forms the beginning moments of authentic existence for Camus is not the logical axiom—"I think, therefore I am"—but the moral commitment: "We rebel against the absurd, therefore we are" ("Camus: Journals," 225).

The Plague's Rieux and Tarrou are Camus's true rebels. In them is the portrayal of true prophetic revolt. As the story of their lives illustrates, the destruction of the absurd can only be accomplished through a revolt based on people's working together in solidarity with others who also see the tragic absurdity of the plague. This loving revolt, the only kind that truly saves, Merton notes, "demands dialogue, openness, speech."[36] This demand highlights the second component in dealing with the absurd: the Camusian revolt is necessarily communicative. In communication revolt finds its prophetic power, said Merton, because it "protests against the conspiracy of silence which, everywhere, both under totalism and under capitalism, seals men's lips so that they do not protest against organized murder but approve it" ("Terror," 243). The great danger, in Merton's reading of Camus's ideas of lucidity and revolt, is absurdity's silent acquiescence: "the homage of unquestioning acceptance which the majority of men offer to the idol" ("Terror," 246). Herein lies the obligation to vocalize resistance.

The resistance of Camus's prophetic revolt was not, for Merton, about the direct accusation of any particular social or economic injustice. Rather, it was about unmasking the fallacy that power actually promotes life when it depends on killing thousands of human beings and relies on policies that ultimately necessitate these deaths. Lucid language is the remedy required to penetrate through the foggy and miasmic rhetoric of the philosophical

---

[36] Merton, "Terror and the Absurd: Violence and Nonviolence in Albert Camus," in *Literary Essays*, 232–51, here 243.

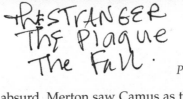
The Stranger
The Plague
The Fall.

justifiers of the absurd. Merton saw Camus as the "human" and "humble" prophet because Camus held that the human task was "a humble and limited one: to find those few words by which to appease the infinite anguish of free souls."[37] Merton, however, admitted that Camus's statement should be read in its broader context: "He was concerned with the power of language—of truth then—to protect man against ferocity, murder, nihilism, chaos. Language used clearly and honestly in the service of a lucid consciousness would protect man against his tendencies to nihilism and self-destruction" ("Three Saviors," 276).

This theme of prophetic communication is a central theme of Camus's final completed novel, *The Fall*. Merton understood the theme of *The Fall* to be summed up "as the total failure of garrulous analytical reasoning as a means of authentic communication" ("Three Saviors," 277). Clamence, Camus's protagonist, is, for Merton, the mythical false-prophet figure—"a sort of feeble twentieth-century John the Baptist preparing the way for nobody, bringing no news except the analysis of his own sins and those of his world, and announcing, with finality, nothing but general and irreversible guilt" ("Three Saviors," 277). One of Camus's goals in *The Fall* is to demolish the barrier that guilt has erected between the one who communicates and the one who is being communicated to. What Camus seeks is a form of communication that is pure and free from individualistic self-awareness. Only then is language safeguarded in the proper sincerity, where authentic love can be expressed. Yet the temptation always remains to pervert language in hateful and violent rhetoric. Such an option nullifies language's prophetic power. Thus Camus, as a wise instructor, offers this prophetic advice: "Over the expanse of five continents throughout the coming years an endless struggle is going to be pursued between violence and friendly persuasion, a struggle in which, granted, the former has a thousand times the chances of success than that of the latter. But I have always held that, if he who bases his hopes on human nature is a fool, he who gives up in the face of circumstances

[37] Cited in "Three Saviors in Camus: Lucidity and the Absurd," in *Literary Essays*, 275–91, here 276.

is a coward. And henceforth, the only honourable course will be to stake everything on a formidable gamble: that words are more powerful than munitions."[38]

Camus's relationship to the church was of particular interest to Merton. He also felt that Camus had important things to say about his own life as a monk. In this regard, David Belcastro notes that "Merton heard in Camus a prophetic voice challenging him to examine critically the Christian faith he professed and the monastic life he lived."[39] Merton explored these themes in his essay "Camus and the Church."

Both the chaplain in *The Stranger* who seeks Meursault's conversion and Père Paneloux in *The Plague* represent Camus's problem with the church. Camus had the opportunity to express this problem to a group of Dominicans when he presented a paper at the Dominican Monastery of Latour-Maubourg in 1948. Camus's basic criticisms were aimed at the church's apparent Pharisaism, by which Merton said that he meant two things: "on one hand the man who thinks that it is enough to *recognize* an obligation by a purely formal and punctilious fulfillment is a Pharisee. On the other the man who detects the failure and points to it, without fulfilling an equivalent obligation himself, is also a Pharisee" ("Camus," 264). The chaplain of *The Stranger* and Paneloux of *The Plague*, as well as Clamence in *The Fall*, are all embodiments of Pharisaism and, instead of healing the world of its nihilism, according to Camus, end up only contributing to it.

In order to substantiate his criticism to the Dominicans, Camus raised the question of why Christians, particularly Vatican officials, had not spoken out more forcefully against the violent aggressions of the Nazis. By citing this lengthy passage in his essay, Merton is also underlining the credibility of Camus's assessment:

---

[38] Albert Camus, "Neither Victims nor Executioners," in *The Pacifist Conscience*, ed. Peter Mayer (New York: Holt, Rinehart and Winston, 1966), 423–39, here 438–39; cited in Merton, "Terror," 251.

[39] David Joseph Belcastro, "Merton and Camus on Christian Dialogue with a Postmodern World," *The Merton Annual* 10 (1997): 223–33, here 223.

nihilism: support of the state in acts of violence against humankind [handwritten annotation]

Why shall I not say this here? For a long time I waited during those terrible years, for a strong voice to be lifted up in Rome. I an unbeliever? Exactly. For I knew that spirit would be lost if it did not raise the cry of condemnation in the presence of force. It appears that this voice was raised. But I swear to you that millions of men, myself included, never heard it; and that there was in the hearts of believers and unbelievers a solitude which did not cease to grow as the days went by and the executioners multiplied. It was later explained to me that the condemnation had indeed been uttered, but in the language of encyclicals, which is not clear. The condemnation had been pronounced but it had not been understood. Who cannot see in this where the real condemnation lies? Who does not see that this example contains within it one of the elements of the answer, perhaps the whole answer to the question you have asked me? What the world expects of Christians is that Christians speak out and utter their condemnation in such a way that never a doubt, never a single doubt can arise in the heart of even the simplest man. *That Christians get out of their abstractions and stand face to face with the bloody mess that is our history today. The gathering we need today is the gathering together of men who are resolved to speak out clearly and pay with their own person. When a Spanish bishop blesses political executions he is no longer a bishop or a Christian or even a man. . . . We expect and I expect that all those will gather together who do not want to be dogs and who are determined to pay the price that has to be paid if man is to be something more than a dog.* (cited in "Camus," 266–67)

It is passages such as this that lead to Belcastro's sobering evaluation: "Merton sets Camus before the church as a prophetic voice challenging Christians to examine their participation in modern nihilism, that is, their support of the state in acts of violence against humankind" ("Merton and Camus," 230). Yet Belcastro admits that Merton sees Camus's reproach in a greater light. Camus was not simply concerned with condemning the church. He was also, Merton said, "a prophet who opens new ways of being in the world that promise new life for the Church" ("Camus," 264).

Two important points should not go unnoticed. First, the proper way to be in the world as a prophetic church is to communicate with the world in a language that is at once understandable and uncompromising. There are moments when nuance and abstract terminology should give way to direct and forceful admonition—hence Merton's emphasis on Camus's notion of *lucidity*.

Yet although Camus does not admit it, communication in nuance and philosophical abstraction is at times necessary for the church. Theological and philosophical sophistication and complexity require it. Logically, this fact means that there are many ways in which the church communicates with the world that are not prophetic. This reality highlights an important question, which Merton implicitly asks by citing the passage above: does the church currently have an adequate platform for effective prophetic communication?

Merton's question leads to the second important point of Camus's admonition to the Dominicans. It pertains to the age-old struggle between institutional bureaucracy and charismatic expression. How effectively can the church *as an institution* prophetically communicate? There seems to be no biblical precedent for institutional prophetic communication. In the Bible, authentic prophecy always occurs by prophets—by individual human beings moved by God's Spirit. In fact, their prophetic messages are often aimed directly against the compromising effects of institutional dependence.[40]

Merton admits that Camus's challenge to the church is nothing new. The sincerest of intentions are always filled with ambiguity and confusion. Much that is said, promised, or rejected in one statement has a way of being negated in the next. The weight of being inoffensive, saving face, and trying to please everyone can easily tempt the church to communicate in uncertainties and obscurities

---

[40] See Isaiah's prophecy against blindness and perversity (Isa 29:9-16), Amos's prophecy against Israel's corrupt worship (Amos 5:21-27), Jeremiah's Temple sermon prophecy (Jer 7:1–8:3), John the Baptist's prophetic denunciation of the Pharisees and Sadducees (Matt 3:7-9), and Jesus' prophetic admonition to the Pharisees and scribes on their dependence on the tradition of the elders (Matt 15:1-20).

and can all too often lead to silence when the world cries out for a prophetic word. Yet Merton recognized that, with a few exceptions, the church has at times spoken "without ambiguity though still in official language."[41] He cites the statement from Vatican Council II's *Gaudium et Spes*, the Pastoral Constitution on the Church in the Modern World: "The arms race is an utterly treacherous trap for humanity and one which injures the poor to an intolerable degree. . . . Divine Providence urgently demands of us that we free ourselves from the age-old slavery of war. But if we refuse to make this effort . . ."[42] Merton also considered Pope John XXIII's *Pacem in Terris* to be a clear, prophetic encyclical. But the problem persisted, as Merton lamented, because "Christians themselves do not pay attention, or simply shrug the whole thing off" ("Camus and the Church," 268).

Merton here defines prophetic effectiveness as being dependent on the prophet's own relevance and value. Implicit is the prophet's own integrity and credibility. What happens when the source of the prophetic voice becomes complicit in the sin that it condemns? Has it forfeited its right to prophesy? These questions arise from the concerns voiced by Camus and echoed by Merton and bespeak the ambivalence of ecclesiastical prophetic communication.

In this ambivalence both Camus and Merton found the need for creative writers and artists. The role of the prophet in modern society is fulfilled most of all, they thought, in these vocations. They are the ones endowed with the gifts of clear and creative communication skills. The select few who are endowed with God's Spirit have the greatest opportunity to be God's prophetic instruments in the world—to sound God's truth in a way that demands attention. Merton understood Camus's message to the church in precisely this way: "It is at this point that we can see what Camus is asking not only of intellectuals but also of the Church: this *purification and*

---

[41] Thomas Merton, "Camus and the Church," 268.

[42] Second Vatican Council, *Gaudium et Spes* (the Pastoral Constitution on the Church in the Modern World), 81, http://www.vatican.va/archive /hist_councils/ii_vatican_council/documents/vat-ii_const_19651207 _gaudium-et-spes_en.html.

restitution of language so that the truth may become once again unambig-uous and fully accessible to all men, especially when they need to know what to do" ("Camus and the Church," 273). For Merton, the whole message of Camus rested on the idea of *"telling the truth"* ("Camus and the Church," 274).

Merton perceived that Camus's prophetic revolt rested on faith in the power of words to lead in what Merton termed "a creative and life-affirming direction" ("Camus and the Church," 274). In his novels, plays, and essays, Camus explored this central theme, and, as Merton noted, everywhere they all reach the same conclusion: "we live in a world of lies, which is therefore a world of violence and murder. We need to rebuild a world of peace. We cannot do this unless we can recover the language and think of peace" ("Camus and the Church," 274).

William Faulkner: *"The* American Prophet of the Twentieth Century"[43]

What has been said about Camus must be put in proper per-spective. John Eudes Bamberger recounts an incident that occurred in the late 1960s when Merton, after giving his series of talks on Camus to the young monks of Gethsemani, "with his usual verve,"[44] rejected his earlier strong endorsement of Camus's views: "Camus is a man of the past and outdated. Forget what I said about him!" (*Prophet*, 26).[45] He then began a series of talks, given with equal verve, on Rainer Maria Rilke and William Faulkner.

William Faulkner (1897–1962) had up to this point had little impact on Merton's thought or spirituality. As a precocious sixteen-year-old, Merton had attempted a reading of Faulkner's then-new book *Sanctuary*, but to no avail. It left him completely befuddled.

---

[43] Thomas Merton, *Learning to Love: Exploring Solitude and Freedom*, ed. Christine M. Bochen, The Journals of Thomas Merton, vol. 6 (New York: HarperCollins, 1997), 171.

[44] John Eudes Bamberger, *Thomas Merton: Prophet of Renewal*, MW 4 (Kalamazoo, MI: Cistercian Publications, 2005), 26.

[45] This is a paraphrase of how Bamberger remembers Merton's comment.

A similar thing happened in the late 1950s with *A Fable*. Not until December of 1966 did Merton mention any interest in the writer whom he would eventually call "*the* American prophet of the twentieth century (or at least the first half of it)," a prophet "too great to be heeded by the nation" (*Learning*, 171).

Merton recorded his thought on Faulkner in two main places: first, a series of conference talks recorded by his novices (two of which have been transcribed and appear in an appendix in *The Literary Essays of Thomas Merton*); second, in two articles, also published in that volume.[46] These works reveal at least some of the reason that Merton considered Faulkner "*the* American prophet of the twentieth century."

On December 2, 1966, Merton declared his admiration for Faulkner in his journal:

> Early morning—reading Faulkner's *The Bear*.[47] Glad the time has come for me to read this. Shattering, cleansing, a mind-changing and transforming myth that makes you stop to think about re-evaluating everything. All great writing like this makes you break through the futility and routine of ordinary life and see the greatness of existence, its seriousness, and the awfulness of wasting it. And how easy it is to waste and trivialize it. Seriousness of my own solitary vocation. Eschatological witness of Ike McCaslin. (*Learning*, 165)[48]

Like Camus, Faulkner wrote mythic stories that explored the existential plight of characters reeling in the drudgery of a fallen world. Unlike Camus, Faulkner imbued his novels with moments

---

[46] Merton originally wrote "'Baptism in the Forest': Wisdom and Initiation in William Faulkner" as an introduction to *Mansions of the Spirit*, ed. George A. Panichas (New York: Hawthorn, 1967); it was reprinted in *Literary Essays*, 92–116. "Faulkner and His Critics" was a review article published in *The Critic*, April–May 1967. Of lesser importance are Merton's comments on Faulkner in *Opening the Bible* (Collegeville, MN: Liturgical Press, 1970).

[47] "The Bear" is here italicized in conformity to its appearance in *Learning*, but it is not a novel, but a story within the novel *Go Down, Moses*.

[48] This is the first mention of Faulkner in Merton's journals.

of hopeful optimism through characters who represented overtly spiritual and biblical themes. Merton was fully alert to Faulkner's spiritual and biblical vision.

As the journal entry makes clear, reading "The Bear" had a tremendous effect on Merton. The following day, he continued his reflections: "Biblical Faulkner. I could write a book on *The Bear* as a basis for contemplative life. The *true* kind. *Theoria*. Freedom. *One* truth" (*Learning*, 166). Again on December 6: "*The Bear* can be read as a perfect tract on the monastic vocation, i.e. especially poverty" (*Learning*, 166). Eventually he developed these initial ideas into the basis for his important essay "'Baptism in the Forest': Wisdom and Initiation in William Faulkner," where he described Faulkner's literary approach as not "religious" or "metaphysical" but *sapiential*:

> Faulkner is typical of the creative genius who can associate his reader in the same experience of creation which brought forth his book. Such a book is filled with efficacious sign-situations, symbols, and myths which release in the reader the imaginative power to experience what the author really means to convey. And what he means to convey is not a system of truths which explain life but a certain depth of awareness in which life itself is lived more intensely and with a more meaningful direction. The "symbolic" in this sense is not a matter of contrived signification in which things point arbitrarily to something else. Symbols are signs which release the power of imaginative communion. ("Baptism," 98)

The value of this *sapiential* approach is in the way it enables readers to apprehend their deepest significance and ultimate destiny. As Merton declared, symbols "seek to help man liberate in himself life forces which are inhibited by dead social routine, by the ordinary involvement of the mind in trivial objects, by the conflicts of needs and of material interests on a limited level" and allow for a life of "poetic and contemplative awareness" where one encounters the truth hidden within "the drama of human existence" ("Baptism," 100). He later elaborates: "Sapiential thinking has, as another of its characteristics, the capacity to bridge the cognitive gap between our

minds and the realm of the transcendent and the unknown, so that
without 'understanding' what lies beyond the limit of human vision,
we nevertheless enter into an intuitive affinity with it, or seem to
experience some such affinity" ("Baptism," 100–1).

In his essay, Merton uses his commentary on "The Bear" to
illustrate this *sapiential* method. "The Bear" as *sapiential* myth, he
writes, is fully steeped in the religious, mythic tradition. Merton
first explains what he means by myth: "A myth is a tale with an archetypal pattern capable of suggesting and of implying that man's
life in the cosmos has a hidden meaning which can be sought and
found by one who somehow religiously identifies his own life with
that of the hero in the story" ("Baptism," 102).

The mythic arc of "The Bear"—indeed, the whole of *Go Down,
Moses*, of which it is a part—is for Merton an account of Ike McCaslin's
spiritual initiation: "It is clearly the story of a disciple being taught
and formed in a traditional and archaic wisdom by a charismatic
spiritual Father who . . . hands on not only a set of skills or a body
of knowledge, but a *mastery of life*, a certain way of being aware, of
being in touch not just with natural objects, with living things, but
with the cosmic spirit, with the wilderness itself regarded almost
as a supernatural being, a 'person'" ("Baptism," 103–4).

Ike's eventual sight of the Bear, named Old Ben, represents the
moment of his spiritual illumination. This is why Ike, the hunter in
constant search for his prey, is never able to see Old Ben until the
moment is right. Not until he is ready to surrender himself entirely
to the wilderness without defensive munitions does he become
properly disposed to come face to face with the one he seeks. This
resolve to approach the wilderness with solely his naked reserves
is the crucial turning point that allows Ike's initiation to take place.
Ike's nakedness is the symbol of his new consciousness, which is
unencumbered by his preconceived notions of how he is supposed
to relate to the world. It is a type of raw and immediate vision
freely opened to the present moment. With this new consciousness,
Merton explains, "He will learn to be not only a wonderful hunter
but a contemplative and prophet, a wise man who has beheld the
real ground of mystery and value which is concealed in the Edenic
wilderness and which others can only guess at" ("Baptism," 104).

The tragedy of the story of "The Bear" is that as an old man, even after his spiritual initiation, Ike finds his prophetic vision to be helpless in preventing a young relative from practicing injustice. Merton aptly summarizes Ike's predicament: "He has seen the inner meaning of the wilderness as an epiphany of the cosmic mystery. He has encountered the Bear and had his 'illumination.' In the light of this he has seen into the religious and historic mystery of the South which lies under judgment and under a curse. Yet there is nothing he can do about it apart from his monastic gesture, which remains ambiguous and abortive" ("Baptism," 104).

This reference to the civil rights problem, "the religious and historic mystery of the South," signals one of the major prophetic themes that run throughout Faulkner's novels. Merton was keenly sensitive to it, along with Faulkner's unpopularity because of it. Merton explained that unpopularity, in fact, as a "penalty for taking a unique personal position and not electing to run with some pack" (*Learning*, 185). As Merton's biographer, Michael Mott, notes, "Faulkner had the added credential of being equally unpopular with both sides on the issue."[49] Of course, the South's particular sin was slavery. But Faulkner's Ike feels that Southerners at least exemplified some forms of compassion toward their slaves.

John Hunt, in his book *William Faulkner: Art in Theological Tension*, offers helpful insights into Ike's "theological" perspective. As Hunt explains, Ike considered that the South was especially dear to God, even with its stain of the sin of slavery on its hands. The sin of the North, however, was worse: "Rugged individualism of the new industrialism expressing itself economically in *laissez-faire* capitalism produced a spiritual arrogance which could not go unpunished. God's purpose was lost in the celebration of the boundlessness of the human spirit, while with ruthless rapacity and greed the North manufactured for a profit the products of the southern society it condemned."[50]

---

[49] Michael Mott, *The Seven Mountains of Thomas Merton* (New York: Harcourt Brace, 1984), 475.

[50] John W. Hunt, *William Faulkner: Art in Theological Tension* (Syracuse, NY: Syracuse University Press, 1965), 148.

Merton reflected on Faulkner's mythic battle between North and South in his journal entry for February 15, 1967. While admitting Faulkner's penchant for "tirade" and "schizoid grandiloquence" in the debate between privacy and government, he insisted that Faulkner's idiosyncrasy and individuality ought to be respected by his readers, not reproved and despised, as was often the case. For Merton, Faulkner's brand of Southern mythology is far more persuasive and compelling than the perspective offered by the North: "The danger of his mythology is precisely that it is convincing, and in many ways better, more coherent, certainly more alive and interesting than Northern liberal mythology. It presents a seemingly plausible case for the contrivance of what is completely finished—and can't get anywhere" (*Learning*, 199). Thus it is in Faulkner's ambivalent and peculiar position toward the South that Merton discerns Faulkner's prophetic vocation. While embracing the South, Faulkner also stands apart from it. He stands apart from it in order to speak his prophetic mythology to it and lead it into a more humane future.

The Faulknerian myth, "The Bear," and Southern mythology are meant to be read, in Merton's view, as narratives that reinforce one another. Merton scholar Thomas Del Prete interprets Merton's reading of Faulkner's program of spiritual formation as set forth in "The Bear" as a story of "learning how to live beyond boundaries."[51] It is a story where the initiated move beyond linear time and enter into an eschatological dimension of reality. It is the place of "nowhere" that is the privileged place of prophetic insight and wisdom. Faulkner's commentary on the South demonstrates that it is only in this place of "nowhere" that the mythic story can be told honestly and accurately. These insights lead Del Prete in his treatment of "The Bear" to observations about Merton himself: "Clearly Merton is challenging boundaries . . . refusing to be bound by certain cultural assumptions and expectations which make a person into an image and reality into a product, and which pigeonhole him in some spiritually stifling place" ("Geography," 6). And later, "There is a hidden geography beyond the boundaries

---

[51] Thomas Del Prete, "The Geography of Nowhere: Living Beyond Boundaries," *Merton Seasonal* 24, no. 3 (1999): 3–8, here 3.

of space and culture, a spiritual geography shaped by compassion, which, with profound implications for Merton's engagement with the social issues of his time, identifies him with the 'struggles and suffering of the world'" ("Geography," 7). Del Prete's insights into Merton's reading of Faulkner highlight the prophetic affinity that existed between these two American writers.

Merton's reading of Faulkner's *sapiential* approach continued with his treatment of Faulkner's 1939 novel *The Wild Palms*. Read as a sort of biblical "meditation,"[52] Merton says, *The Wild Palms* is a "symbolic presentation of deep, classic truths about man and human values" ("Faulkner Meditations," 515). Merton notes that Faulkner's approach is highly individual. It combines two apparently unrelated stories ("Old Man" and "Wild Palms"), told in alternating fashion.[53] This approach, which Merton defines as "counterpoint" ("Faulkner Meditations," 517),[54] has the effect of taking the reader more deeply into the meanings Faulkner was trying to convey—more deeply, Merton mentions, than could have been grasped by reading the stories independently of one another.

The two stories "Old Man" and "Wild Palms" are, as Merton notes, "pitched on entirely different levels" ("Faulkner Meditations," 516) but have one underlying theme in common: "each is the story of a man and a woman thrown into situations where they are completely alone and isolated from the rest of the world, engulfed in a flood, a 'tidal wave' that threatens to destroy them" ("Faulkner Meditations," 517). On one level, the novel is about the social and psychological situation of modern people. On another level, it is about the wisdom of "preternatural" people told in mythic form. The significance of this juxtaposition, for Merton, is that as the two

---

[52] Merton, "Faulkner Meditations: *The Wild Palms*," in *Literary Essays*, 515–36, here 515.

[53] Merton consistently refers to the story of "Wild Palms" as "The Wild Palms," but both the original 1939 publication and other commentators lack the article. He is consistent, however, in referring to the novel as *The Wild Palms*.

[54] Merton points out that *counterpoint* was the word Faulkner himself used to describe what he was trying to do in "Wild Palms."

stories move along, the characters in the mythological tale end up being depicted as more human than those in the modern tale. As Merton explains, "In them Faulkner seems to be presenting a sort of quintessential humanity: *they* are man-and-woman and the other two, the moderns, are simply a couple of poor, beat-up, ruined people" ("Faulkner Meditations," 517).

"Old Man" is about a "tall convict" who finds himself swept out of his penitentiary (which Merton likens to a monastery) by the flooding of the Mississippi River in 1927. The goal of this "tall convict" is to return to the penitentiary and escape from the chaos that confronts him at every turn out in the world. After he rescues a woman whom he encounters while being swept along the river in his rowboat, they together are hurled down the Mississippi, ending up in the Cajun country of the Louisiana delta. One life-threatening incident after another occurs, yet nothing prevails over the "tall convict" and the woman he saved (who has by now even had a child amid the surrounding chaos). When after months battling the primal chaos of the Mississippi the convict returns finally to the security and solitude of his "monastic" penitentiary, he proudly hands over the woman he saved along with her newborn baby.

The modern tale told in "Wild Palms" seems wholly different. A man meets a married woman with whom he falls in love. They each believe that the greatest value in life is the love that they share. They do not see any value in marriage but see it only as an obstacle to their life together. All that matters is what they call love. Their so-called love leads to the conception of a child and a botched abortion that leaves the woman, Charlotte, bleeding in the hands of a doctor whom the male character, Harry, has found by chance. Charlotte is taken to the nearby hospital, where she undergoes an operation to restore her to health, but to no avail. She dies on the operating table. Harry is hauled off to the penitentiary. Their enmeshment in each other results in the destruction of each.

Merton's interpretation of the novel hinges on the significance of the mythic power of the river, which is for him a "symbolic expression of the tragedy of life" ("Faulkner Meditations," 519). This motif of the river as "deluge" ties the stories together and imbues them with multiple layers of meaning. Merton comments:

> Where the novel gets interesting is in the correspondence
> between the material on a cosmic scale in "Old Man" and
> the modern man and woman in "The Wild Palms" who are
> also engulfed in a flood, a deluge, a tragedy of their own
> making, but they don't realize it. They are typical, modern
> people who don't believe in anything, are convinced that
> death is the end of it, we live our lives since that's all there
> is. This is the basic faith of modern man! This is what peo-
> ple today think! I want to get something out of life before
> it's too late! This faith is what Faulkner's two-level novel
> finally torpedoes as he describes its shallowness and stu-
> pidity: That's not the way to live! People who try it let loose
> in their lives a titanic flood, a tremendous force, without
> even knowing what they are doing, without even knowing
> they are also in a "flood." ("Faulkner Meditations," 519)

Of the many corresponding themes between the cosmic descriptions in "Old Man" and tragic descriptions in "Wild Palms,"
the most significant is the theme of life and death. "Old Man"
depicts life that comes forth out of chaos. "Wild Palms" depicts
the denial of life and the imprisonment that allegiance to modern
values brings. As Merton notes, Faulkner has embedded throughout *The Wild Palms* biblical symbolism. He sees the symbol of the
flood as an "eschatological symbol": "Faulkner is saying that *our
life* is like being in the flood. *We are in the deluge*" ("Faulkner Meditation," 520). This interpretation of *The Wild Palms* leads Merton to
this bold statement: "[Faulkner's] novels and stories are far more
prophetic in the Biblical sense than the writings of any theologian
writing today (at least, any that I know!). . . . I am convinced that
we have before us a better idea about man and nature and values
and God than can be found in the whole Spiritual Directory, and
everything else on the Mystical Theology Shelf as well" ("Faulkner
Meditations," 520–21).

Of course, Merton did not have any intention of baptizing
Faulkner and forcing on his thought a Christian interpretation.
He intended his reference to Faulkner's prophetic writing "in the
Biblical sense" to be understood not as if Faulkner himself were
intentionally proclaiming the faith of Abraham, Isaac, and Jacob

or that of Jesus Christ. Merton took Faulkner's writing to be prophetic "in the Biblical sense" because Faulkner boldly and vividly
put forth myths that were pervaded with biblical symbolism and
wisdom. Faulkner was a religious humanist, not a Jew or Christian. He desired to explore the mythical, symbolic, religious, and
sapiential meanings of reality.

Faulkner's approach to literature was much like that of Joyce,
Proust, Camus, and the other modernists of his era: truth is known
only in vague shadows, life is permeated with doubt and frustration, hope and understanding come only when one approaches
life with authenticity and radical honesty. According to Merton's
interpretation, for Faulkner, like Camus, the ideal way to communicate in such a philosophical atmosphere was through mythic
storytelling informed by *sapiential* content.

Thus Merton's provocative assertions that Faulkner was "*the*
American prophet of the twentieth century" and that his writings
were "far more prophetic in the Biblical sense than the writings
of any theologian writing today" find their legitimacy only when
understanding them in light of the value he places on Faulkner's
sapiential-mythic approach to storytelling. The prophet, then,
emerges in Merton's interpretation of Faulkner as the wise man
or woman, endowed with penetrating insight into the reality of
things. Such people have a remarkable ability to recognize the social
and cultural flaws in popular consciousness and possess the gift
of bringing these flaws to awareness through symbolic narratives
that not only condemn but also—through wise admonition—point
toward a more life-giving way of being in the world.

Merton scholar Patrick O'Connell explicates this connection between wisdom and prophecy in his article "Wisdom and Prophecy:
The Two Poles of Thomas Merton's Mature Spirituality." Interestingly, he is able to substantiate his thesis without any mention of
Faulkner's influence.[55] Nevertheless, his conclusions are applicable
here and informative:

---

[55] Other scholars place more emphasis than O'Connell on Faulkner's
formative influence on Merton's understanding of a *sapiential* reading of
fiction. See e.g., George Kilcourse in *Ace of Freedoms: Thomas Merton's Christ*

In Merton's mature spirituality the sapiential is balanced by the prophetic. If wisdom recognizes how creation already manifests the presence of God, prophecy calls attention to the gaps between divine design and human realization, the personal and social failures and consequent brokenness that obscure or interfere with the unfolding of God's will for the creation. Hence Merton's attentiveness to the ruptured bonds between creation and Creator, the alienation and isolation caused by the rejection of wisdom, the violation of the divine image through violence and war, racial and religious prejudice, and the exploitation of the poor. But for Merton, as for Jeremiah, the prophetic calling is not just to "root up and to tear down" but "to build and to plant" (cf. Jer. 1:10), not just denunciation but annunciation, a bringing of the future into the present, a call to model God's covenantal love and justice here and now. . . . Without the leaven of prophecy, wisdom might tend to overlook the problems and contradictions of the concrete human condition. . . . Conversely without the grounding of wisdom, prophecy could become shrill, harsh

---

(Notre Dame, IN: University of Notre Dame Press, 1993); and "Spirituality and Imagination: Thomas Merton's Sapiential Thinking," in M. Basil Pennington, ed., *Toward an Integrated Humanity: Thomas Merton's Journey*, CS 103 (Kalamazoo, MI: Cistercian Publications, 1988), 114–31; Ross Labrie, in "Thomas Merton on Art and Religion in William Faulkner," *Religion and the Arts* 14 (2010): 401–17. Kilcourse, however, makes no connection between wisdom and prophecy, and Labrie does so only cursorily. Michael Mott alludes to the connection: "With a careful reading of the works of Camus and Faulkner, Merton was coming to a new sense of the power of certain writers to reach a hidden level of truth through fictional models" (*Seven Mountains*, 477). O'Connell, even while failing to mention the influence of literary figures on Merton's understanding of wisdom or prophecy, remains the only scholar to place such an important emphasis on the symbiotic relationship between the two. He sees the primary influences of wisdom as coming from the Bible and Eastern religions, and the primary influences of prophecy as coming from the Old Testament prophetic tradition and the monastic movement within Christianity. See also Patrick O'Connell, "Prophecy" in *The Thomas Merton Encyclopedia*, ed. William H. Shannon, et al. (Maryknoll, NY: Orbis Books, 2002), 372–74.

and self-righteous: it could degenerate into what Merton calls the "frenzy of the activist," which "destroys the fruitfulness of his own work, because it kills the root of inner wisdom which makes work fruitful."[56]

Concluding Remarks

Merton's early love for literature and his faith in it to communicate important truths of life became a central interest in his final ten years. Dismayed by the confusion prevalent in the philosophical and theological discourse of his day, Merton was finely attuned to the resulting void left in the consciousness of a world in desperate need of meaning and direction. Renewed hope was enkindled with his reading of three novelists whose prophetic writings he found endowed with profound significance.

Of the three, Boris Pasternak is the only writer with whom Merton had a personal correspondence, however brief. Merton's affection for this "prophet of a new age" was profound. Unlike Camus and Faulkner, about whose personal lives Merton made little comment, Pasternak embodied for him the life of a prophet. In Pasternak he saw one whose life was in complete conformity with his writing. Pasternak, he thought, lived prophetically, and his *Doctor Zhivago* should therefore be understood as the fruit of his prophetic existence. In this novel, he said, Pasternak offered a penetrating example of prophetic fiction.

Characterized by a narrative imbued with symbolic imagery and humanistic themes, the novel was an indictment of shallow, materialistic philosophies that reduce the human person to a social organism. Through its utilization of multiple contrasts (person vs. social organization, true vs. false humanism, spirituality vs. materialism), Pasternak had constructed a work of prophetic protest, in which peace and love triumph over violence and hatred. The hero of the novel, however flawed, is the artist and symbolist

[56] Patrick O'Connell, "Wisdom and Prophecy: The Two Poles of Thomas Merton's Mature Spirituality," *American Benedictine Review* 60, no. 3 (2009): 276–98, at 277–78. The Merton words come from *Conjectures*, 86.

whose *gadavardic* life and sacramental poetry offered the healing and transforming love necessary to save the whole human family. His prophetic art, proclaiming the triumph of the spirit, thus inaugurated the "new age" of Boris Pasternak.

The prophet as artist is also a central theme in Albert Camus's self-understanding as a writer of fiction. Through his mythical novels, Camus demonstrates that the prophet is the one who humbly comes to reconcile a fallen world, lost in the chaos of nihilism, back to the human values from which it fell. Camus's program of prophetic revolt begins in one's decision to live authentically, separated from the mass consciousness that is bent toward a nihilistic void. Arising in one's alienated solitude are the "prophetic flutters" that both give evidence to one's authentic existence and witness to human truth ("The Plague," 196).

Camus's prophet of revolt, rather than being a sanctimonious herald of righteousness, is the relentless and self-sacrificial worker who never tires of resisting the void of the absurd. This resistance requires a commitment to bold and lucid communication, at whatever cost. Merton gravitated toward Camus's criticism of the church in this regard, highlighting the need for better and more effective means of ecclesiastical prophetic communication.

The novel as mythic storytelling took center stage in Merton's reading of William Faulkner. Although Faulkner used a methodology similar to that of Camus, Merton was finally able to articulate what he called a *sapiential* approach to writing only in Faulkner. Through commentary on "The Bear" and *The Wild Palms*, Merton explicated a theory that provided the basis for his bold assertion that Faulkner was "*the* American prophet of the twentieth century." Through his *sapiential*-mythic storytelling, Merton thought Faulkner perceptively analyzed the race problem in American culture and shone a light on the many ways in which Americans continued to persist in living with corrupt and deceitful motivations. From Faulkner Merton learned that the prophet is the one whose choice to live in simple solitude, dependent on nature, yields the lessons of wisdom, from which flow the mythic narratives that provide for human redemption.

In reading Pasternak, Camus, and Faulkner, Merton arrived at an understanding of authors as prophets, with their prophetic role beginning in their being fundamentally artists. They are artists who write with a particular ability to define the symbolic, the poetic, and the mythological. Through their *sapiential* storytelling, such authors compassionately yet resolutely expose the social injustices and cultural maladies of the world around them. Their inward drive urges them to write with forceful and lucid protest, through courageous, selfless communication. They write with a cause—the cause of restoring human values back into public consciousness.

As Merton recognized, the humanism of all three authors, while not overtly Christian, was deeply religious. They were fearless advocates of the human spiritual dimension and saw solitude as the atmosphere necessary to form the prophetic consciousness. While Camus's prophet is of a particularly philosophical bent, Pasternak's and Faulkner's prophet is more *sacramental*, emphasizing a transformative encounter with sacred images and symbols. Yet all three writers—prophets, in Merton's understanding—were gifted with deeply perceptive wisdom and insight, enabling them to be liberators of those caught in the muddle of existential chaos and confusion.

PART TWO

The Existentialist as Prophet

Chapter 5

A Prophecy of Faith and Hope
Thomas Merton and Christian Existentialism

My whole life is an epigram calculated to make people aware.[1]
—Søren Kierkegaard

Between 1958 and 1965, among the predominant themes of Thomas Merton's letters and journals were the insights he garnered by wrestling with the existentialist thinkers of the nineteenth and twentieth centuries. Merton's attraction to philosophical existentialism appears in his esteem for Albert Camus, who while rejecting the existentialist label certainly promoted existentialist themes in his novels. Yet Merton had a more direct engagement with the leaders of the existentialist movement.

In 1940, at the age of twenty-five, Merton purchased his first book by Søren Kierkegaard (1813–1855). Its title, *Fear and Trembling*, appropriately signifies its effect on him in his initial reading. He quickly developed a fascination for Kierkegaard, copying excerpts of Kierkegaard's works in the Boston Public Library and in Harvard's Widener Library when he made a brief excursion to Boston in late 1940. Merton's adolescent enthusiasm for Kierkegaard, however, was short-lived. He did not mention him again for about sixteen years. In the late 1950s, however, when Merton began engaging the popular philosophical and cultural voices of the world, he once again picked up Kierkegaard and began to read him anew. By this

---

[1] Cited in H. J. Blackham, *Six Existentialist Thinkers* (New York: Harper & Row, 1959), 6. This quotation is taken from Søren Kierkegaard, *Journals and Papers*, trans. and ed. Howard V. Hong and Edna H. Hong, vol. 5 (Bloomington, IN: Indiana University Press, 1978), 435.

time, though, his enthusiasm for the existentialist approach had become much broader. Along with Kierkegaard, he had come to value Gabriel Marcel (1889–1973), Karl Jaspers (1883–1973), Martin Heidegger (1884–1976), Jean-Paul Sartre (1905–80), and theologians who drew significant inspiration from existentialist ideas, namely, Nicolas Berdyaev (1874–1948) and Rudolf Bultmann (1884–1976). Like the poets and novelists Merton was also reading at this time, much of these existentialists' writing struck him as having a definite prophetic character, both in content and, in some cases, in expression.

The fruit of Merton's grappling with existentialist ideas resulted in his essay "The Other Side of Despair: Notes on Christian Existentialism," first published in the October–November 1965 issue of *The Critic*. It later appeared in his book *Mystics and Zen Masters*, published in 1967. In it he not only expounds the major themes in existentialist thought—themes like freedom, authenticity, dread, despair, commitment, and fidelity—but also offers original insights from the vantage point of a Christian contemplative. This essay offers a worthy framework in considering what Merton understood to be the prophetic dimension of existentialism, both in a general sense and, more pointedly, in the sense of Christian existentialism.

The essay begins with Merton's situating the then-current responses given to the century-old existentialist movement, noting in particular the conservative reaction, whose appellation "the existentialist revolt" expressed conservatives' perspective on how the peculiar religious overtones of Kierkegaard inevitably led to Sartre's outright rebellion against the decency and sanity of his era. Merton also noted the church's cautious response, along with Gabriel Marcel's eventual repudiation of the "existentialist" label. The so-called revolt was primarily aimed toward the popular notion of the existentialist movement as articulated by the French literary figures (mainly Camus and Sartre).

Yet this form of existentialism was not that which most interested the church. Rather, the church found of most interest the existentialism of Heidegger, which had come to have such a deep influence on Christian theology, both Catholic and Protestant.

Many who did not know what to make of Heidegger's secular approach to the sacred sciences considered his disciples, such as the Roman Catholic theologian Karl Rahner and the Protestant biblical scholar Rudolf Bultmann, dangerous. Such ambivalence was still in the air in the mid-sixties when Merton wrote his article, which can be understood as his effort to bring clarity to the theological confusion.

The first task in Merton's attempt at clarification was to find an adequate description of existentialism. In his article he described it as "an experience and an attitude, rather than a system of thought."[2] As an example, he specified the area where he thought existentialism had been most unambiguously expressed: in literature. Ironically, his representative was not Camus but an American fiction writer, Flannery O'Connor. Merton offered this description of O'Connor's existential approach:

> The first thing that anyone notices in reading Flannery O'Connor is that her moral evaluations seem to be strangely scrambled. The good people are bad and the bad people tend to be less bad than they seem. . . . Her crazy people, while remaining as crazy as they can possibly be, turn out to be governed by a strange kind of sanity. In the end, it is the sane ones who are incurable lunatics. The "good," the "right," the "kind" do all the harm. "Love" is a force for destruction, and "truth" is the best way to tell a lie. (*Mystics*, 259)

What results, he continued, is an unsettling feeling that comes over the reader: "we are on the side of the fanatic and the mad boy, and we are against this reasonable zombie. We are against everything he stands for. We find ourselves nauseated by the reasonable, objective, 'scientific' answers he has for everything. In him, science is so right that it is a disaster" (*Mystics*, 260).

Existentialism as defined here is the case against the gods of science and sociology in a positivist society, or, stated positively, "It

[2] Thomas Merton, *Mystics and Zen Masters* (New York: Farrar, Straus and Giroux, 1967), 258.

is a brief for the person and for personal, spiritual liberty against determinism and curtailment" (*Mystics*, 261). Merton thus argues that existentialists, seeing the gross limitations of positivist know-how that results from only asking the questions *how* and *what*, insist on asking the questions *who* and *why*. Only then can the concrete personal subject be discovered, as well as the proper use of that person's authentic freedom—and that is the goal of the existentialist.

Merton then brought into the discussion Kierkegaard's *The Present Age*, a book he described as "completely prophetic,"[3] introduced to substantiate the chief existentialists' complaint against the positivists. In Merton's words, this complaint runs as follows: "the claim of science and technology to expand the capacity of the human person for life and happiness is basically fraudulent, because technological society is not the least interested in values, still less in persons: it is concerned purely and simply with the functioning of its own processes. Human beings are used merely as means to this end" (*Mystics*, 263). Merton highlights a certain "prophetic page" (*Mystics*, 263) from the book to demonstrate that Kierkegaard was already exposing this philosophical problem a hundred years earlier. The ideas that interested Merton are represented by Kierkegaard's terms *leveling* and *reflection*, terms that more recent existentialists had replaced with *alienation* and *estrangement*. By *leveling* Merton interprets Kierkegaard to mean the process by which "the individual person loses himself in the vast emptiness of a public mind" (*Mystics*, 263). In equating this abstraction of the public mind with the truth, he said, people forfeit their own experience and intuition and lose their own conscience. This abdication of the self into pure abstraction is the exchange of the soul for the "public void" of a collective myth (*Mystics*, 264). In so explaining the process and its effects, Merton relies on Kierkegaard's explanation in his book *The Present Age*: "More and more individuals, owing to their bloodless indolence, will aspire to be nothing at all—in order to become the

---

[3] Thomas Merton, *Dancing in the Water of Life: Seeking Peace in the Hermitage*, ed. Robert E. Daggy, The Journals of Thomas Merton, vol. 5 (New York: HarperCollins, 1997), 275.

public."[4] Kierkegaard goes on to liken such leveling to a "hopeless forest fire of abstraction" (*Present Age*, 81): "The abstract leveling process, that self-combustion of the human race produced by the friction which arises when the individual ceases to exist as singled out by religion, is bound to continue like a trade wind until it consumes everything" (*Present Age*, 55–56).

This danger of losing one's soul to the public void of abstract myth was the central idea of which the existentialist was most intimately aware and most concerned to prevent. For this very reason, the existentialist faced condemnation, as Merton noted, from both the capitalist positivism of America and the Marxist positivism of the Communist countries. This condemnation came, he said, for one principal reason: "he is a rebel, an individualist, who, because he withdraws from the common endeavor of technological society to brood on his own dissatisfactions, condemns himself to futility, sterility, and despair. Since he refuses to participate in the glorious and affluent togetherness of mass society, he must pay the price of fruitless isolation" (*Mystics*, 265). Merton admitted that this description was a particular kind of caricature—mainly the overly negative and dissolute kind that characterized Sartre. Nevertheless, he thought that it demonstrated an important reality that faced the existentialist movement as a whole: its orientation was basically prophetic in nature, and existentialists had to be willing to pay the price for their prophetic stance against mass society.

Although Merton ended his discussion of *The Present Age* at this point, a few other aspects of Kierkegaard's book probably led to Merton's response to it as "completely prophetic" (*Dancing*, 275). Kierkegaard opened his book with a description of the present age as filled with numbing apathy and endless reflection. What was missing in society, he said, was passion and creative energy, which provide the fuel for social revolutions and society's transformation. Kierkegaard lamented, "A revolutionary age is an age of action; ours is the age of advertisement and publicity. Nothing ever happens

---

[4] Søren Kierkegaard, *The Present Age*, trans. Alexander Dru (New York: Harper and Row, 1962), 64.

but there is immediate publicity everywhere. In the present age a rebellion is, of all things, the most unthinkable" (*Present Age*, 35). The human person, he went on, had forgotten how to grow and engage his or her social environment because human spontaneity and vitality had been sacrificed to the god of reason. All that remained were sudden outbursts of enthusiasm that quickly withered and faded back into apathetic reflection.

Kierkegaard rooted his idea of passion within the moral subject. For him, morality was a character engraved deep within the human soul. The problem with the present age was that it was morally ambiguous, and ambiguity enters into life when the qualitative distinctions of good and evil are weakened by a gnawing reflection; hence the need for a "revolt of the passions" (*Present Age*, 43). As he explained, "The springs of life, which are only what they are because of the qualitative differentiating power of passion, lose their elasticity" (*Present Age*, 43). What results is the person's inability to act with passion.

Continuing his analysis of the existentialist protest against mass society, Merton cited two other works that had contributed to the discussion: Karl Jasper's *Man in the Modern World* and Gabriel Marcel's *Man against Mass Society*. These works had this in common: they both demonstrated that authentic existence is much more than *Dasein*, the inert being-there-in-the-world in a state of alienated passivity. The human person is more than a die in a crap game thrown into being. Rather, the person bears the power to make a decision to exist truly even in his or her own finiteness and "nothingness." As Merton explains, when one approaches nothingness from a matter of personal choice and not as a "vast, formless void of the anonymous mass" (*Mystics*, 266), one discovers it to be "a presence, a voice, an option in the actions of the real world" (*Mystics*, 266).

For Merton, existentialism was a philosophy of life that found its fulfillment in its engagement with mass society. It was not a form of monastic withdrawal. One of the goals of the existentialist movement was to create and foster authentic community. Authentic community can only happen in a group of authentic *people*. In order to experience one's own authentic personality, which is suitable for true community, Merton argued that a certain posture toward oneself and the other is required, namely *openness*: "True openness means the acceptance of one's own existence and one's own possibilities in confrontation with, and in free, vital relation with, the existence and potentialities of the other. It means genuine acceptance, response, participation" (*Mystics*, 267–68).

What the existentialist seeks to combat are the falsifications rampant in mass society that produce a personality closed off to authentic freedom—both within oneself and toward the other. Merton saw that "The freedom by which one delivers oneself from the tyranny of the void is the freedom to choose oneself without being determined beforehand by the public, either in its typological fantasies or in its sociological pressures. What then is the basis of this choice? In what sense can it be called unconditional? In the sense that it is made in and proceeds from the inviolate sanctuary of the personal conscience" (*Mystics*, 268).

Merton considered this free choice of the personal conscience to be the aspect of existentialism that separated atheistic existentialism from its more religious form. Jaspers and Marcel, the main proponents of religious existentialism, both demonstrated that conscience was incomprehensible apart from its interpretation as an aspect of the voice of the "transcendent Ground of being and freedom" (*Mystics*, 269). Merton offered additional clarification of their views: "the basic choice by which one elects to have one's own personal, autonomous existence is a choice *of oneself as a freedom that has been gratuitously given by God*. It is acceptance of one's existence and one's freedom as pure gift" (*Mystics*, 269). For the religious existentialist, he said, even Sartre's blank nothingness became "the luminous abyss of divine gift" (*Mystics*, 269). In this sense, he noted, even the more nonreligious forms of existentialism were unconsciously oriented toward a religious worldview.

The popular criticism of existentialism as a philosophical movement leading to negativism, disillusionment, and immorality was rejected by these religious proponents. Christian existentialism, Merton showed, was grounded in the concrete and personal and articulated mainly through a biblical mode of expression. Citing Karl Adam, "whom," Merton quipped, "no one would think of calling an existentialist" (*Mystics*, 270), he demonstrated the effectiveness that existentialism can have in theology: "Every 'Credo,' if said in the spirit of the church, ought to be an act of complete dedication of the entire man to God, an assent springing from the great and ineffable distress of our finite nature and our sin."[5]

Such faith, much more than a mental assent to religious doctrine, however sincere, issues from "the intimate spiritual ground of one's own existence" (*Mystics*, 271). It is total assent, not partial. The Bible, in Merton's view, demonstrated that humankind is, without equivocation, fallen and alienated, estranged in the delusion of its own existence apart from God. What was required, Merton insisted, was repentance and a complete overhaul of consciousness in order for one to be set on the right course. A false optimism about humankind's condition that undermines the effects of evil on both the human person and the human community is something that theological existentialism exposes and seeks to overcome. As he argued, "We must reemphasize the call of the Gospel to healing and to hope, not merely reaffirm that everything is going to be all right because man is smart and will meet the challenge of evil with the best possible solutions" (*Mystics*, 273). Without this oppositional stance toward evil and its dehumanizing effects, religion loses its relevance and simply becomes just another social movement—one that is impotent to instigate real change. Merton explains the consequence of this idea for religious understanding:

> If organized religion abdicates its mission to disturb man in the depths of his conscience, and seeks instead to "make converts" that will smilingly adjust to the status quo, then it deserves the most serious and uncompromising criticism. Such criticism is not a disloyalty. On the contrary, fidelity to truth and to God demands it. One of the most important aspects of our current biblical-existentialist theology is precisely the prophetic consciousness of a duty to question the claims of any religious practice that collaborates with the "process of leveling" and alienation. (*Mystics*, 273)

[5] Karl Adam, *Two Essays by Karl Adam: Christ and the Western Mind; Love and Belief*, trans. Edward Bullough (New York: Macmillan, 1930), 41; cited in *Mystics*, 270–71.

The concept of fidelity to which Merton alludes in this passage carries great significance in his understanding of prophecy, as appears in a number of other passages from his writings, especially his personal correspondence. To Mother Coakley, a Religious of the Sacred Heart, Merton wrote, "For we are called above all to be signs of His mercy in the world, and our fidelity will in its turn be a small sign to others of His fidelity, not that our fidelity has any value in itself, but it enables Him to give us richer blessings and to manifest Himself in doing good to us who are nothing."[6] To Mr. Donn he wrote, "The Prophets have taught us that Israel is a great sign of the fidelity of God to His promises and His revealed plan for mankind."[7] After reading Abraham Heschel's *The Prophets*, he wrote to Heschel, "They offer us examples of fidelity to Him and patterns of suffering and faith which we must take into account if we are to live as religious men in any sense of the word."[8]

Most important and comprehensive of these comments is a passage from *The Springs of Contemplation*, the text of a set of retreats given to contemplative nuns toward the end of his life and posthumously transcribed and published. Merton's perspective was distinctive: "We just let Christ be faithful to us. If we live with

[6] Merton to Mother Coakley, January 3, 1965, in Thomas Merton, *The School of Charity: The Letters of Thomas Merton on Religious Renewal and Spiritual Direction*, ed. Patrick Hart (New York: Farrar, Straus and Giroux, 1990), 261–62.

[7] Merton to Mr. Donn, September 23, 1966, in Thomas Merton, *Witness to Freedom: The Letters of Thomas Merton in Times of Crisis*, ed. William H. Shannon, Thomas Merton Letters, vol. 5 (New York: Farrar, Straus and Giroux, 1994), 326. Little is known about the identity of Mr. Donn (no first name is ever mentioned). All that is known is that he sent Merton a copy of the quarterly publication *Israel's Anchorage: The Voice of Messianic Judaism*.

[8] Merton to Heschel, January 26, 1963, in Thomas Merton, *The Hidden Ground of Love: The Letters of Thomas Merton on Religious Experience and Social Concerns*, ed. William H. Shannon (New York: Farrar, Straus and Giroux, 1985), 431. The subject of Merton and Heschel's friendship and correspondence has been studied by Edward K. Kaplan in "Abraham Heschel and Thomas Merton: Prophetic Personalities, Prophetic Friendship," *The Merton Annual* 23 (2010): 106–15, where he states, "The human responsibility to the living God is a foundational element of their alliance" (108).

that kind of mind, we are prophetic. We become prophetic when we live in such a way that our life is an experience of the infallible fidelity of God. That's the kind of prophecy we are called to, not the business of being able to smell the latest fashion coming ten years before it happens. It is simply being in tune with God's mercy and will."[9] He continued: "In other words, if we trust God to act in us, God will act in us. This is how our lives become prophetic. Prophecy is not a technique, it is not about telling someone else what to do. If we are completely open to the Holy Spirit, then the Spirit will be able to lead us where God wants us to go. Going along that line, our lives will be prophetic" (*Springs*, 74).[10]

Merton's line of thought here proceeds along the way of the development of faith in the life of the Christian. The spiritual life is understood as the nexus for prophetic activity because of its environment, which fosters the maturation of fidelity to God. Prophetic activity does not present itself as a goal for which the Christian must strive but as a fruit of a life lived in the Spirit. Merton's favored interpretation of prophecy was the one presented by the prophets of the Hebrew Scriptures, whose tenacious faith in God led them to be moved with both passion and compassion for the wayward Israelites and for their reconciliation to God.[11] Total allegiance to God, then, he believed, leads to a way of living in the world that is a sign of God's faithfulness to his people. The prophets' unfailing commitment to the well-being of the Israelites at whatever cost expressed the depth of God's loving-kindness toward his people and the extent to which he was willing to go in order to remain

---

[9] Thomas Merton, *The Springs of Contemplation: A Retreat at the Abbey of Gethsemani*, ed. Jane Marie Richardson (Farrar, Straus and Giroux, 1992), 73.

[10] For a fuller treatment of prophecy in *The Springs of Contemplation*, see chap. 8.

[11] Merton's own prophetic passion at times found expression in the following manner: "When I am most sickened by the things that are done by the country that surrounds this place I will take out the prophets and sing them in loud Latin across the hills and send their fiery words sailing south over the mountains to the place where they split atoms for the bombs in Tennessee" (*Dancing*, 240).

true to his covenantal promises. Our faithfulness in return will inevitably make us prophetic.

Yet Merton's interpretation of prophecy in terms of fidelity intimated a concern that he shared with the Christian existentialists, especially that of Gabriel Marcel. Merton was aware of this concern and struggled with it in a journal passage from early 1963:

> The great trial of fidelity in Christian life—a trial which springs from the fact that we too closely identify *fidelity to God* and *fidelity to external organization* in the Catholic Church. Hence there is invariably a great trial when an apparent conflict is precipitated (and it is easily precipitated). There are times when it seems that fidelity to God is *not* compatible with mere obedience to an external norm, where fidelity to God requires something else: certainly not revolt or disobedience, but a presentation of alternatives and deeper views. A "fidelity" which *always* demands the sacrifice of the interior and the more perfect in order to conform to an external norm that is mediocre, and requires of us only passivity and inertia, is an infidelity to God and to His Church. Yet at the same time we must not make a fetish out of autonomy and be "faithful" only to our own will, for this is the other way to infidelity. The answer is in the Church considered less as an organization than as a living body of interrelated freedoms. Fidelity belongs not so much to the realm of Law as to the realm of love. But it presupposes obedience and self-sacrifice.[12]

Merton's struggle with authority, especially the authority of his abbot, James Fox, is well documented.[13] A number of Merton scholars have referred to him as a "rebel."[14] His prophetic writings

[12] Thomas Merton, *Turning Toward the World: The Pivotal Years*, ed. Victor A. Kramer, The Journals of Thomas Merton, vol. 4 (New York: Harper-Collins, 1996), 289–90.

[13] See especially Merton's journals.

[14] Two popular titles make obvious reference to this view: William Shannon's *'Something of a Rebel': Thomas Merton, His Life and Works: An Introduction* (Cincinnati, OH: St. Anthony Messenger Press, 1997); and

on peace and non-violence show his intense frustration at how he thought authoritative figures in the church failed to oppose what were to him obvious ethical infringements on human rights and justice. But to paint Merton simply as a rebellious prophet angrily flailing invectives against ecclesiastical powers is a gross oversimplification of a man who deeply and genuinely cared, to his dying day, about the well-being of the Roman Catholic Church and his monastery. He especially demonstrated this deep attachment in his efforts to come to a mature understanding of obedience in the Christian life in general, and in his monastic life in particular.[15]

Merton experienced a breakthrough in this regard when in 1958 he read Gabriel Marcel's *Homo Viator*. In his journal he wrote of at once coming upon the essay "Obedience and Fidelity" in the book. This essay, in essence, helped to bring clarity to much of the confusion surrounding his relationship with his abbot. The journal entry of early 1963 quoted above demonstrates the result of implementing many of the insights Marcel voiced in his book.

This existential wrestling with the reality of a person's freedom and loyalties within the institutional confines and limitations of a spiritual community formed a sort of crucible through which Merton saw a person's faith being purified and perfected. The prophet, he thought, was one who persevered through this purifying process and became a beacon of the resulting holiness. Faith is truly purified not by a passive acquiescence to the purifying flames of God's love but only through a total engagement with the dread of one's own finite existence in the face of divine mystery. Like Jacob, Job, and Jeremiah, one dares to confront God for meaning and insight into the absurdities and mystifications of one's own existence. Only then does one truly come to know God and have something meaningful to communicate to others. Only then does one come to know the true meaning of faith and obedience: "The

---

Michael Higgins's *Heretic Blood: The Spiritual Geography of Thomas Merton* (Toronto: Stoddart Publishing, 1998).

[15] Michael Mott writes, "Dom James told many in Merton's lifetime that Father Louis was 'a most faithful monk, a most obedient monk.'" See *The Seven Mountains of Thomas Merton* (New York: Houghton Mifflin, 1984), 279.

prophet is a man of God not only in the sense that he is seized and controlled passively by God, but much more truly in the sense that he is consciously and freely obedient to the Holy Spirit, no matter what the price may be. And this presupposes fidelity in all the obscure mysterious trials by which his soul is purified so that he may become a divine instrument."[16]

Merton uses the final pages of his essay to demonstrate that the Christian existentialist's prophetic living of fidelity to God and to the *koinonia* of the church is the only true hope for calling modern humanity out from its estranged alienation and isolating subjectivism. He defined *existential theology* as the proper orientation for the existentialist movement and the prophetic signpost that could guide those forms of existentialism, an orientation that leaves its adherents standing outside and apart from the mass mind, directed toward a meaningful existence beyond the void. He describes existential theology's several components: (1) openness to the other in creative dialogue, (2) an emphasis on the formation of conscience, (3) its focus on grace and love as opposed to nature and law, and (4) its concern with the world and the time in which humankind finds itself.

Merton rejected the myth that existentialism necessarily leads to a "liberal and rationalistic dilution of the Gospel message" (*Mystics*, 277). Rather, because of its strong biblical content, it insists on the obedience of faith as the only path to freedom in Christ. This grace, which is the source of humankind's only true liberation, is an event, "an ever renewed encounter with God and one's fellow man *now*, in present reality, in dynamic acceptance and availability" (*Mystics*, 278). By retreating into a static past, one only confines oneself within one's silent recollection and prevents an authentic encounter with God, the source of grace.

This emphasis on grace as event came to Merton through Rudolf Bultmann's *Essays*, which he was reading in the early days of 1964, as he recorded in his journal: "Bultmann's *Essays* have been a revelation to me, so powerful, so urgent, so important that every sentence stops me and I don't seem to get anywhere. I am

---

[16] Thomas Merton, *Disputed Questions* (New York: Harcourt Brace Jovanovich, 1960), 223–24.

snowed under by it" (*Dancing*, 55). He continues, "Fantastically good. How many of my own ideas I can now abandon or revise. He has revealed to me the full limitations of all my early work, which is utterly naive and insufficient, except in what concerns my own experience" (*Dancing*, 55). He was particularly moved by the following words by Bultmann: "God's grace is to man grace in such a thoroughgoing sense that it supports the whole of man's existence, and can only be conceived of as grace by those who surrender their whole existence and let themselves fall into the unfathomable, dizzy depths without seeking for something to hold on to."[17]

Yet Merton was quick to point out the shortcomings of Bultmann's existential approach. His criticisms revolved mainly around Bultmann's ecclesiology, or lack thereof, and revealed one of the greatest concerns and frustrations in his efforts in promoting ecclesial and monastic renewal, along with an important insight into his own self-awareness:

> Bultmann's inadequate notions of the Church. Good to see clearly where his existentialism falls short of genuine Christianity. This is of course a danger for me too. There is no question I think individualistically, to a great extent. But I also realize the insufficiency of this. At the same time a superficial inadequate communal spirit will only make things worse for me, not better. There is no question of the deep inauthenticity of the common life in this monastery, in most religious communities, and in the Church. It is due in part to the way authority is conceived and exercised (to the great psychological and spiritual harm of many) and to the fact that this can hardly be remedied as matters stand (at least here). The "new" approach, however, seems to me to be equally inauthentic, for reasons that are more obscure. I think the relationships set up are based more on insecurities and superficial needs than on the Spirit and on faith. They do not spell authenticity. (*Dancing*, 270)

---

[17] Rudolf Bultmann and James C. G. Greig, *Essays: Philosophical and Theological* (New York: Macmillan, 1955), 136; cited in Merton, *Dancing*, 59.

Merton understood that the church as a fellowship of faith bore within herself the particular task of bearing witness to the love of God—a task that only she could fulfill. Existential theology, revolting against the mass mentality that had infiltrated the church and religious communities, sought to make authentic, free persons for authentic, free relationships. The danger, of which Merton was well aware, was failing to follow through to the end to which this particular brand of theology led and to remain in one's isolated individualism. Renewal meant, then, a continual struggle toward true *koinonia*, wholly dependent on the Spirit of God and His sustaining power.

Thus an existential theology speaks, Merton thought, to the inner hopelessness of modern humanity, whose despair and confusion had left it wallowing in its own isolation and loneliness. By succumbing to the secular and positivist illusions of the fallen world, modern humanity faced only death. The Gospel of the Christian existentialist, on the other hand, Merton argued, opened the modern person up to a genuine future—"a future liberated from the facticity of life in a depersonalized mass, free from the care and concern with the mere 'objects,' free at last even from death" (*Mystics*, 279).

Concluding Remarks

Merton's natural response to the causes of the existentialist movement is apparent in many ways. Existentialism gave him a philosophical framework from which he sought to live out some of his spirit's most pressing urgencies: the need for authenticity, unwavering fidelity, obedience properly understood, true freedom, and life-giving *koinonia*. In his essay "The Other Side of Despair: Notes on Christian Existentialism," Merton set out to chronicle the major themes of the existentialist movement and sought to clarify their proper integration within Christian theology and life. For him, the existential experience and attitude of life was aimed at recovering life's most fundamental reality—one's own sense of personhood. He defined this effort as requiring the monumental task of uncovering the many layers of illusion that mass society had amassed upon one's authentic self. It required a Kierkegaardian "leap of faith."

Kierkegaard's *The Present Age* offered Merton many insights into the prophetic nature of the existentialist movement. What modern society needed above all, he thought, was the passion that could motivate humankind toward the ethical imperative and help it break free from its apathetic, reflective subjectivism. The "leveling" of society was the result of this reflective consciousness trapped within itself. What was needed, besides passion, was the restoration of the *principle of contradiction*, whose vital distinctions give to life the necessary energy that makes possible authentic communal experience. Only then can the falsifications of mass society be eradicated. The secret ingredient that allows for these vital distinctions is *openness*, both toward oneself and toward the other.

Christian existentialism offered Merton the insights that allowed him to form his ideas about prophecy primarily in terms of fidelity—both in the sense of God's fidelity toward humankind and humans' fidelity toward God. Merton considered that prophecy happens as the fruit of a life lived in total faithfulness to God. Being fully committed to God will make one prophetic. This view led him, however, to an existential predicament within his own vocation. How does one maintain fidelity to God and fidelity to one's faith community when they seem to contradict one another? Mainly through his reading of Gabriel Marcel, he began to refine his understanding of the proper place of obedience in his own Christian life within the church and within his monastic life at Gethsemani, an understanding that led him to greater freedom in both regards. Merton found that the proper response to this existential predicament lay in a healthy balance between understanding the church primarily as a community of free persons and understanding the need for personal obedience and self-sacrifice.

Rudolf Bultmann's notion of grace as event helped to catapult Merton's existential theology toward a radical reunderstanding of the extent of God's desire to refashion the self according to his divine will. Until God alone becomes one's source of dependence through faith, Merton argued, life's falsifications will persist. Yet Bultmann left Merton longing for the true experience of *koinonia*—the experience of a life-giving community of persons who are truly free. True Christian existentialism is not satisfied with leaving Christians rejoicing in their own individual freedoms. Rather, its ultimate goal is found in the formation of authentic community. Only then are existentialism's prophetic endeavors fulfilled.

Chapter 6

The Role of Authenticity in Thomas Merton's Prophetic Spirituality

A prophet is one who cuts through great tangled knots of lies.[1]

—Thomas Merton

The trajectory of Thomas Merton's spiritual journey can be mapped out as one extended expedition aimed toward the discovery of the ground of reality. In Merton's outlook, the greatest roadblocks to this spiritual expedition are the many illusions that present themselves as the really real but that, when embraced, prove to be only vain and empty fabrications of authentic existence. The result of this most fundamental of sins is a life enslaved to unreality—most often without the awareness that one's life is enslaved at all—caught in the web of an illusory existence. Often, he thought, it is not until one is made to come face to face with one's superficial life in a forceful confrontation that one will finally begin to see the illusions for what they really are. Here is found the moment of decision and grace and the possibility of the transformation of human consciousness.

Merton's spiritual writings revolve around this core moment as a central theme expressed in many variations. It is not too bold to assert that what mattered most to Merton was the discovery of truth and the freedom found hidden within it. One of the distinctive

---

[1] Thomas Merton, *Turning Toward the World: The Pivotal Years*, ed. Victor A. Kramer, The Journals of Thomas Merton, vol. 4 (New York: HarperCollins, 1996), 27.

features of his spiritual search was his insistence that the ultimate confrontation with truth be grounded in a personal appropriation and assimilation of its realities. That insistence explains why he found the existential writers so convincing. They were articulating many of the same ideas about the need for this personal encounter in order to authenticate existence. As the previous chapter shows, many of these writers, while offering Merton insight into the path of human transformation, ultimately proved unsatisfactory (with the possible exceptions of Kierkegaard and Marcel).

Yet Merton considered the existential writers to be prophetic mainly because of their outspoken resistance against anything they felt robbed the human person of really living. For many of the existentialists, authenticity was the ultimate goal of life. For Merton, rather than being the ultimate goal, authenticity was a proximate end for the truly ultimate goal of life in God. The special role that authenticity plays in his prophetic spirituality appears in two interdependent aspects of his writings on the spiritual life: the transformation of self-consciousness and the transformation of social consciousness.

The prophetic function of the transformation of both self-consciousness and social consciousness can be understood in terms of the unmasking of illusions in order to reveal the really real. In this sense the prophet is the one who has developed an eye for truth and seeks to expose the lies that entangle and oppress. The prophet is a liberator. Merton insisted that this prophetic function, in order to be truly authentic, must begin with the liberation of one's own self. Until one achieves such liberation, at least to a significant degree, one will not be able to see clearly through the tangled knots of lies in others to be effectively prophetic. Further, the trust needed to bring about change in others, he argued, would not be earned without the manifestation of genuine authenticity in one's own life. For Merton, only the authentic could make authentic.

Authenticity and the Transformation of Self-Consciousness

The road to personal authenticity is an arduous one. It involves the very stripping away of the only existence with which one is familiar. It requires supernatural faith and perseverance, and it often takes many years before significant change is accomplished. In order to attain to one's own truth, one must first confront one's own lies. This confrontation is the task of the contemplative. Henri Nouwen supported this view of the contemplative endeavor: "Merton understood that the unmasking of illusion belonged to the essence of the contemplative life. The many years of prayer and solitude had confronted him with his own illusions. But through this he was also prepared to show himself and his fellow human beings that which they would rather keep hidden. This unmasking is not a game that one can choose to play or not to play. It is a sacred duty, and regards the here and now of what occurs in this world."[2]

Merton knew that this sacred duty began with one's self, and that his was no exception: "What I find most in my whole life is *illusion*."[3] What was true of him, he believed, was also true of the modern person in general. In a letter of July 10, 1965, he explored this theme in response to a letter from Charles Anthony Wainwright.[4] It offers insight into how Merton related the particular theme of authenticity to existentialism in general:

> It comes quite natural to us, doesn't it, to think that "modern man" is a man who faces a "moment of truth" once, several times, often in his life. . . . For my own part, I think that life turns out to be a continual series of moments of

[2] Henri Nouwen, *Thomas Merton: Contemplative Critic* (Ligouri, MO: Ligouri/Triumph, 1991), 54.

[3] Thomas Merton, *Dancing in the Water of Life: Seeking Peace in the Hermitage*, ed. Robert E. Daggy, The Letters of Thomas Merton, vol. 5 (New York: HarperCollins, 1997), 198.

[4] Only one letter to "Mr. Wainwright" is published in the collection of Merton letters. Merton's response to C. A. Wainwright's letter (which is not extant) was incited by Wainwright's project of writing a number of famous people asking about their "moment of truth" in the face of adversity. Wainwright began this project as therapeutic writing after the death of his daughter and the loss of his job. After beginning a career in advertising, he had been involved in business leadership and served on the board of many charities.

untruth in which (when the going gets sufficiently ghastly) a moment of truth finally appears in the midst of all the mess. This I suppose reflects the existentialist type of thinking that has become more and more common with me, and which does not by any means prevent me from living a happy sort of life. In any case, I think it is important to face the fact that modern man, whether he likes it or not, leads a life that is low in authenticity. Things are decided for him, foisted on him, and even experienced for him by others. His existence is more and more secondhand, and even his moments of truth tend to be fabricated for him. That is the problem. I would say that as a result of this, the real moments of truth that do obviously occur (since where there is life there is resistance to inauthenticity) appear at first to be quite other than they are.[5]

This particular problem was for Merton also a reality in religion. Continuing along the same lines in his letter to Wainwright, he referred to the modern Christian:

I can say as a Christian, and an existentialist Christian, that I have often experienced the fact that the "moment of truth" in the Christian context is the encounter with the inscrutable word of God, the personal and living interpretation of the word of God when it is lived, when it breaks through by surprise into our own completely contemporary and personal existence. And this means of course that it breaks through conventional religious routines and even seems in some ways quite scandalous in terms of the average and accepted interpretation of what religion ought to be. Hence, those for whom religion constitutes in effect a protection against any real moments of truth are people I cannot understand. (*Witness*, 254)

Merton believed the contemplative life to produce the necessary disposition for the sacred "encounter with the inscrutable word of

[5] Merton to Mr. Wainwright, July 10, 1965, in Thomas Merton, *Witness to Freedom: The Letters of Thomas Merton in Times of Crisis*, ed. William H. Shannon (New York: Harcourt Brace, 1994), 253–54.

God." He held that the liberation of the true self can only occur in the atmosphere of solitude and that it happens through the grace of divine affirmation. It is only after people develop the ears to hear God speak the truth of who they really are that they truly come to be. And this coming to be, for Merton, was not simply to be alone with one's newfound freedom—rather, it was the prerequisite for authentic love. Yet even in this love is found the threat of illusion: "Often our need for others is not love at all, but only the need to be sustained in our illusions, even as we sustain others in theirs. But when we have renounced these illusions, then we can certainly go out to others in true compassion. It is in solitude that illusions finally dissolve."[6]

In *The Climate of Monastic Prayer*,[7] Merton made important connections between contemplative prayer and its function in transforming the self. He drew one significant line of connection between the existentialist thinkers like Heidegger, Camus, and Sartre, with their insistence on the need for humankind to probe its own inauthenticity and enter uncompromisingly into the abyss of its own emptiness, and the life of the contemplative, who, in essence, does the same thing:

> After all, some of the basic themes of the existentialism of Heidegger, laying stress as they do on the ineluctable fact of death, on man's need for authenticity, and on a kind of spiritual liberation, can remind us that the climate in which monastic prayer flourished is not altogether absent from our modern world. Quite the contrary: this is an age that, by its very nature as a time of crisis, of revolution, of struggle, calls for the special searching and questioning which are the work of the monk in his meditation and prayer. (*Climate*, 34–35)

[6] Thomas Merton, *Honorable Reader: Reflections on My Works*, ed. Robert E. Daggy (New York: Crossroad, 1989), 117.

[7] *The Climate of Monastic Prayer*, CS 1 (Kalamazoo, MI: Cistercian Publications, 1969) was republished in 1971 under the title *Contemplative Prayer* in order to appeal to a wider audience.

Existentialists describe coming face to face with one's own inauthenticity in solitude as an experience of dread. Connecting this existentialist theme to the spirituality of Saint John of the Cross, Merton explored this idea in the context of contemplative prayer: "This deep dread and night must then be seen for what it is: not as punishment, but as purification and as grace. Indeed it is a great gift of God, for it is the precise point of our encounter with his fullness" (*Climate*, 136). The insecurity of human inauthentic existence finds its security only in the realization of one's life in God, he declared, stating that the transition from one way of being to the other is often only traversed through this dark night of dread. Dread, indeed, was Merton's remedy for the sickness of inauthenticity, on both the communal and the personal levels:

> It is precisely the function of dread to break down this glass house of false interiority and to deliver man from it. It is dread, and dread alone, that drives a man out of this private sanctuary in which his solitude becomes horrible to himself without God. But without dread, without the disquieting capacity to see and to repudiate the idolatry of devout ideas and imaginings, man would remain content with himself and with his "inner life" in meditation, in liturgy or in both. Without dread, the Christian cannot be delivered from the smug self-assurance of the devout ones who know all the answers in advance, who possess all the clichés of the inner life and can defend themselves with infallible ritual forms against every risk and every demand of dialogue with human need and human desperation. (*Climate*, 145–46)

Embracing one's sense of dread is coming face to face with one's sense of alienation. For Merton, alienation is what occurs to a person when he or she begins to assume roles assigned by the dictates of society. Without realizing it, such people often begin to identify with that role and soon lose touch with their own authentic selves. They believe that they are the mask they are wearing. What results is a "painful, sometimes paranoid sense of being always under observation, under judgment, for not fulfilling some role or other we have forgotten we were supposed to fulfill."[8] Merton's remedy is severe: "It is not enough to complain about alienation, one must exorcise it" ("Why Alienation," 382).

This transformation from inauthenticity and alienation through dread to communion with God in an authentic existence expressed in genuine love of neighbor is also a frequent topic of *Conjectures of a Guilty Bystander*. Here it becomes clear that humble self-transformation is the prerequisite for effective prophetic activity: "If we really sought truth we would begin slowly and laboriously to divest ourselves one by one of all our coverings of fiction and delusion: or at least we would desire to do so, for mere willing cannot enable us to effect it. On the contrary, the one who can best point out our error, and help us to see it, is the adversary whom we wish to destroy. This is perhaps why we wish to destroy him. So, too, we can help him to see his error, and that is why he wants to destroy us."[9]

Only after this humble acceptance of one's own truth does the face of the true prophet appear:

> In the long run, no one can show another the error that is within him, unless the other is convinced that his critic first sees and loves the good that is within him. So while we are perfectly willing to tell our adversary he is wrong, we will never be able to do so effectively until we can ourselves appreciate where he is right. And we can never accept his judgment on our errors until he gives evidence that he really appreciates our own peculiar truth. Love, love only, love of our deluded fellow man as he actually is, in his delusion and in his sin: this alone can open the door to truth. (*Conjectures*, 69)

What makes this self-transformation in truth and the development of an authentic concern for others so difficult is the way people

---

[8] Thomas Merton, "Why Alienation Is for Everybody," in *The Literary Essays of Thomas Merton*, ed. Patrick Hart (New York: New Directions, 1981), 381–84, here 382.

[9] Thomas Merton, *Conjectures of a Guilty Bystander* (1966; New York: Image Books, 1989), 68.

convince themselves that they genuinely seek the truth when, in actuality, their search for truth is fraught with subtle and hidden motivations of self-interest. As Merton writes, "what we desire is not 'the truth' so much as 'to be in the right' . . . What we seek is not the pure truth, but the partial truth that justifies our prejudices, our limitations, our selfishness" (*Conjectures*, 78). Freedom from prejudice, limitation, and selfishness is one of the premier goals of the contemplative life. Stated positively, the contemplative seeks a pure and whole existence free from the dark undercurrents of a wounded ego. For Merton, it is not simply truth that will free the modern person but only truth expressed in genuine love.

An added obstacle to authentic prophetic expression is the baggage that has been attached to language through so much of its misuse. Words, so often manipulated, are more often sources of fear and mistrust than catalysts for real change. Merton examines this problem with a particular cogency: "There have been so many words uttered in contempt of truth, in despite of love, honor, justice, and of all that is good. Even these concepts themselves (truth, honor, goodness) have become sick and rotten to us, not because they are defiled, but because we are" (*Conjectures*, 92). What is the modern prophet to do in such a linguistically convoluted situation? Merton's advice is clear and forceful: "Nevertheless, we must risk falsity, we must take courage and speak, we must use noble instruments of which we have become ashamed because we no longer trust ourselves to use them worthily. We must dare to think what we mean, and simply make clear statements of what we intend. This is our only serious protection against repeated spiritual defilement by the slogans and programs of the unscrupulous" (*Conjectures*, 92–93). This is precisely what the gift of solitude enables—a lucid consciousness that cuts through ambiguous manipulations: "What the solitary renounces is not his union with other men, but rather the deceptive fictions and inadequate symbols which tend to take the place of genuine social unity—to produce a façade of apparent unity without really uniting men on a deep level."[10]

[10] Thomas Merton, *Disputed Questions* (New York: Harcourt Brace Jovanovich, 1960), 188.

Merton understood that modern people were situated in a certain existential predicament that implicated the totality of their lives. Participation in the delusions and illusions of existence is a part of the reality of sin in which all participate. If people desire to be authentic Christians, they must make a fundamental choice against this participation. For them, there really is no middle path of compromise. The world is too infected with sin. This perspective of Merton's does not change even with his "befriending" the world in the 1960s. His motive to engage the world was not founded on a desire to become a part of it but to help save it. The risk was great. It would have been much easier for him to continue the tradition of monastic isolation and insulation from the world and seek to protect himself from its illusions.

Perhaps one of the greatest motivating forces for Merton's eventual engagement with the world was the realization that any existence apart from the world and its illusions is itself an illusion. His encounter with the world in the monastery, in a sense, gave him no other option than to fight against the world. That predicament gave rise to this assessment: "The priest, the religious, the lay-leader must, whether he likes it or not, fulfill in the world the role of a prophet. If he does not face the anguish of being a true prophet, he must enjoy the carrion comfort of acceptance in the society of the deluded by becoming a false prophet and participating in their delusions."[11]

Thus the transformation of self-consciousness according to Merton's understanding begins in a humble acknowledgment of the many ways in which sin has distorted the human vision of reality—both of oneself and of the reality all around—and culminates in prophetic self-expression in genuine care and compassion. He laid out the course of this transformation in *The New Man*, a work published in 1961, whose working title, "Existential Communion," communicates something of the nature of the goal of this transformation. The descent into unreality, he writes, commenced at the very beginning of human existence:

---

[11] Thomas Merton, *Faith and Violence: Christian Teaching and Christian Practice* (Notre Dame, IN: University of Notre Dame Press, 1968), 68.

> Adam's fall was therefore the willful acceptance of unreal-
> ity, the consent to receive and even prefer a lie to the truth
> about himself and about his relationship to God. This lie
> robbed him of the innocence by which he saw nothing but
> good in himself, in things and in God and endowed him
> with the power to know evil, not only speculatively but
> by experience. The experience of falsity destroyed in him
> the instinctive taste for spiritual truth. Illusion entered in
> to spoil the existential flow of communication between his
> soul and God.[12]   •

Hope is not lost, however, since a possible return to God and a reversal of Adam's sin has been made possible in Christ. Merton highlights what is required: "The first step in all this is to recognize our true condition. Before we can ever hope to find ourselves in God, we must clearly recognize the fact that we are far from Him. Before we can realize who we really are, we must become conscious of the fact that the person we think we are, here and now, is at best an impostor and a stranger. We must constantly question his motives and penetrate his disguises" (*New Man*, 119). Recognizing one's true condition is the essence of the meaning of humility, and it is the work of humility that brings humans ever closer to their own truth and reality.

Merton allows for no evasions: this is an arduous journey, one that requires much grace and discipline: "This demands an ascetic struggle, in which our spirit, united with the Spirit of God, resists the flesh, its desires and its illusions, in order to strengthen and elevate us more and more, and open our eyes to the full meaning of our life in Christ" (*New Man*, 157–58).[13] Humility and asceticism, the hallmarks of monastic and contemplative spirituality, enable the integration of truth into one's life, thereby setting it free from illusion and sin. This encounter with the truth of one's existence authenticates one's life and rids it of obstructions to the existential

---

[12] Thomas Merton, *The New Man* (New York: Farrar, Straus and Giroux, 1961), 77.

[13] Merton also emphasized the need for asceticism to unmask illusions in his novitiate conference tape *True Freedom* (Credence Cassettes AA2803).

flow of God's Spirit within. In this existential communion with God, one becomes transparent—a type of mirror reflecting divine goodness, love, and truth. This is the spiritual authenticity that allows the "new man" to come into existence.

As the previous chapter shows, Merton held that becoming prophetic is a result of fidelity to the call of God. By persevering in faith through the existential demands of Christian discipleship, one's true self emerges, and one becomes a reflection of the life of God in the world. For Merton, prophecy is, in its most fundamental sense, this reflection of the transformed self.

Authenticity and the Transformation of Social Consciousness

Merton discovered that the God whom he encountered in his solitude as a monk was preeminently a God overflowing with love and compassion for all humankind, who had fallen into the alienation perpetuated by an illusory existence. The final decade of Merton's life was marked by a type of contemplation that made little distinction between solitude and service. In a sense, a life of service to those in need demonstrates that one's solitude is real. For Merton, the call to be a monk had become most fundamentally a call to transform society, not by going out into the world and pastoring churches or preaching missions, but by offering the distinctive gift of the monk: spiritual insight into the reality of things. By being firmly rooted in a life of contemplation, he understood, the monastic vocation blossoms into a prophetic witness to the kingdom of God.

Writings on Mohandas Gandhi

Authenticity played a formidable role in the manner in which Merton exercised his social concerns in the 1960s. In Mohandas Gandhi (1869–1948), the revolutionary Indian religious and national leader, Merton found both the model and inspiration for what he considered to be the most effective way to cut through the many-tangled knots of lies embedded in the consciousness of any given society. This way, *satyagraha*, of which the root meaning is "holding on to truth," refers to the Hindu insistence that the illusory existence of injustice and violence could only be fought and over-come with the weapons of non-violent resistance. Gandhi's wit-ness of "active non-violence" had a profound impact on Merton's thinking in the mid-sixties and informed the way in which he sought prophetically to resist the injustices of racism and war in his own day. Gandhi's witness led Merton down a distinctive and controversial path for a Trappist—writing about issues that his superiors thought were inappropriate for a monk. Eventually they suppressed his work in promoting non-violence, but not before he published his basic ideas on the subject in his meaningfully titled *Seeds of Destruction*, the 1964 companion volume to his widely read *Seeds of Contemplation*.[14] In the same year he also published his tribute to his mentor in non-violence as a type of Gandhian catechism, *Gandhi on Non-Violence*.[15] Both texts bear witness to the way in which Merton learned the prophetic power of authenticity of life from the Indian sage.

In *Seeds of Destruction*, Merton forcefully asserts his idea of the prophetic nature of the contemplative life in the first line of his author's note: "The contemplative life is not, and cannot be, a mere withdrawal, a pure negation, a turning of one's back on the world with its sufferings, its crises, its confusions and its errors. First of all, the attempt itself would be illusory. No man can withdraw completely from the society of his fellow men; and the monastic community is deeply implicated, for better or for worse, in the economic, political, and social structures of the contemporary world."[16]

A monk, above all things, is a person moved by compassion, Merton argues. In his chapter "A Tribute to Gandhi," he offers the Hindu leader as a prime example of how contemplative life flowers

[14] Thomas Merton, *Seeds of Destruction* (New York: Farrar, Straus and Giroux, 1964). Merton, dissatisfied with the insulated idea of contemplation suggested in *Seeds of Contemplation*, seems to have intentionally adapted the earlier title in order to express contemplation's fuller, prophetic dimension.

[15] Thomas Merton, *Gandhi on Non-Violence* (New York: New Directions, 1964).

[16] Thomas Merton, "Author's Note," in *Seeds of Destruction*, xiii–xvi, here xiii.

into prophetic witness. He makes this point by relating the central place authenticity holds in Gandhi's philosophy: "The vow of *sat-yagraha is the vow to die* rather than say what one does not mean" (*Seeds*, 230). A life of non-violence is completely dependent on the full acceptance and integration of the truth into one's life: "Gandhi's religio-political action was based on an ancient metaphysic of man, a philosophical wisdom which is common to Hinduism, Buddhism, Islam, Judaism, and Christianity: that 'truth is the inner law of our being'" (*Seeds*, 231). This inner law of our being, he went on, is a law based more on experience of truth than on logic.

So, he wrote, the wisdom of Gandhi teaches that "the way of peace is the way of truth, of fidelity to wholeness and being, which implies a basic respect for life not as concept, not as a sentimental figment of the imagination, but its deepest, most secret and most fontal reality. The first and fundamental trust is to be sought in respect for our own inmost being, and this in turn implies the recollectedness and the awareness which attune us to that silence in which a lone Being speaks to us in all its simplicity" (*Seeds*, 232). Fidelity to the Word of God again appears as Merton's pattern for prophetic living. Merton concludes his chapter on Gandhi with these words of admonition: "A Christian can do nothing greater than follow his own conscience with a fidelity comparable to that [with] which Gandhi obeyed what he believed to be the voice of God. Gandhi is, it seems to me, a model of integrity whom we cannot afford to ignore, and the one basic duty we all owe to the world of our time is to imitate him in 'disassociating ourselves from evil in total disregard of the consequences'" (*Seeds*, 234).

In the introductory essay to *Gandhi on Non-Violence*, entitled "Gandhi and the One-Eyed Giant," Merton offers one of his most perceptive insights into the nature of truth. Henri Nouwen, writing on Gandhi's influence on Merton in this regard, captures the essence of this truth: "the spirit of truth is the spirit of non-violence."[17] According to Merton, the non-violent spirit springs

---

[17] Henri Nouwen, *Thomas Merton: Contemplative Critic* (Ligouri, MO: Ligouri/Triumph, 1991), 64.

Truth is the inner-law of our being

"from *an inner realization of spiritual unity*" (*Gandhi on Non-Violence*, 10). He insisted that overcoming inner division is the prerequisite for the inner freedom required for meaningful social influence. The social dimension of the spiritual life, Merton argued, becomes accessible only in the realization of this spiritual unity and thus an ability to recognize the spiritual life is much more than a private affair. As Merton notes, "The spiritual life of one person is simply the life of all manifesting itself in him" (*Gandhi*, 11). Insight into Gandhi's integrated and communal spirituality demonstrated to Merton that Gandhi's political involvement was fundamentally a religious duty, with the liberation of India but one step toward the liberation of all of humankind. Merton noted that for Gandhi, there was no such thing as a secular public sector. All sectors of society were sacred and bore the special concern of God and, therefore, warranted human concern as well.

Yet, Merton went on, society bears within itself so-called secular structures that are basically irreligious and are to be rejected as dehumanizing. That reality was a particular symptom of the affluent industrial society whose organized greed tended intrinsically toward violence because of its structural disorder and moral confusion. So Merton declared, "The first principle of valid political action in such a society then becomes *non-cooperation* with its disorder, its injustices, and more particularly with its deep commitment to untruth" (*Gandhi*, 15). *Satyagraha*, he argued, plays a vital role in this *non-cooperation*. It fastens the *satyagrahi* to the truth and integrity of his or her own authentic existence, through which he or she becomes a witness to truth in society: "The first job of a *satyagrahi* is to bring the real situation to light even if he has to suffer and die in order that injustice be unmasked and appear for what it really is" (*Gandhi*, 16). It was precisely the way in which Gandhi existentially identified himself with the helpless and vulnerable that, in Merton's view, gave him the power to expose injustice and reveal truth. This Christlike condescension led Merton to write, "In Gandhi the voice of Asia, not the Asia of the Vedas and Sutras only, but the Asia of the hungry and silent masses, was speaking and still speaks to the whole world with a prophetic message. This message, uttered on dusty Indian roads, remains more meaningful

Satya graha: holding on to truth

than those specious promises that have come from the great capitals of the earth" (*Gandhi*, 16).

This message also appeared in the extent to which Gandhi embodied his own belief in *satyagraha.* His famous fast unto death on behalf of the *Harijan*—the outcasts or untouchables—was a prophetic action that he hoped would help to integrate them into the social life of Indian culture. For Merton, what made this symbolic gesture so prophetic was its effectiveness in overcoming the reality of sin entrenched in society: "He did not seek to reproach and confound others with the spectacle of his own penitence for their sin. He wanted them to recognize from his example that they could learn to bear and overcome the evil that was in them if they were willing to do as he did" (*Gandhi*, 25).

The non-violent approach to prophetic witness in Gandhi was, therefore, unlike that of the scolding Hebrew prophets, whose aggressive invectives often fell on deaf ears. Gandhi had the particular Christian insight, according to Merton, that true power lay in weakness and humility. He also had the particular Christian insight that only a transformed self, made alive in the embrace of truth, can really transform others. Merton expressed this insight and its effectiveness:

> Gandhi's symbolic acts (which were meaningful as symbols only because they marked his own flesh with the stamp of their acute reality) were aimed at three kinds of liberation. First, he wanted to deliver Indian religious wisdom from the sclerosis and blindness into which it had sunk by reason of the gross injustices of a system which had become untrue to itself. Second, he wanted to liberate the untouchables, the *Harijan*, not only from political and economic oppression, but also from the incubus of their own self-hate and their despair. And, finally, he wished to liberate the oppressors themselves from their blind and hopeless dependence on the system which kept things as they were, and which consequently enslaved everybody both spiritually and materially. (*Gandhi*, 25)

What struck Merton most about Gandhi's approach to active non-violence was how comprehensive it was in "its breadth, its integrity, and its unity" (*Gandhi*, 25). Fighting violence with violence was for Gandhi the greatest of illusions preventing true peace in the world. Merton summed up Gandhi's legacy to the world in this observation: "The evils we suffer cannot be eliminated by a violent attack in which one sector of humanity flies at another in destructive fury" (*Gandhi*, 25).

In Gandhian teaching, Merton saw that the truth of the situation is that everyone without exception shares in a common evil. The solution, therefore, is also common. The reason that most people do not undertake this common task of active non-violence, Merton said, is "because we are not ourselves" (*Gandhi*, 25). Thus, he pointed out, "the first duty of every man is to return to his own 'right mind' in order that society itself may be sane" (*Gandhi*, 25).[18] Thus the cure of society's insanity according to Gandhian principles of non-violence may come about primarily through the prophetic witness of individuals who humbly and radically embrace the self-sacrifice that makes authentic mercy and compassion possible. So Merton noted, following the line of thought presented by Ananda Coomaraswamy, that the prophetic witness of the *satyagrahi* was aimed above all at the restoration of humankind's "right mind." The "vow of truth" that Gandhi professed, Merton said, was "the *necessary preamble to the awakening of a mature political consciousness*," or a "right mind" (*Gandhi*, 30). Without the full embrace of one's authentic existence in peaceful truth, there will never be peace on earth.

Writings on Monastic Renewal

Authenticity is also the central theme in Merton's writings on monastic renewal. Notably considered one of the primary ways in

[18] Merton took this idea of "right mind" from Ananda Coomaraswamy's article "On Being in One's Right Mind," *Review of Religion* 7 (1942): 32–40. Merton writes, "Coomaraswamy, in an important article, once outlined the meaning of the process called *metanoia*, or recovery of one's right mind, the passage from ignorance of self to enlightened moral awareness" (*Gandhi*, 25–26).

which he functioned prophetically,[19] Merton's writings on monastic renewal have garnered much attention in postconciliar monasticism as religious communities have sought to adapt and acclimate themselves to the modern situation. These writings offer another dimension to Merton's conception of the prophetic power of authenticity, a conception whose goal was both the restoration of spiritual vitality in religious life and, thereby, the restoration of the "right mind" in society.

In an article on Aelred of Rievaulx posthumously published in *Cistercian Studies* in 1985, Merton shared his ideas about the true spirit of the Cistercian reform: "At the roots of the Cistercian reform was a hatred of artificiality and an intense impatience with the illogical compromises into which monks are led when they yield to the obscure enticements of the world, the flesh and the devil, and live like worldlings under a religious disguise. Saint Stephen Harding and his monks were consumed by the passionate desire for truth."[20] Merton went on to explain that the early Cistercian writers interpreted the monastic goal of purity of heart mainly in terms of living an authentic existence free from the false self that identified itself with an artificial reality. In the recovery of the true self one discovers one's pure heart, Merton declared. His efforts at monastic renewal must, therefore, be understood predominantly in terms of *renewal* or *aggiornamento* rather than in terms of a radical departure from the Cistercian tradition. In this respect, his prophetic role mimicked that of the Hebrew prophets, whose vocation was to call God's people back to covenantal faithfulness.

The problem with which Merton came face to face, especially in his dealing with monks in formation was that, as he saw it, the then-current structure of his order was inadequately aligned with the true spirit of the early Cistercian reform. For Merton, the early Cistercians were convinced that their monastic vocation bore within

---

[19] The most important study on this perspective to date is John Eudes Bamberger's *Thomas Merton: Prophet of Renewal*, MW 4 (Kalamazoo, MI: Cistercian Publications, 2005).

[20] Thomas Merton, "Saint Aelred of Rievaulx and the Cistercians," *Cistercian Studies* 20 (1985): 212–23, here 214.

it a definite prophetic role. This prophetic dimension, he argued, was one of the essential elements of the Cistercian vocation that had been lost and was in need of recovery if true renewal was to take place. For John Eudes Bamberger, what was true of the Cistercian fathers was also true of Merton. In his *Thomas Merton: Prophet of Renewal*, he stated, "Thomas Merton contended that bearing prophetic witness to the transcendent holiness of God continues to be a major function of all Cistercian communities true to their vocation" (*Thomas Merton: Prophet of Renewal*, 16).

Merton's remedy, according to Bamberger, was to begin by reforming the program of monastic formation. Essential in this reform was Merton's insistence on authenticity of life. Bamberger writes, "Merton's desire for the authentic, for truth, and for a radical transformation motivated Merton's concern for reforming the studies in the Order" (*Thomas Merton: Prophet of Renewal*, 40). The foundational issue for him in the reform of monastic formation was found in the development of "a more personal and authentic spirituality that gave greater scope for individuals and for the individual communities of the Order to respond to their monastic charism with a larger measure of personal responsibility and creativity" (*Thomas Merton: Prophet of Renewal*, 36). The recovery of the prophetic dimension in monasticism, Merton believed, began with the authentication and personalization of each individual monk. Fidelity to the monastic way of life would then lead to the recovery of monasticism's prophetic dimension.[21] Such fidelity, which Bamberger saw in Merton, led Bamberger to this assessment: "His perceptiveness, his courageous persistence, and his loyal fidelity in spite of misunderstandings and frustrations, places Merton among the prophetic voices that called the Order to follow in the footsteps of the holy Fathers, and the Church to return to the wholeness of the Gospel" (*Thomas Merton: Prophet of Renewal*, 47).

In his writings on monastic renewal, Merton was cautious about the efforts being made and believed that much that was being hailed as *aggiornamento* was little more than a superficial reconfiguration.

---

[21] For a fuller treatment of Merton's understanding of the prophetic dimension of monasticism, see chap. 7.

The test of authentic renewal would be found precisely in the integration of the prophetic role in contemplative life: "the contemplative orders must take special care to avoid a superficial adjustment which, in the name of a poorly understood *aggiornamento*, would end by depriving them of the authentic riches of their mystical and prophetic traditions."[22] Elsewhere he stated, "it is misleading to talk so much of the *contemplative* life in a way that obscures the fact that what we need to renew is not so much the 'contemplative' and enclosed and abstract dimension of our life, as the *prophetic and eschatological* witness of our silence, poverty, etc."[23] What monasticism suffered, for Merton, was only a microcosmic representation of the ailment found in Catholicism at large. Writing to Colman McCarthy, a former monk from Holy Spirit Abbey in Conyers, Georgia, Merton referred to Carl Amery's idea of "milieu Catholicism." His comments succinctly assess his sense of the problem causing the inauthenticity found in religious life and the price being paid for it:

> Milieu Catholicism is Catholicism which is so completely committed to a social and cultural established milieu that when there arises a choice between the Gospel and the milieu, the choice is not even visible. The milieu wins every time, automatically. In such a situation there may perhaps be saints and even prophetic individuals. But the institution will strive in every way either to suppress them or to absorb them. Instead of exercising a prophetic and iconoclastic function in the world, instead of being a dynamic and eschatological sign, such monasticism is occupied entirely in constructing a respectable and venerable image of itself, and thus ensuring its own survival as a dignified and established institution.[24]

[22] Thomas Merton, *Mystics and Zen Masters* (New York: Farrar, Straus and Giroux, 1967), 214.

[23] Merton to Mother C, April 14, 1968, in Thomas Merton, *The School of Charity: The Letters of Thomas Merton on Religious Renewal and Spiritual Direction*, ed. Patrick Hart (New York: Farrar, Straus and Giroux, 1990), 377. "Mother C" is a reference to Mother Mary Consolata, a Clarissine Abbess of the Madres Clarisas monastery in La Paz, Bolivia.

[24] Merton to Colman McCarthy, August 15, 1967, in *School*, 341–42.

Merton's criticism of the tendency for institutional self-preservation found in monasticism is also the central critique of his book *Contemplation in a World of Action*. In the introduction to the 1971 edition, Jean Leclercq cites a letter that Merton had written to him shortly before he was to embark on his Asian journey, where he was to meet his death:

> Thanks for your good letter about the arrangements for Bangkok. I will be glad to give the talk on Marxism and so on. Important indeed!! I've familiarized myself pretty well with Herbert Marcuse, whose ideas are so influential in the "student revolts" of the time. I must admit that I find him closer to monasticism than many theologians. Those who question the structures of contemporary society at least look to monks for a certain distance and critical perspective. Which alas is seldom found. The vocation of the monk in the modern world, especially Marxist, is not survival but prophecy. We are all busy saving our skins. . . . Do I speak in English or French?[25]

Echoing his letters, Merton, in *Contemplation in a World of Action*, expressed his concerns about the superficial reforms that he saw being lauded by many leaders as authentic renewal. Leaders who were not open to the "full dimension—the mystical and prophetic"[26] of monasticism, he thought, would simply replace inauthentic old structures with inauthentic new ones. In his chapter entitled "The Identity Crisis," Merton, after mentioning modern thinkers whose work highlighted the dehumanizing tendencies found in human consciousness since the industrial revolution, thinkers like Marx, Freud, Jung, Darwin, and the existentialists, exposed what he believed to be the root sickness in the production of these inauthentic social structures: "Right or wrong, these prophets are all concerned with the main problem that faces us: Man is not himself. He has lost himself in the falsities and illusions of a massive

[25] Merton to Dom Jean Leclercq, July 23, 1968, in *School*, 392.
[26] Thomas Merton, *Contemplation in a World of Action* (Notre Dame, IN: University of Notre Dame Press, 1998), 27.

organization. How can he recover his authenticity and his true identity? All these thinkers, even the Christians, tend to regard conventional forms of religion as being in league with the forces which have diminished and depersonalized man" (*Contemplation,* 60). Thus, he stated, "Monastic renewal must now more than ever aim at authenticity" (*Contemplation,* 74). Related to this admonition is an assessment that expressed the root cause of what he saw as monasticism's floundering: "We are failing in the prophetic aspect of our vocation" (*Contemplation,* 215).

Merton was not completely pessimistic in his critique of monasticism's current situation. He was hopeful that genuine renewal was possible, and he was realistic about the limitations that face any form of organized religious life. He also admitted that responsibility for renewal rests with each individual monk and that undue expectations of others are only evasions of this fact: "Thus, my new life and my contribution to a renewal in monasticism begin within myself and in my own daily life. My work for renewal takes place strictly in my own situation here, not as a struggle with the institution but in an effort to renew my life of prayer in a whole new context, with a whole new understanding of what the contemplative life means and demands. Creativity has to begin with me and I can't sit here wasting time urging the monastic institution to become creative and prophetic" (*Contemplation,* 222).

Rembert Weakland substantiated this perspective of the prophetic dimension of the renewal of monasticism in his foreword to *Survival or Prophecy? The Correspondence of Jean Leclercq and Thomas Merton*: "Finally, both authors, but especially Merton, saw their roles as prophetic witnesses. . . . The prophetic stance was one of the enduring and most attractive aspects of the monastic renewal in the last half of the twentieth century; and both Merton and Leclercq, cognizant that the Christian monastic tradition had first emerged as a form of prophetic witness against the ever more worldly Church, brought it to bear on the Church of their own day."[27] Michael Casey,

---

[27] Rembert Weakland, foreword to *Survival or Prophecy? The Correspondence of Jean Leclercq and Thomas Merton,* ed. Patrick Hart, MW 17 (Collegeville, MN: Cistercian Publications, 2008), ix–xv, here xiv.

in his afterword to the same book, draws attention to the ambivalent nature of Merton's and Leclercq's protests against religious institutionalism. On the one hand, he writes, "In a sense it was because they were not institutionalized that they were able to operate as prophets."[28] On the other hand, speaking particularly of Merton, he offers this nuanced perspective in regard to Merton's persistent flirtation with leaving Gethsemani for a less-institutionalized form of monasticism: "If Thomas Merton had left Gethsemani to go into deep solitude, he could have operated as a prophet only if . . . he had capitalized on his status as an ex-Trappist. This dubious distinction would not for long have provided him with the pulpit he needed. And so he stayed at Gethsemani" (*Survival or Prophecy?*, 142).

Casey's intuitive reading of Merton's vocational motivations gives proper priority to the centrality of prophecy in Merton's spiritual impulses. He continues: "Rather than opposing prophecy and institution, it probably needs to be said that prophecy needs the survival of the institution if it is to exist. There is a certain symbiosis, a love-hate relationship. The institutions simultaneously supported Jean Leclercq and Thomas Merton in their activity as prophets and simultaneously provided them with accessible targets for their criticism. May monasteries long continue to survive— because monastic survival is the matrix of prophecy" (*Survival or Prophecy?*, 142).

With the retirement of Abbot James Fox and the election of Flavian Burns as Fox's successor, Merton was allowed more freedom from what he considered to be the unnecessary and overly restrictive constraints of his monastic pursuits—in other words, he was freer to live his monasticism more prophetically. Although some have suggested that Merton would have left monasticism had not it been for his fateful trip to Asia, his journals and letters attest to the contrary. What he desired was a hermitage away from Gethsemani yet connected to it in affiliation. His new abbot supported this wish, and it formed part of the agenda of Merton's itinerary abroad.

---

[28] Michael Casey, afterword to *Survival or Prophecy? The Correspondence of Jean Leclercq and Thomas Merton*, ed. Patrick Hart, MW 17 (Collegeville, MN: Cistercian Publications, 2008), 131–42, here 142.

What Merton desired was not an institution*less* monasticism but a simpler and more authentic one—a monasticism with its institutional and charismatic components properly integrated. Yet there is no doubt that for Merton, the institutional component had always to be at the service of the charismatic, as is evident in the final statement of his conference in Bangkok on "Marxism and Monastic Perspectives": "If you forget everything else that has been said, I would suggest you remember this for the future: 'From now on, everybody stands on his own feet.' . . . We can no longer rely on being supported by structures that may be destroyed at any moment by a political power or a political form. You cannot rely on structures."[29]

Concluding Remarks

Thomas Merton's passionate concern for an authentic life found both validation and added impulse in his encounter with the writers of existentialism. The boldness of their conviction that life's illusions must be unmasked at whatever price inspired Merton to come face to face with the illusions within himself, with illusions in the church, and with the illusions in the world. Existentialism also gave Merton a paradigm for understanding authenticity as a type of catalyst in the transformation of the self and in the world around. The personal and social dimensions of authenticity's aims were, for Merton, interdependent and complimentary. Through the transformation of the self into an authentic existence, the transformation of the world becomes possible, he thought. The two transformations together form Merton's integrated vision of God's desire for re-creating the world in God's image and likeness—of reconciliation.

Merton was not too modern to admit that it is sin that leads to an inauthentic life and to its fabrication—and ultimately to its destruction. Salvation from the lie of sin comes through the grace of God, which effects humankind's authentication as truly human. Using language from the existentialists, Merton asserted that this transformation most often occurs when one freely accepts the dread

[29] Thomas Merton, *The Asian Journal of Thomas Merton* (New York: New Directions, 1973), 338.

of one's current situation in all its limitation and brokenness. This dark night is the seedbed for faith's birth and maturation and for the ultimate victory over illusion. It is where one can finally meet one's true self. Solitude is the atmosphere that provides the necessary clarity and grace to admit one's complicity in illusion and to see with the eyes of faith the pure self of God's divine intention.

Prophecy, in this context, arises in one's fidelity to God in the midst of the experience of the dread of this dark night. Prophecy is an overflow of one "vowed" to authenticity of life—to one's true self. By being faithful to one's deepest truth as a child of God, one becomes prophetic.

The authentic life that results from the unmasking of illusions liberates others, Merton held, because it is grounded in selfless concern and compassion—a willingness to suffer with others. Authenticity was his answer to the problem of modernity's distortion of language. An authentic life speaks a language that is pure and lucid, he said: prophecy is the language of a transparent life.

The life of Mohandas Gandhi was of great inspiration to Merton precisely because it contained this type of transparency. He was an example, thought Merton, of a contemplative prophet whose authenticity of life, grounded in *satyagraha*, offered a model for effective social transformation. His obdurate non-cooperation in the social injustices of his day coupled with his willingness to bear the pain of the oppressed demonstrated a prophetic resistance that was, in Merton's eyes, most robust.

Authenticity also formed a central component of Merton's writings on monastic renewal. At the heart of monasticism's problems, Merton believed, was an overdependence on its institutional element, a dependence that resulted in either a complacent or an overrestricted form of life. What was needed was an authentic *aggiornamento* that recovered monasticism's original spirit. At the heart of the original spirit of monasticism, according to Merton, was monasticism's charismatic dimension—and at the heart of monasticism's charismatic dimension was the prophetic spirit that bore witness to the world of the reality of God's kingdom on earth.

For Merton, God acts and speaks to the modern world through life made authentic.

PART THREE

The Contemplative as Prophet

Chapter 7

Prophetic Monasticism

I am even more convinced of the role of monasticism in today's world. A prophetic and even charismatic role.[1]

—Thomas Merton

The sources from which Benedictine monasticism sprang in the early sixth century are identified in the final chapter of the rule that Saint Benedict wrote for the monks living under his tutelage. What can be discerned are two traditions, each stamped with Saint Benedict's seal of approval and offered as valuable guides in the monk's further growth along the monastic way. One tradition, represented by "the *Conferences* of the Fathers, their *Institutes* and their *Lives*,"[2] and the other, by "the rule of our holy father Basil" (RB 297), have been largely understood to represent two distinct streams of the monastic spirit: the former representing the more eremitical life of the Egyptian desert, reaching Saint Benedict mainly through the writings of John Cassian, and the latter representing the more coenobitical life of Saint Basil's *koinonia* as depicted in his longer and shorter rules.[3] Monks following the Rule of Saint

[1] Merton to Dom Ignace Gillet, September 11, 1964, in Thomas Merton, *The School of Charity: The Letters of Thomas Merton on Religious Renewal and Spiritual Direction*, ed. Patrick Hart (New York: Farrar, Straus and Giroux, 1990), 235. Dom Ignace Gillet was elected Abbot General of the Cistercian Order in early 1964, following the death of Dom Gabriel Sortais.

[2] *The Rule of St. Benedict*, ed. Timothy Fry (Collegeville, MN: Liturgical Press, 1981), 297 (hereafter RB).

[3] The value of Saint Benedict's synthesis of these two streams has been widely acknowledged in recent decades. Claude Peifer's article "The Rule of St. Benedict" in *The Rule of St. Benedict* highlights this important point:

Benedict throughout the centuries have found their monastic identities somewhere along this fluid continuum between solitude and community.

Merton's monastic identity is undoubtedly grounded within the more eremitical tradition of the Egyptian desert, as is manifested in more than his eventual life as a hermit in the final years of his life at Gethsemani. That grounding is also seen in his many years of restlessness within community life, his attraction to the Desert Fathers, his interpretation of the Cistercian tradition and his writings on monastic renewal in light of that tradition, his experience of God in solitude and nature, and, most notably, the way he began to articulate monasticism as a form of prophetic ministry to the world.

A number of sources inspired Merton's interpretation of monasticism as a form of prophetic witness. Most foundational was the witness of the Desert Fathers, whose marginal existence offered Merton a wisdom inaccessible to life in the world. Merton also saw in the Cistercian reformers, especially Saint Bernard, a prophetic spirit in keeping with the monks of the Egyptian desert. Merton's attraction to the original Carmelite spirit was likewise based on an attraction to monasticism that he interpreted as prophetic withdrawal. His profound respect for Russian monasticism of the nineteenth century derived mainly from his esteem for its prophetic and charismatic spirituality. Finally, the Vietnamese Buddhist monk Thich Nat Hahn embodied for Merton the ideal integration of the contemplative and prophetic streams of monastic spirituality. Each of these monastic sources offers meaningful insight into Merton's developing notion of the monk as a prophetic witness to the modern world.

"The disparate branches of the monastic tradition are brought together and harmonized, correcting and completing one another, so that the richness of the whole deposit may be preserved without loss. Diverse elements are not merely juxtaposed but fully assimilated, so that they find their rightful place in a larger unity" (Claude Peifer, "The Rule of St. Benedict," in Timothy Fry, *The Rule of St. Benedict*, 65–112, here 90).

Desert Monasticism

The spirit that drew the early monks into the Egyptian desert in the fourth century manifested itself in an exterior response that sought to fulfill two primary spiritual needs. The first need was distance from superficial society and tepid religious life, and the second was the atmosphere of solitude conducive for seeking God. This process of withdrawal and attachment defined the early monastic movement. According to Merton, this process did not mean that the monks of the desert lost all concern for the world that they left behind. Rather, they sought a new way of being in the world that, in a certain sense, simultaneously transcended it and made it into what God intended it to be. Going out to seek God apart from society was not a compassionless neglect of social responsibility, leaving the problems burdening humanity to fix themselves. Merton understood the primitive monastic motive more positively. In his book of translations of sayings of the Desert Fathers, *The Wisdom of the Desert*, he explained his understanding: "The Desert Fathers did, in fact, meet the 'problems of their time' in the sense that *they* were among the few who were ahead of their time, and opened the way for the development of a new man and a new society."[4]

Merton argued that what these early monks resisted was "the herd mentality" and the passivity that sucked vitality out of the human spirit. This impulse against spiritual superficiality and for spiritual vitality was in Merton's view prophetic because it presented to the world a way of life that made the human person more fully alive—more fully human. The transformation of life happening in the desert through solitude and labor, poverty and fasting, charity and prayer, was a program of life that allowed for the purging of the superficial self and the emergence of the true, real self who is found hidden with Christ in God. The models for these spiritual pioneers, in Merton's opinion, were other prophetic desert dwellers like Saint John the Baptist, Elijah, Elisha, and the apostles. These prophets were seized with a similar spiritual urgency that

[4] Thomas Merton, trans., *The Wisdom of the Desert: Sayings from the Desert Fathers of the Fourth Century* (New York: New Directions, 1960), 4.

demanded a similar radical response. The early martyrs also gave inspiration to the monks of the desert. And for Merton, the Christian martyr of the early church assumed the mantle of the prophets of Judaism. He was able to identify a connection between the Desert Fathers and the prophets: "Not only are the Desert Fathers heirs to the vocation of the martyrs, but the martyrs are the heirs of those pre-desert fathers, the prophets. In either case, {there is} the idea of {the} *prophetic* vocation of the Christian saint as witness to the presence of Christ in the world (classic example—St. John {the} Baptist—model of martyrs, of monks, and of prophets)."[5] Here the monk is prophetic because with his life he testifies to Christ alive in the world.

In his book *Contemplation in a World of Action*, Merton offers an extensive exploration of his ideas on monasticism's history, essence, and future. In reflecting on the initial call of the monk, he emphasizes the inner need for a life of freedom and detachment, "a 'desert life' outside normal social structures."[6] This countercultural stance of the monk, he held, is a prophetic witness bearing a prophetic character—the monk is a witness to freedom. Monastic freedom is freedom from "the massive automatic functioning of a social machine that leaves nothing to peculiar talent, to chance, or to grace" (*Contemplation*, 179). It is directed, on the other hand, to a particular end—namely, the experience of the grace of God: "The monastic vocation calls a man to desert frontiers, beyond which there are no police, in order to dip into the 'ocean of unexploited forces which surrounds a well-ordered society and draw from it a personal provision' of grace and vision" (*Contemplation*, 179).[7]

---

[5] Thomas Merton, *Cassian and the Fathers: Initiation into the Monastic Tradition*, ed. Patrick F. O'Connell, MW 1 (Kalamazoo, MI: Cistercian Publications, 2005), 11. Words in braces were supplied by the editor of the volume in accordance with Merton's instructions to Thérèse Lentfoehr, who typed his "Monastic Formation" lectures (*Cassian and the Fathers*, lxiii, n68).

[6] Thomas Merton, *Contemplation in a World of Action* (Notre Dame, IN: University of Notre Dame Press, 1998), 8.

[7] Merton here quotes from Claude Lévi-Strauss's *Tristes Tropiques*, trans. John and Doreen Weightman (New York: Penguin Books, 1974).

As a place of prayer and witness, the monastery in Merton's vision is not only a place for the development of the contemplative ideal but also a place for the development of a life of prophecy. The contemporary monastery ought, then, to have a distinct desert quality conducive for prophetic formation: "The monastic life is not only contemplative but prophetic. That is to say, it bears witness not only to a contemplative mystique of silence, enclosure and the renunciation of active works, but it is alive with the eschatological mystery of the kingdom already shared and realized in the lives of those who have heard the Word of God and have surrendered unconditionally to its demands in a vocation that (even when communal) has a distinctly 'desert' quality" (*Contemplation*, 194). The monastic community by living and being formed in the presence of God becomes a living sign of God's presence in the world. This is its primary prophetic function.

Monastic freedom also testifies that "God is on the side of freedom" (*Contemplation*, 216). Merton admitted that this idea was "scandalous," yet one charged with great significance for the modern world. By being for freedom, the monk reassures the modern world that in the struggle between thought and existence the monk is firmly on the side of existence and not simply on the side of an ideological abstraction. As a being for existence, the monk seeks to testify that "God is the source and the guarantee of our freedom and not simply a force standing over us to limit our freedom" (*Contemplation*, 216). For Merton, this idea is the witness of the Gospel as articulated in the New Testament, and it is in this "scandalous gospel" that the monk is confronted with the seriousness of his prophetic calling. Of this "scandalous gospel," Merton remarks, "Surely this is the 'message' the monk should give the world" (*Contemplation*, 216).

The distinctive desert quality of monasticism is also a predominant theme in a lecture Merton gave, "The Monk: Prophet to Modern Man."[8] In this lecture, Merton used the writings of Rufinus (340/345–410), the monk, historian, and theologian who spent a

---

[8] "The Monk: Prophet to Modern Man" is side B of the tape *Life and Prophecy* (Chappaqua, NY: Electronic Paperbacks, 1972).

number of years learning the monastic way in the Egyptian desert, to articulate the prophetic component of monastic life. For Rufinus, one of the central images for monastic life was the prophet—the one who manifests the truth of the Word of God to the world. Merton saw that what was distinctive about this ideal of the monk as prophet was that it was an ideal that made itself real. The ideal and the real are both present at the same time, he said, in the life of the monk-prophet. Merton likened the prophetic ideal of the monk to a type of Jungian archetype, with the prophet an archetype for the monk. Archetypes shape a person's mind in a way that, because of the grace embedded within the particular symbol, enables a certain response. Through reading the prophets, the monk learns how to be prophetic. He then becomes a "sign of contradiction"—one who contains a word of truth that calls others to that truth. He is a sign of Christ in the world. Merton notes that it is psychologically impossible to see Christ in ourselves. We see Christ in others, and they see Christ in us. One of the goals of monks is to see Christ in all things. If they can accomplish that, then Christ will live in them. The monk's approach to living Christ in the world must be modest yet assured, since, as Merton noted, people come to the monastery to see Christ in the monks.

Elsewhere, Merton utilizes Rufinus's Latin translation of the *Historia Monachorum*[9] to make a similar point. In his novitiate lectures posthumously published and entitled *Pre-Benedictine Monasticism: Initiation into the Monastic Tradition 2*, Merton quotes Rufinus: *Vere vidi thesaurum Christi in humanis absconditum vasculis.*[10] Merton's reflection on this text highlights the transparent nature of the monk's prophetic witness: "It is the triumph of Christ's grace that makes the virtues of the Desert Fathers possible. . . .

---

[9] The *Historia Monachorum* is a translation of an unknown original account of a journey to the desert; it became one of the main sources of Antonian spirituality.

[10] Thomas Merton, *Pre-Benedictine Monasticism: Initiation into the Monastic Tradition 2*, ed. Patrick F. O'Connell, MW 9 (Kalamazoo, MI: Cistercian Publications, 2006), 29. O'Connell provides the translation in a footnote: "I have truly seen the treasure of Christ hidden in human vessels."

In making this treasure known to others the writer brings them salvation and also saves his own soul. This implies a very clear notion of the monastic vocation and {its} charismatic place in the Church" (*Pre-Benedictine Monasticism*, 29).[11] Merton goes on to list a number of general points about the monastic life and virtues. His second point is another sentence from Rufinus: *Novos prophetas, tam virtutibus animi, quam vaticinandi officio suscitatos* (*Pre-Benedictine Monasticism*, 29).[12] Merton follows this sentence with the admonition, "[Note the] trope of the 'prophetic' life of the monk: a living witness to the truth of God's word, of His promises, and of His demand for penance. The monk is the man who has taken the word of the Lord literally" (*Pre-Benedictine Monasticism*, 29).

The monk, then, Merton implies, remains a sign of contradiction to the modern world just as Christ was to his. The monk's silent witness forms the heart of his prophetic power as a sign of contradiction. As Merton puts it, "The lone man remains in the world as a prophet to whom no one listens as a voice crying in the desert, as a sign of contradiction."[13] Monastic silence was for him one of the most potent forms of prophetic communication to the modern world, as he said in a letter to Allan Forbes, Jr.: "Yet as you say, if there is anything of the prophetic spirit left in us, it can find something to do while we are here in silence. And I myself do not underestimate the power of silence either. I know that as a matter of fact I can do much more for peace here, in silence, than I can by coming out and showing my head above ground so to speak. This is just another way of saying that there are many, many unexplored aspects of resistance and of witness."[14] The prophetic silence of the monk, Merton thought, was a sign of contradiction

[11] Words in braces were supplied by the editor of the volume.

[12] O'Connell's translation reads, "new prophets, raised up by the virtues of their souls as much as by the function of prophesying."

[13] Thomas Merton, *Disputed Questions* (New York: Harcourt Brace Jovanovich, 1960), 204.

[14] Merton to Allan Forbes, Jr., early April 1962, in Thomas Merton, *Witness to Freedom: The Letters of Thomas Merton in Times of Crisis*, ed. William H. Shannon, Thomas Merton Letters, vol. 5 (New York: Farrar, Straus and

to the modern world because, as the monk was wholly devoted to the eschatological kingdom of God, his prophetic silence was a sign of a different world—the world to come. The desert spirituality of the monk ensures that the world to come may come in actuality for the one who values listening over speaking, obedience over rebellion, humility over pride.

Saint Bernard of Clairvaux and Primitive Carmelite Spirituality

Monasticism in the eleventh and twelfth centuries was characterized by numerous reform movements that sought to revitalize the spiritual ethos of increasing institutionalization and secular dependency. Two such movements had particular significance for Merton. The Cistercian reform, mainly under the inspiration of Saint Bernard of Clairvaux, and the primitive Carmelite movement were two separate yet similar responses to the spiritual needs of religious life at the time. Both of these movements, Merton noted, owed much to the desert spirituality of early Egyptian monasticism. Like their forebears, the Cistercians and Carmelites sought a way of life that was simultaneously contemplative and prophetic. It was not isolationism that the early Cistercians sought in building their monasteries in remote locations; rather, it was the atmosphere of solitude that would be conducive to spiritual transformation, enabling the monastery to become a witness of the kingdom of God alive in the world. Again, it was not absorption into God that the early Carmelite hermits sought, but the spiritual center of existence from which they could make the Gospel known. Merton writes in his introduction to Amédée Hallier's *The Monastic Theology of Aelred of Rievaulx*, "The aim of medieval monasticism was not simply to gain heaven by rejection of the world . . . but a positive witness to the presence of Christ in the world. The monastic witness was not so much ascetic as eschatological. Not so much a denial of man and the flesh as an affirmation of the Word made Flesh, taking

---

Giroux, 1994), 48–49. Allan Forbes, Jr. (1921?–2006) was a documentary filmmaker, writer, and peace activist.

created things to himself, in order to transform and fulfill them in himself."[15]

This particular orientation of medieval monasticism owed its greatest influence to one of the towering figures of medieval Christendom: Saint Bernard of Clairvaux (1090–1153). Merton's writings on Saint Bernard, which include two books[16] and a number of articles, forewords, and introductions, attest to his esteem and affection for one who was decisively formative for his monastic identity. Saint Bernard's influence on Merton is especially obvious in Merton's developing relationship with the world. In Bernard, Merton found more than a justification for his concern for the world: he found a model. As he explained in his foreword to Henri Daniel-Rops's book, *Bernard of Clairvaux*, "Bernard of Clairvaux was plunged deep in the mystery of the Cross, which was the mystery of God's will for his world and ours. He who had left the world to become a monk was thrown back into the world to be an apostle, a worker of miracles, a peacemaker and a warmaker, the reformer of abbeys, the monitor of Popes and a prophet sent to alarm kings."[17]

Yet for Merton, Saint Bernard's concern for the spiritual well-being of Europe in no way compromised his monastic disposition. Instead he judged that what Bernard gave to Europe was the fruit that issued forth through his years of living "deep in the mystery of the Cross." In Bernard's contemplative orientation as a monk, Merton located the effectiveness of his charismatic ministry. The Spirit, he argued, draws humans into the life of God only to draw them out into the life of the world, in a continuous action that knows no end in human life here on earth. Contemplation and

---

[15] Thomas Merton, introduction to Amédée Hallier, *The Monastic Theology of Aelred of Rievaulx: An Experiential Theology,* CS 2 (Shannon, Ireland: Irish University Press, 1969), vii–xiii, here viii.

[16] *The Last of the Fathers: Saint Bernard of Clairvaux and the Encyclical Letter* Doctor Mellifluus (New York: Harcourt, Brace and Company, 1954); and *Thomas Merton on Saint Bernard,* CS 9 (Kalamazoo, MI: Cistercian Publications, 1980).

[17] Thomas Merton, foreword to Henri Daniel-Rops, *Bernard of Clairvaux,* trans. Elisabeth Abbott (New York: Hawthorn Books, 1964), 5–7, here 5.

action coexist and are interdependent. Merton made this point explicitly with regard to Bernard: "Bernard, the contemplative, was a great man of action because he was a great contemplative. And because he was a contemplative he never ceased fearing to be a mere man of action. . . . The natural sincerity and the supernatural zeal for divine truth that burned within him could not help showing him the faults of frailty and passion which even a saint could commit in the heat of ruthless and energetic action. . . . Bernard is sent to instruct us how human a saint must be, to forge out the will of God in the heat of the affairs of men" (*Bernard of Clairvaux*, 5–6).

Merton made it a point to highlight what is not altogether obvious in the character of Saint Bernard, namely, his humility. Even in the midst of his grandiose dealings with the most notable of European society, along with his trenchant self-confidence, he had the humility, Merton noted, to be himself in all circumstances. Monastic humility did not for Bernard mean inaction and passivity in the face of injustice when one had the capacity to be a voice for the will of God. In embracing the righteous indignation of the prophets, Bernard has at times acquired a reputation of possessing a self-righteous egotism. Merton rejected such views as based on only one aspect of Bernard's character: "Bernard, the passionate Bernard, who even in his anger and in his passion was a saint, will not blind everyone to the merciful Bernard, the gentle and longsuffering monk who could be as tender as a mother to anyone who did not give evidence of being a hardened Pharisee, and who had in his heart something of Christ's unending patience with the weak sinner and his compassion for the publican" (*Bernard of Clairvaux*, 7).

Fidelity to the holiness of God is also the subject of Merton's article "St. Bernard, Monk and Apostle," published in *Disputed Questions*. The discussion begins by commenting on the prophetic nature of sanctity, with Saint Bernard the exemplary personification. Merton describes a saint as "a sign of God": "His life bears witness to God's fidelity to promises made to man from the beginning. He tells us who God is by fulfilling God's promises in himself and by being *full of God*" (*Disputed*, 274). Here again Merton connects prophecy with fidelity. With his or her life, he says, the saint becomes an "irrefutable witness of the mystery of God with us" (*Disputed*, 276). The sanctity that revealed itself in the witness of Bernard's life and apostolic ministry, Merton said, must be understood in this existential light. The passion that moved Bernard beyond the walls of his cloister was for Merton not born from a call to teach or pastor. It was above all the charismatic call to be apostle and prophet, like Isaiah. Indeed, he likened Bernard's holiness to Isaiah's: "It is like the flame of sanctity that burned the lips of Isaias in his vision of God flaming forth in a fire of love and truth, radiant with prophetic vision coruscating with miracles and other charisms, imparting the substance of its own life to other men and making them share in something of the apostle's own vision of eternity" (*Disputed*, 282). The prophet is one who coruscates—who shines and glitters with the glory of God. As Merton attested, the surest sign of God alive in the world is the evidence of his presence on the faces of his people. Bernard illustrated Merton's idea that prophecy is most profoundly spiritual embodiment.

Merton's article "The Primitive Carmelite Ideal," also published in *Disputed Questions*, contains one of his most comprehensive discussions on the nature of prophecy. In the first section, titled "The Prophetic Spirit," Merton analyzes the spiritual motivations that formed the beginning of the primitive Carmelite movement. Unlike the earlier monastic communities, the first Carmelites formed loose-knit communities of hermits with openness to occasional apostolic service. Merton called attention to the purpose of the Carmelites' vocation in the words of their Rule: "Let each one remain in his cell or near it, meditating day and night on the Law of the Lord, and vigilant in prayer, unless he is legitimately occupied in something else"[18] (cited in *Disputed*, 220). What appealed to Merton was the simplicity and flexibility of this primitive approach to religious life: "The purpose of the life was solitude and contemplation, but within a framework that allowed complete liberty for the individual development of each one under the guidance of the Holy Spirit" (*Disputed*, 220). These words sum up in a nutshell all that Merton was advocating in his writings on monastic renewal. This

[18] http://carmelnet.org/chas/rule.htm (see chap. 10).

charismatic, prophetic dimension was the key to the revitalization of monasticism and was the only way for monasticism to bestow upon the world its peculiar gift.

Ironically, Merton traced the early Carmelite lineage to the devastating crusade preached by Saint Bernard, as the first Carmelites were those who followed Bernard's promptings, becoming warrior-pilgrims. In the end, they renounced the world with its ambitions and wars to live lives consecrated to God in solitude on Mount Carmel. Merton declares, "It is certain that Bernard himself must first have communicated to them something of the spirit and power of Elias, the burning and shining light that was in him" (*Disputed*, 228–29).

It is significant to note that Elijah is broadly considered to be the founder of the primitive Carmelite movement. More than anything, this claim acknowledges the inspiration that the first Carmelites attributed to the great desert-dwelling prophet. Merton acknowledged this significance: "The first Carmelites then were not only hermits and descendants of the early desert fathers, but they were also very conscious of a certain *prophetic* character about their vocation. This meant of course that they were inclined to give precedence to what we would call the 'mystical' side of their vocation over the ascetic, never of course neglecting or excluding that latter" (*Disputed*, 222).

Reflection on this prophetic character of the Carmelite vocation led Merton to articulate in great detail his understanding of the prophetic vocation. For him, the prophet in the traditional sense was much more than one who under divine inspiration foretold future events. He preferred to understand the prophet as a witness, just as a martyr is a witness. Yet one element of a prophet's witness is distinct from a martyr's. While the martyr suffers death,

> The prophet suffers inspiration, or vision. He shoulders the "burden" of vision that God lays upon him. He bows under the truth and the judgments of God, sometimes the concrete, definite historical judgment pronounced on a given age, sometimes only the manifestation of God's transcendent and secret holiness, which is denied and opposed by

> sin in general. But above all the prophet is one who bears
> the burden of the divine mercy—a burden which is a gift
> to mankind, but which remains a burden to the prophet
> in so far as no one will take it from him. (*Disputed*, 222–23)

This understanding of prophecy as bearing the burden of divine
mercy is reminiscent of Abraham Heschel's notion of prophecy
as sharing in the divine *pathos*.[19] Merton, while very impressed
with Heschel and his writings, had not yet read *The Prophets* or
any of his other books that he would soon come to regard highly.[20]
Nevertheless, similar to both writers is the priority of divine *hesed*
over divine judgment in the prophetic ministry. This point became
poignantly clear early in Merton's writing career, toward the end
of *The Sign of Jonas*: "The Voice of God is heard in Paradise: 'What
was vile has become precious. What is now precious was never
vile. I have always known the vile as precious: for what is vile I
know not at all.' 'What was cruel has become merciful. What is now
merciful was never cruel. I have always overshadowed Jonas with
My mercy, and cruelty I know not at all. Have you had sight of Me,
Jonas My child? Mercy within mercy within mercy.'"[21]

So Merton perceived that the Hebrew prophets, especially Elijah,
offered the early Carmelite Fathers their greatest inspiration in forming their rule of life. A foundational text that he noted was 1 Kings
17:1-4: "Elijah the Tishbite, from Tishbe in Gilead, said to Ahab: 'As
the LORD the God of Israel lives, before whom I stand, there shall
be neither dew nor rain these years, except by my word.' The word
of the LORD came to him, saying, 'Go from here and turn eastward,
and hide yourself by the Wadi Cherith, which is east of the Jordan.
You shall drink from the wadi, and I have commanded ravens to

[19] For Heschel's treatment of prophecy, see his *The Prophets* (New York:
Harper and Row, 1962).

[20] For Merton's correspondence with Heschel, see Thomas Merton, *The
Hidden Ground of Love: The Letters of Thomas Merton on Religious Experience
and Social Concerns*, ed. William H. Shannon (New York: Farrar, Straus and
Giroux, 1985), 430–36.

[21] Thomas Merton, *The Sign of Jonas* (New York: Harcourt Brace and
Company, 1953), 362.

feed you there.' " Carmelites thus interpret their entire vocation in light of this event in the life of its prophetic founder. Its prophetic spirituality, Merton said, issues forth from the primary position of standing in the presence of God and listening to his Word, with an obedient response in humble service following God's request. The divine summons is to "hide" and "drink." Merton notes what this summons meant for the Carmelite: "To hide in the torrent of Carith is to embrace the ascetical life, which leads to the perfection of charity by one's own efforts, aided by the grace of God. To drink of the torrent is to passively receive the secret light of contemplation from God and to be inwardly transformed by His wisdom" (*Disputed*, 225–26).

What these desert-dwelling contemplative prophets offered the church, Merton thought, was a paradigm of religious life that expressed itself in a spiritually integrated fashion. Contemplation and prophecy, as Merton envisioned them, form the pillars of a way of being simultaneously toward God and toward the world. Their lives proclaim the message that "we do not have on this earth a lasting city, and that we are pilgrims to the city of God" (*Disputed*, 226). The goal of their message is even more direct. Through witness and preaching the Carmelite seeks "to lead others in the ways of prayer, contemplation and solitude" (*Disputed*, 226).

Merton concludes this section of "The Prophetic Spirit" by drawing attention to another inspiration for the early Carmelites, the Blessed Virgin Mary. He saw Mary as embodying the perfection of the Carmelite ideal, "beyond prophecy" (*Disputed*, 227). As Mary, he wrote, was the symbol of hiddenness, ordinariness, and perfect humility, there is nothing pretentious about Marian spirituality: it listens and obeys. Merton draws a parallel between Mary and Saint John of the Cross, whose spirituality, he said, "goes to great lengths to exclude everything that savors of heroic show and mystical display" (*Disputed*, 227). Merton offered this insight into the Marian, Juanist disposition because he believed it necessary to root the prophetic spirit in humility and egoless concern. As he pointed out, "It would therefore be a tragic mistake to look at the Carmelite ideal too exclusively from the prophetic viewpoint. This would lead to distortion and dramatization, to violence and ultimately to a kind of pharisaical pretense" (*Disputed*, 227). The proper relationship between his understanding of contemplation and prophecy comes into clearer focus with this analogy. Prophetic expression as he defined it was just that—an expression of what one has heard and seen in the Spirit. He brings these ideas together in his concluding paragraph: "It can be said that the Carmelite spirit is essentially a 'desert' spirit, a prophetic ideal. And that Elias represents the exterior, the more material aspect of that ideal. But that the Virgin Mary is the symbol and source of the interior spirit of Carmel. Which means that in the long run, the desert spirit and prophetic ideal of Carmel are understood most perfectly by those who have entered into the 'dark night' of Marian faith" (*Disputed*, 228).

Saint Seraphim of Sarov
and Nineteenth-Century Russian Monasticism

Beginning in the late 1950s and continuing well into the 1960s, Merton explored the world of Russian theology and spirituality, whose monasticism, he came to see, had a particularly mystical-prophetic bent. Russian mysticism can largely be traced to the center of Orthodox spiritual life, Mount Athos. From there flowed the springs of liturgy, asceticism, and mysticism that have shaped Russian monasticism until the present day. One of the most notable mystical influences that rapidly spread throughout Russian monasticism and Russian laity alike was that of the Greek Hesychast way of prayer, whose mantra-like "Jesus Prayer" solidified Russian spirituality in a contemplative ambiance.

Like monasticism in the West, Russian monasticism also underwent numerous renewal movements that sought to maintain the spiritual vitality so integral to its charismatic identity. One such movement held particular significance for Merton: the movement of the *startsy*, or charismatic, prophetic monks of the nineteenth century. *Startsy*, specialists in asceticism and Hesychast prayer who offer spiritual direction to those seeking spiritual wisdom, became the pillars of Russian mysticism in the nineteenth century and helped make it the golden age of Russian spirituality.

Merton took interest in the *startsy* influence on Russian monasticism because of its charismatic, prophetic nature and the evidence of renewal that took place through their leadership. As he wrote in his journal in March 1960, "More and more impressed by the seminal and prophetic stuff of Russian nineteenth century. If there was something I intended to study I think it would be that."[22]

Saint Seraphim of Sarov (1759–1833) was one of the most significant and best known of the Russian mystics and *starets* of the nineteenth century. From living his own "desert" life in the Russian forest, his spirituality is original and authentic. In an article entitled "Russian Mystics," published in *Mystics and Zen Masters*, Merton noted how many post-medieval desert dwellers suffered from mimicry and artificiality in their approach to seeking God in solitude, even to the point of obsession. Their approach often led to what he called "a negative, gloomy, and tense spirituality in which one is not sure whether the dominant note is hatred of wickedness or love of good."[23] And, he pointed out, "hatred of wickedness can so easily include hatred of human beings, who are perhaps less wicked than they seem" (*Mystics*, 181). Saint Seraphim, on the other hand, moved in a different direction. Characterized by a spiritual spontaneity, his life in the forest was marked by an effusion of joy that poured forth from his austere and simple life, revealing a gentle and compassionate concern for those in need of spiritual guidance. Likened to the spirituality of Saint Francis of Assisi and Saint Anthony of the Desert, Saint Seraphim's mysticism was for Merton a mysticism of light. Merton tellingly compared Saint Seraphim to another of his favorite mystics: "The only contemporary figure in the West who speaks so eloquently and with such ingenuous amazement of the divine light shining in darkness is the English poet William Blake" (*Mystics*, 182).

In the mysticism of Saint Seraphim, Merton observed the two defining streams of Christian spirituality, *apophaticism* and *kataphaticism*, perfectly wedded. With Russian mysticism in general, Saint

---

[22] Thomas Merton, *A Search for Solitude: Pursuing the Monk's True Life*, ed. Lawrence S. Cunningham, The Journals of Thomas Merton, vol. 3 (New York: HarperCollins, 1996), 380.

[23] Thomas Merton, *Mystics and Zen Masters* (New York: Farrar, Straus and Giroux, 1967), 181.

Seraphim's integrated approach to life in God appealed to Merton precisely because its negative and positive aspects are so interdependent: light shines out of darkness and makes known what is hidden. Yet Russian mysticism is much more than an intellectual apprehension of hidden truth come to light; it is, in Merton's view, primarily transfiguration. Its goal is not only to reveal truth but also to make true all that has fallen into the disfigurement of untruth. Grounded in the mysterious unknown, the mystical approach of Saint Seraphim and the nineteenth-century Russian monks demonstrated a spiritual vitality that Merton described as "unquestionably prophetic" (*Mystics*, 184). Usually, he noted, spiritual vitality implies a certain variety that can often lead to conflict. There was something special, however, he thought, about nineteenth-century Russian monasticism:

> In nineteenth-century Russian monasticism we find darkness and light, world-denial and loving affirmation of human values, a general hardening of resistance to forces of atheist humanism and revolution, and yet an anguished concern at the sinful oppression of the poor. We cannot with justice dismiss the whole Russian monastic movement as negative, pessimistic, world-hating. Nor can we identify its deep and traditional contemplative aspirations with mere political or cultural conservatism. There was an unquestionably prophetic spirit at work in the movement, and St. Seraphin is only one among many examples that prove this. (*Mystics*, 184)

What Merton found in the mysticism of these Russian monks was not only a legitimization of a monastic, prophetic spirituality but also an effective paradigm whereby the prophetic spirit could express itself both through individual monks and through a monastic movement. The Russian paradigm was also a paradigm based on an embrace of God through the negative theology passed down from Pseudo-Dionysius and Saint Maximus the Confessor, which was completely compatible with the positive theology of a mysticism of light that saw no compromise in manifesting itself in merciful and compassionate concern for the world.

Merton wrote of a "less prophetic" (*Mystics*, 184) spirit active in the golden age of Russian monasticism that nonetheless carried deep implications in regard to social influence and national aspirations. This spirit, characterized, he said, by "ascetic fervor, of discipline, of order" (*Mystics*, 185), asserted itself in a more aggressive contempt for the world: "The ascetic who renounced the city of man in order to lament his sins in the *poustyna* (desert) may well have been giving his support to a condition of social inertia by implicitly affirming that all concern with improvement was futile and even sinful" (*Mystics*, 185). In this comparison of "prophetic" and "less prophetic" spirits in Russian monasticism, an important aspect of Merton's understanding of prophecy comes into focus as he ties prophecy integrally together with concern. One's way of life may influence and effect change in the world, but not all ways of life would be considered a form of prophetic living. Prophetic living, he insisted, involves *a disposition of concern toward the world*. What was unique about nineteenth-century Russian monasticism and its particular brand of mysticism was that, like the Carmelites, it possessed dual dispositions: one toward God, the other toward the world. The antinomy between these two dispositions, which has been a significant theme in the Western monastic tradition, played only a minor role in the monasteries of nineteenth-century Russia. Saint Seraphim and the other *starets* of nineteenth-century Russian monasticism clearly made an indelible impression on Merton by modeling for him the type of monasticism he was seeking to live.

Thich Nhat Hanh

On May 28, 1966, Thich Nhat Hanh, a Vietnamese Buddhist monk who had become well known for his non-violent resistance to the Vietnam War, visited Merton at Gethsemani. In Nhat Hanh, Merton found more than just a friend or brother; in many ways he found a soul mate. Writing a few days after their meeting, Merton described Nhat Hanh as "a true monk; very quiet, gentle, modest, humble, and you can see his Zen has worked. Very good on Buddhist philosophy and a good poet."[24] He expressed his view of the significance of the relationship he formed with Nhat Hanh in greater depth in a short essay called "Nhat Hanh Is My Brother," first published in *Jubilee* in August 1966. In this heartfelt tribute and plea on Nhat Hanh's behalf, Merton expressed a form of compassion that he did not reveal in any of his other relationships. It also contained a meaningful statement about the prophetic ministry he saw Nhat Hanh embodying. In a lecture entitled "Reflections on a Buddhist Monk," Merton described Nhat Hanh as a prophet called to a prophetic ministry, using him as a template in discussing the prophetic function of monastic life. In the lecture, Merton stated, "The monk should be able to stand up and say that in the name of truth this is wrong. Or I say that in the name of God this should not be done."[25] That was precisely what Nhat Hanh was doing and why his life was in great danger. Merton's plea in "Nhat Hanh Is My Brother" was written to try to protect his friend from harm.

In "Nhat Hanh Is My Brother," Merton sought to provoke not a political response but a human one. In order to accomplish this goal, he first made explicit his complete and total acceptance of Nhat Hanh and the way he as a monk was resisting the social injustices he felt compelled to reject. Merton's radical compassion and unwavering conviction are clearly heard in his statement honoring Nhat Hanh: "He is more my brother than many who are nearer to me by race and nationality, because he and I see things exactly the same way. He and I deplore the war that is ravaging his country. We deplore it for exactly the same reasons: human reasons, reasons of sanity, justice and love. We deplore the needless destruction, the fantastic and callous ravaging of human life, the rape of the culture and spirit of an exhausted people."[26]

---

[24] Thomas Merton, *Learning to Love: Exploring Solitude and Freedom*, ed. Christine M. Bochen, The Journals of Thomas Merton, vol. 6 (New York: HarperCollins, 1997), 76.

[25] Thomas Merton, *Life and Contemplation* (Chappaqua, NY: Electronic Paperbacks, 1972). "Reflections on a Buddhist Monk" is located on side B.

[26] Thomas Merton, *The Nonviolent Alternative*, ed. Gordon Zahn (New York: Farrar, Straus and Giroux, 1980), 263.

In his defense of his Vietnamese brother, Merton explains Nhat Hanh's position as being completely free from ideological persuasion, saying that he represented neither a political nor a religious movement. Rather, "He represents the young, the defenseless, the new ranks of youth who find themselves with every hand turned against them except those of the peasants and the poor, with whom they are working" (*Nonviolent Alternative*, 263). For Merton, Nhat Hanh was giving voice to new insights and judgments swelling up in the social consciousness of Vietnam. He was the one who was courageously standing up, risking his life to make that new voice heard.

Nhat Hanh's favorable reception in his visit to the United States demonstrated for Merton that Americans still desired the truth when truth was made known to them and still had the sense in most cases to favor the human person over the political machine. But Nhat Hanh did not seek refuge in the United States; he went back to his home in Vietnam, where he once again faced the death threats of the Viet Cong. This move, more than any other, prompted Merton to write "Nhat Hanh Is My Brother." The heart of Merton's message to his fellow Americans appears in his passionate appeal:

> We cannot let him go back to Saigon to be destroyed while we sit here, cherishing the warm humanitarian glow of good intentions and worthy sentiments about the ongoing war. We who have met and heard Nhat Hanh . . . must also raise our voices to demand that his life and freedom be respected when he returns to his country. Furthermore, we demand this not in terms of any conceivable political advantage, but purely in the name of those values of freedom and humanity in favor of which our armed forces declare they are fighting the Vietnam war. (*Nonviolent Alternative*, 264)

In this statement, one prophetic voice risked his reputation in advocacy for another. For Merton, the prophetic ministry of Nhat Hanh was that important, and so was the cause of Nhat Hanh's prophetic ministry: life and freedom.

For Merton the prophetic character of Nhat Hanh was most vividly expressed in the freedom in which he lived his life. His life in the midst of the precarious situation in Vietnam proved and revealed the depth of his personal freedom. As Merton wrote, "Nhat Hanh is a free man who has acted as a free man in favor of his brothers and moved by the spiritual dynamic of a tradition of religious compassion" (*Nonviolent Alternative*, 264). This tradition, Zen Buddhism, was in Merton's mind perfectly expressed in Nhat Hanh's life: "More than any other he has shown us that Zen is not an esoteric and world-denying cult of inner illumination, but that it has its rare and unique sense of responsibility in the modern world" (*Nonviolent Alternative*, 264). Merton concluded that it was precisely because of Nhat Hanh's grounding in Zen that his prophetic spirit was able to take flight: "Wherever he goes he will walk in the strength of his spirit and in the solitude of the Zen monk who sees beyond life and death" (*Nonviolent Alternative*, 264).

Concluding Remarks

Merton's interpretive lens for the monastic vocation was the spirit that inspired the first monks to separate themselves from the superficialities of Egyptian culture and to seek a more meaningful existence in the solitude of the desert. Through his writings on the Desert Fathers, Merton overtly traced this spiritual impetus to the prophetic ethos of the Hebrew prophets, and preeminently to John the Baptist. This desert motif became the predominant and persistent element in the development of his ideas of a prophetic monasticism.

Merton believed that the Desert Fathers had developed a countercultural society in the desert for the express purpose of bearing witness to the principles of the kingdom of God. Their motive was not simply to lose themselves in the contemplation of God. In order to establish the kingdom of God on earth, they believed, two spiritual movements were necessary: withdrawal and attachment. In these movements the transformation of the monk from worldly to eschatological took place. Whether one was alone or in a community, this transformation gave birth to prophetic monasticism.

The witness of the kingdom of God in a transformed life is a witness to freedom. It is significant that Merton seldom makes reference to peace or joy as characteristic signs of the presence of the kingdom of God in the world. More than anything, the monk's witness is a witness to freedom. With the freedom of a transformed life, the monk witnesses to the Transcendent alive and present in the world, testifying to an existence different from what most people are used to. In a sense, the monk's life is shocking to modern sensibilities—and for Merton, this reality is as it should be. One of the monk's prophetic tasks, he thought, is to shock the modern person into a new consciousness. Through his or her life of silence, poverty, simplicity, humility, and obedience, the monastic becomes a prophet pointing toward eternal realities.

Saint Bernard's Cistercian reform and the primitive Carmelite movement were for Merton two significant renewal movements of the twelfth century that reinvented many of the spiritual impulses of desert monasticism and brought them to bear in medieval religious life and society. These two movements modeled a vocation in which the contemplative and prophetic ideals were wedded in an exemplary way. Bernard helped Merton form a more nuanced way of relating the active life to the contemplative as well as helping to justify a prophetic form of contemplative living from within his own monastic tradition. From Bernard, Merton learned that monastic, prophetic activity must remain true to the monastic principles of spirituality, especially humility, but that the monk need not be afraid to embrace a passion for justice. Yet this passion must be controlled, free from egocentric self-righteousness. Thereby monastic passion radiates the reality of one's intimate life with God and becomes a sign of divine love for the world.

Merton further explored the relationship of prophetic action and contemplation in his discussion of the primitive Carmelite ideal in "The Prophetic Spirit." Dependence on the Holy Spirit made early Carmelite spirituality vital and prophetic, he argued; continued dependence on the Holy Spirit was the key to maintaining the charismatic element of the desert spirituality that marked the primitive Carmelite spirit. For Merton, recognizing Elijah as founder of the Carmelites established the prophetic nature of the Carmelite vocation and led him to speak of the prophet as one who suffers the burden of inspiration, vision, and divine mercy. Further, he said, Mary is the archetypal symbol that grounds the prophetic spirit in egoless concern.

Nineteenth-century Russian monasticism also interested Merton for its admirable integration of contemplation and prophetic witness. The charismatic, prophetic monks who characterized this era of Russian monasticism, of whom Saint Seraphim of Sarov was the most popular, saw no threat to the contemplative ideal in exercising the apostolate of spiritual direction and wisdom formation. Saint Seraphim presented a mysticism of light, spontaneity, joy, and compassion that Merton found compelling. In Saint Seraphim, Merton found the perfect integration of the spiritual streams of darkness and light along with the necessary dual disposition toward God and toward the world that makes monasticism prophetic.

In Thich Nhat Hanh, Merton found another model of the prophetic monk, one who admirably, even heroically, integrated the contemplative spirit with the prophetic. Above all, Merton admired Nhat Hanh for his witness to freedom—his freedom from ideology and fear—his being alive to the truth of conscience in total allegiance. In many ways, "Nhat Hanh Is My Brother" communicates how much Merton desired to be like Nhat Hanh, as he poignantly conveys in the essay's final plea: "If I mean something to you, then let me put it this way: do for Nhat Hanh whatever you would do for me if I were in his position. In many ways I wish I were" (*Nonviolent Alternative*, 264).

The prophetic monasticism for which Merton became an ardent advocate through both his writings and his own monastic life did not go unnoticed, either in his lifetime or in the decades following his death. In a 1978 article entitled "Merton and History," Jean Leclercq summed up the way prophecy formed one of the central components of Merton's monastic vocation:

> He did not play the prophet, but was a member of a body—
> monasticism—which, because it does not aim at immediate
> action, can look far ahead, foresee and foretell. He felt that
> this was not restricted to Christian monasticism. In other
> religious traditions, what interested him was not so much
> the lofty and subtle doctrines, as the monks themselves,
> those who today, as in the past centuries, live according

to these doctrines, thus attesting to their practicality. In
such action fired by contemplation, Merton discerned an
energy capable of changing the course of history. . . .
A prophet is a person of neither vague ideas nor ready-
made solutions. He or she is a person who, by reason of the
vigor of his or her concepts and the intensity of his or her
contemplation, compels other persons to act, giving them
worthy reasons for doing so. Because he was a person of
vision—not of "visions"—and a powerful catalyst, Merton
was a prophet, and there is nothing to say that he was the
last of the prophets.

That a country like the United States should produce
someone of such wealth, and continue to listen attentively
and so broadly to his message, augurs well for the future of
the Church and the world. Is there any reason not to hope
that God will raise up at all times other such witnesses of
his own eternal contemplative action, Love?[27]

[27] Jean Leclercq, "Merton and History," in *Thomas Merton: Prophet in the Belly of a Paradox*, ed. Gerald Twomey (New York: Paulist Press, 1978), 213–31, here 230–31.

Chapter 8

The Contemplative-Prophetic Vocation in *The Springs of Contemplation*

We have a prophetic task. We have to rock the boat, but not like the hippies.[1]

—Thomas Merton

Merton heard the Second Vatican Council's call for the renewal of religious life as a confirmation of his personal concerns and efforts in the revitalization of monasticism and its contemplative ideal. As contemplation and prophecy and their mutual interdependence formed the heart of his conception of an authentic monastic renewal, Merton invited a group of contemplative nuns to his hermitage once in December of 1967 and again in May of 1968 to search for ways to aid in this renewal process and to have a creative interchange of ideas about the issues facing female contemplative communities. He facilitated these informal gatherings, beginning each session by initiating a particular topic for discussion; they often, however, took on a life of their own through the interchange that took place.

These discussions left a significant mark on Merton's spirit. After the completion of the first gathering, he commented, "The last four or five days have been quite fantastic: among the most unusual in my life. I hardly know how to write about them. There should

---

[1] Thomas Merton, *The Springs of Contemplation: A Retreat at the Abbey of Gethsemani*, ed. Jane Marie Richardson (New York: Farrar, Straus and Giroux, 1992), 80.

be a whole new key—and a kind of joy unusual in this journal."[2] The fifteen nuns present on this occasion caused Merton to rethink some of the "superficial ideas and judgments" he had made about contemplative religious life (*Other Side*, 20). They gave him an un-expected sense of hope that a remnant of genuine contemplative life was alive and well in North America. Merton's comments after the second retreat in May of 1968 were more sober: "Once again, realization of the paralyzing problems of these contemplative con-vents and of their need. . . . Many of the convents were afraid of any change, don't know what to do, preserve silly or inhuman regulations and customs, are under attack from all sides, and see hope only in utter conservatism—which means purely and simply their extinction. Others want to develop and are prevented from doing so" (*Other Side*, 123).

The Springs of Contemplation consists of transcriptions of these two retreats.[3] The themes explored there all examine in some way the nature of contemplative life and its relevance (or irrelevance) to the contemporary church and society. Merton drew inspiration and insight from Che Guevara and Malcolm X, from Zen masters and Teresa of Avila, from Martin Buber and Herbert Marcuse. He highlighted the tension between solitude and community, between charism and institution, between fidelity to tradition and adapt-ability to modernity. Perhaps the predominant and overarching theme that runs throughout the conferences, though, is the pro-phetic aspect of the contemplative vocation. Many of Merton's ideas presented in the course of this study resurfaced and found

[2] Thomas Merton, *The Other Side of the Mountain: The End of the Jour-ney*, The Journals of Thomas Merton, ed. Patrick Hart, vol. 7 (New York: HarperCollins, 1998), 20.

[3] Patrick O'Connell, "The Springs of Contemplation: A Retreat at the Abbey of Gethsemani," in *The Thomas Merton Encyclopedia*, ed. William H. Shannon, et al. (Maryknoll, NY: Orbis Books, 2002), 451–52. O'Connell notes that Jane Marie Richardson, the editor of *The Springs of Contempla-tion*, attributed one of the conferences to the first retreat, "Contemporary Prophetic Choices," though it was actually given at the second, referring to both the assassination of Martin Luther King, Jr., and the Catonsville Nine draft board raid, events that postdated December 1967.

their summation in the two retreats, representing Merton's most mature conceptualization of a prophetic spirituality.

The opening sessions directed the conversation toward the themes of the essential nature of the contemplative life and the possibilities of adaptation to a post–Vatican II church. Merton introduced the topic of contemplation by drawing on its dynamic significance: "In the contemplative life we all face the question 'What are we supposed to do?'" (*Springs*, 3). One obvious and practical answer for Merton was to gather in informal meetings with other contemplatives to explore issues facing contemplative life in church and society. Being present to one another, he thought, should be a priority for contemplative communities. Such time together was of special importance amid the sweeping changes taking place in the church in the wake of the Second Vatican Council, and also of special importance for any community seeking to live in the creative power of the Holy Spirit. As Merton noted, Pentecost means 'new life,' which means frequent change.

The issue of *silence* was offered by Merton as an example of a theme in transition in many contemplative communities. On the one hand, it is essential to contemplative life; on the other, instead of promoting presence in a contemplative community, it can promote absence through evasion and avoidance. The job of the contemplative, then, is to cultivate a silence that fosters communion. Such a fostering of communion happens when each member of a community contacts the ground of his or her being and accesses the streams of spiritual activity that constantly flow deep within. Drawing on an article by Joost A. Merloo, a Dutch psychoanalyst, Merton spoke of various "modulations" of silence: "Silence can carry many different messages; it can be a powerful form of communication" (*Springs*, 7). What is most important for a contemplative community, he said, is that silence communicates "a loving presence" (*Springs*, 7).

More than that, Merton said, silence carries with it the unique abilities of spiritual intuition and discernment. In reference to a Muslim Sufi he once met whom he described as being as much a "finished product" as anyone he had ever met, he shared how impressed he was in the way this Sufi was able to answer a question with such depth and insight that he addressed what the person asking the question really wanted to know. For Merton, this response showed how a true spiritual master teaches.

Merton also insisted on the communicative aspect of silence: "I am against reducing silence to muteness, against depriving individuals of their right to a many-voiced silence, their right to hear both on the level of grace and on the level of nature" (*Springs*, 14). In keeping with the Rule of Saint Benedict, he felt, silence is for listening—for hearing and being moved to obey what is heard with the utmost concern. Contemplative communities gathering together for spiritual discussions offer one significant way of collectively listening to what the Spirit is saying and fostering mutual compassion from the Spirit's leading—of dreaming out loud and purifying the air.

Merton also explored the idea of presence and authentic communal living. He spoke of renewal as probing the basic form and truth of a particular vocation and insisting on an institutional paradigm that nurtures genuine personal development: "Wherever there is human presence, we have to be present to it. And wherever there is a person, there has to be personal communication. There Christ can work. Where there is presence, there is God. A Christian is one who continues to communicate across all the boundaries, a sign of hope for a convergence back to a kind of unity" (*Springs*, 31). What was paramount for vibrant contemplative communities in Merton's mind was the life of the community itself rather than the institutional structure on which it was based, since community is the place where God is present and the place where the Spirit works.

In these retreats Merton also introduced the theme of the prophetic vocation. Warning against the tendency in some communities to make themselves look dynamic for the sake of being "with it" and ending up being outdated in only a few years, Merton said that a true contemplative community must instead respond to the Word of God at whatever cost. In addition to this requirement, he declared an obligation "to a prophetic call" (*Springs*, 37)—including an obligation for centuries-old forms of religious life: "even in our somewhat rigid institutions, I think we can be prophetic" (*Springs*, 37–38).

After being asked to elaborate on the charismatic, prophetic element in contemplative communities, Merton explained that something charismatic is a gift from God that fosters a special kind of freedom. This freedom of the contemplative makes one fully accessible to God's initiative and inspiration. Merton held that for that reason it is essential that those in contemplative life not be tied down to routine duties such as parish work. In his view, such duties restrict spiritual spontaneity and availability and have the potential to stifle the flow of prophetic inspiration that becomes accessible in a contemplative stance toward God: "An inspiration of the Holy Spirit may have nothing to do with anything terribly important in itself, but it gives us the conviction that when we follow through on this ordinary thing, we are on the right track. We need to be free for that. We are not in our monasteries simply saying prayers. We are remaining open to something, the unexpected. Something is going on at a deep level" (*Springs*, 46).

What gives access to the spiritual churnings at this deep level, he goes on, is prayer: "Prayer is where charism operates. And prayer and charism lead to a pure heart" (*Springs*, 48). Contemplative prayer, then, is marked by a certain emptiness—a freedom from egocentric concern, which gives way to a state in which God can move freely in and through the contemplative. This is what purity of heart meant for Merton and why he considered it a requisite for genuine prophetic activity. This contemplative way is prophetic, "not in the sense of sudden illuminations as to what is going to happen at some future moment, but in the sense that we are so one with the Holy Spirit that we are already going in the direction the Spirit is going. You can, in some way, anticipate things in the Church and you're ready for what is coming along. . . . Our life is meant to give us that kind of sensitivity and that kind of atmosphere, a state of real humility and peace and simplicity" (*Springs*, 49).

Merton describes the function of the contemplative life here as putting one into contact with the Spirit of God that is as intimate as possible and finding ways to be sustained in this distinctive relationship. In this spiritually charged atmosphere arises the prophetic ministry that intuits and anticipates the movement of the

Spirit in the world. The prophet is the one who leads others in the way of the Spirit.

This contemplative-prophetic vocation is therefore crucial for the well-being of the church, according to Merton. Without it, the church becomes stagnant, overly dependent, and perhaps even fixated on institutional propagation. Merton's ecclesiology was essentially charismatic in nature. Although he never denied the significance and necessity of the institutional aspect, he held that in order for the church to fulfill its mission, it must be led by charismatic leaders.

In these retreats Merton called attention to the way contemplative life helps one to see what is artificial—how it helps one to discriminate and make critical judgments. This ability was of particular value in American culture, Merton thought, since in his estimation Americans, and Western culture in general, had fallen deeply into the sin of artificiality. For this reason, he noted, Americans have trouble understanding the relevance of the contemplative life. A pragmatic, materialistic society sees no purpose in such a life.

With this perspective in mind, Merton referred to Robert A. Heinlein's 1961 best-selling science fiction novel *Stranger in a Strange Land*. It tells of a human child who visits Mars and brings back a new religion that is a kind of parody of modern, popular religion in America. A major part of the spiritual discipline of this new religion is learning the Martian language. One Martian word, *grock*, is of particular interest for the discussion. Merton explains its meaning: "*Grocking* is really a form of prophetic intuition which is able to project forward and to anticipate what's coming, so that people in this religious elite, by virtue of their discipline and their study of the Martian language, are *grocking* what's ahead" (*Springs*, 66).

Merton mentions one unidentified book that applies *grocking* to Christianity. The book suggests that the Christian should be able not only to be orthodox but also to see what is going to happen and to make it happen. Merton's response to such a suggestion is not favorable: "This is the Marxist view of things: you get in the know about the laws of history and you are so smart and so disciplined that you can make things move in that direction" (*Springs*, 66). Young Americans were favorable to it, he mentioned, because they had grown weary of a faith that was used as an excuse to evade hard questions and one that no longer required discipline for its members. What they wanted was human responsibility in religion—they wanted an elite group of contemplatives who *grocked* the future. While Merton admitted that this depiction might be silly, he also acknowledged that it reflected something very real about the modern world and its relationship to religion—about how the world continued to look to contemplatives, not just for some peace and solace when the world became too chaotic, but for direction and meaning for the most fundamental aspects and pressing needs of life.

Merton also spoke of vocation as a creative possibility, leading to things never suspected. What is essential to communities and individuals alike, he said, is to keep as open as possible to these possibilities—never to close one's self off to vital potential. What threatens such radical openness, he goes on, is the desire for security and not wanting to be bothered by "nitwit ideas" (*Springs*, 68). A community that wants to live in the dynamism of the Spirit must develop a patient tolerance for sifting through mediocre possibilities, much as a composer does when fashioning a *magnum opus*. The creative process can be tedious. As an example, Merton mentions Native American rituals that form young people into spiritually sensitive adults. Crucial to such a vocational formation are the moments of crisis, which help develop personal realization and in turn foster authentic community life.

With particular concern for Christian contemplative communities, Merton cites First Corinthians 1:26–2:5, where Saint Paul mentions that not many wise were called by God, but the foolish were called to confound the wise. The passage was significant for Merton, because it stands in direct contradiction to the idea of *grocking*. The purpose of life, he asserted, was not to form elite communities separated from the realities of the contemporary world. Authentic religious community is based on poverty and humility, not on Gnosticism and elitism. The genesis of religious community is located in the simple obedience to the call of God to follow him in a certain way. Such fidelity to the call of God is the sustenance of a prophetic vocation.

Merton led the discussion to the topic of the prophetic task incumbent on both the church at large and contemplative communities in particular. Prophetic action, he said, would often be met with misunderstanding and confusion—and when its message is fully comprehended, with outright hostility. He cited a specific case to illustrate his point. Dan Berrigan's conscientious objection to the Vietnam War and his willingness to go to jail because he considered that living in the world was a form of imprisonment was for Merton a symbolic, prophetic action, which he recognized as being difficult for most people to accept. Part of the reason, he argued, for the lack of clarity in prophetic communication is living "in a society where everything is so predetermined that being prophetic is simply not going to fit anybody's preconceived ideas" (*Springs*, 79). As a result, the contemplative life, as long as it is true to its prophetic vocation, will never find much approval from the world—even from those who look to those living it for guidance and direction. Thus, the motivation of contemplative communities can never be the support of society. Their prophetic vocation embraces a marginal position in relation to the world—and even, to a certain degree, in relation to the church.

The prophetic stance of contemplative communities that Merton advocated has not been for the most part held over the course of the church's history. He noted that contemplative communities had in large part been seen as made up by conservatives who acquiesced to ecclesiastical power through humility and obedience. But, according to Merton, such a stance was a hindrance to the church, which needs healthy argumentation, criticism, and dialogue for its growth and development. Such a posture is part of the prophetic role of contemplative communities. Yet Merton once again cautioned against an overzealous "prophetism" that led only to revolution. For that reason, he was critical of French Catholic liberals whose social criticism was basically Marxist.

Merton offered Che Guevara and Malcolm X as two examples of men whose prophetic lives provided exemplary patterns for social transformation. By being "mystery men," both fulfilled the desire for a prophet common among young people. Che, by laying his life on the line—even without achieving much with his life—inspired the young with his death. Malcolm X, by liberating himself from an oppressive social system, demonstrated how to make choices that give honor and dignity to one's own "soul." According to Merton's assessment, both men introduced a type of prophetic formula: "If we cannot be like that, we should at least be followers of people like that" (*Springs*, 86). Merton also mentioned Martin Luther King as an example of one who acted unequivocally, a kind of action that Merton asserted to be necessary for the prophetic vocation.

Pointing out that contemporary prophetic movements failed because they fit too cozily into society, Merton explained such failure as caused by society's having adapted in such a way as to incorporate dissent into itself:

> In other words, the thesis behind this position is that we're living in a totalitarian society. . . . It's organized for profit and for marketing. In that machinery, there's no real freedom. You're free to choose gimmicks, your brand of TV, your make of new car. But you're not free not to have a car. In other words, life is really determined for everybody. Even the hippies in their dissent are living a predetermined kind of life, although they are trying to get out of it. They rock the boat, there's a splash, everybody is suitably shocked and scandalized, a bit titillated by it. After three years the whole thing vanishes and another fashion starts. It all means nothing. (*Springs*, 129–30)

This situation, Merton warned, required a genuine prophetic response.

Merton located the solution to this problem in the Old Testament history of prophecy, beginning when God told Abraham to leave his people. Thus the prophet, Merton noted, must get out of a certain kind of society or social structure, and that departure requires that the prophet put total trust in and dependence on God for provision and sustenance. God also told Moses to leave the oppressive Egyptian structure, because Egypt had robbed the Jews of their freedom to have God determine the totality of their lives, which, instead, the Egyptians determined. Merton perceived that these scenarios led to a form of alienation that prohibited authentic human existence. Here again he showed that the goal of the prophetic vocation was human liberation and authentic human living.

Other prophetic instances that Merton cited included Elijah, John the Baptist, and Saint Francis. God compelled Elijah to stand against the whole structure of the kingdom in which he lived, whose king and queen wanted him dead. He responded by escaping into the desert and hiding in a cave where he could assert his own prophetic choices. Merton saw that the same pattern appeared in the lives of John the Baptist and Saint Francis of Assisi, who also made radical breaks from the world so that they could be free to make their own choices not determined by outside sources. Merton explained the essential aspect of the prophetic vocation in this way: "Whenever you make a choice from your own deepest center, you are not being predetermined by somebody else" (*Springs*, 133). This mature sense of autonomy often leads, Merton argued, to the proclamation of a subversive message that is unacceptable to most people: the prophetic task is not to tell slaves to be free but to tell people who think they are free that they are slaves.

The great challenge to the integration of the prophetic element in contemplative life, as Merton saw it, was the manner in which contemplative life had evolved to become not only non-prophetic but also anti-prophetic. As he lamented, "It's designed to block any kind of prophetic reaction at all" (*Springs*, 134). Speaking of his own monastery, Merton quipped, "If someone did something prophetic around here, it would upset the whole place, the community would be shocked. We'd have no way of handling it" (*Springs*, 134). Merton offers a difficult solution to this difficult problem: ideally, contemplative communities should not just produce prophetic individuals but should become themselves prophetic. The task of the contemplative community, then, he held, was "not to produce prophetic individuals who could simply end up as a headache, but to be a prophetic community" (*Springs*, 134).

This last comment provoked one sister to ask, "Then we don't try to identify with the people of our time?" (*Springs*, 134). Merton's response removed any suspicion about his interest in relating to contemporary society. He was emphatic: contemplatives must relate to the society in which they find themselves as "a sign of contradiction which reminds them of the freedom they've forfeited" (*Springs*, 134). As an example of a prophetic community, he offered the creators of jazz, some of whose forms were largely conceived as protest music. He contrasted such protest with what the racial majority of America had produced: "It's completely different from the innocuous Muzak, accepted by white society, that you hear in the dentist's office, totally the opposite" (*Springs*, 135).

Thus Merton explained that the prophetic community witnesses on the one hand against unjust social or religious structures and, on the other hand, warns against an unhealthy dependence on any structure whatsoever. The prophetic community is, therefore, a mature community—one that has learned how to ride without training wheels. It is made up of authentic human beings who are comfortable existing on the margins of a given structure—"who can create their own existence, who have within themselves the resources for affirming their identity and their freedom in any situation in which they find themselves" (*Springs*, 136). These ideas reiterate Merton's approach to early desert monasticism as essentially a non-conformist movement.

What the contemplative-prophetic vocation seeks is *qualitative* change, Merton went on to say, while what society seeks is *quantitative* change. As he observed, "New products, new gimmicks are everywhere. We can buy more and different things and replace them quickly because they get obsolete so fast. The human race has never been so standardized and so bound to a predetermined situation as it is today" (*Springs*, 138). But contemplative vision, he insisted, sees beyond the changing fads of superficial, materialistic fluff and searches for what life offers as its most meaningful and permanent values. The contemplative heart is so fully set on the truth of these values as not to be swayed by the lure of the desire to be relevant. In Merton's view, unlike the modern age, the Middle Ages, although often referred to as an age of unfreedom, provided societies where people were generally able to choose for themselves.

Merton also judged that the church was largely failing, and had for most of its history failed, to provide adequate structures for this prophetic vocation. Prophecy had thus become an activity aimed not only at the reformation of society but also, in a more pressing sense, at the reformation of the church itself. Further, Merton saw it as an activity aimed not simply at ill behavior but, more specifically, at the ill structural systems at the root of sick societies and unhealthy forms of religious life. Living through a system was the antithesis of living prophetically, in Merton's mind. Dependence must be on God, the conscience, and the community of faith. These were Merton's pillars for prophetic living, and because he depends on all three of these combined, the prophetic life as he defines it is difficult to maintain. It requires that people really live. Merton noted that to do so "may be a much less spectacular thing than protesting" (*Springs*, 141).

In a later session, Merton made a bold assertion about the place of the prophetic vocation in the contemplative life: "Yesterday we talked about the prophetic aspect of our vocation. I wanted to get down to the most fundamental root of our life—the prophetic function" (*Springs*, 143). By describing prophecy as the "fundamental root" of contemplative life, he asserted that it is a nonnegotiable aspect of that life—what is most essential and basic to it. It plays the central role in the formation and well-being of a particular life—the key to its flourishing. For Merton, neither conservatives nor progressives were functioning prophetically. Each was missing the mark when it came to genuine prophetic activity: "The conservative approach wants to fit us into a medieval society; the progressive, into modern society. Neither of these is prophetic. So we're caught between two traps. This is hardly ever talked about" (*Springs*, 143).

Merton's critique once again revealed that freedom was his interpretive key in assessing genuine prophetic activity. In setting forth the contemplative's answer to the problems of the alienated and spiritually enslaved society he had described, Merton spoke of the basic purpose for monastic, contemplative communities. Those who had come to seek God behind the walls of a cloister, he said, had come to the realization that "in following the ordinary approved paths, you cannot live your own life" (*Springs*, 147). They had the keen insight of the contradictions embedded within a predetermined society. But in fact, he went on, the cloister was meant for more than simply "skipping movies because they're no good or giving up dancing because it's frivolous" (*Springs*, 148); it was meant to reorient one's life toward its deepest center so that one could follow one's deepest needs and desires. In his mind, much of religious life had been watered down and was heading toward disrepair precisely because this insight was being neglected and compromised. In such an atmosphere, religious life loses one of its fundamental reasons for being, "to provide a place where people can find something that they cannot find elsewhere" (*Springs*, 148).

One of the most pressing needs of a society that had become, in Herbert Marcuse's words, "one-dimensional," was for such people living in such a society to have the opportunity to experience life being lived in multidimensional forms. In Merton's mind, the monastery should provide this opportunity. A one-dimensional society, he explained, "makes people need things and need them so badly that everything is put aside for the sake of fulfilling these needs" (*Springs*, 151). It was therefore an addicted society—addicted to an illusive promise of fulfillment. The contemplative, prophetic community sees through these illusive promises and testifies to the true reality of human fulfillment. The contemplative-prophetic community is truly itself when it is most free.

Taking his cue from Marcuse, Merton asserted that the major source of illusion in one-dimensional societies is the misuse and distortion of language. Changing times contribute to the changing of the meanings of words. Technology, especially mass media, contributes to that change. Thus it becomes incumbent on contemplative-prophetic communities to raise their level of awareness of the "factors behind the facts" (*Springs*, 155–56): "To live prophetically . . . You've got to be aware that there are contradictions. In a certain sense, our prophetic vocation consists in hurting from the contradictions in society. . . . And the contradictions in our own background and in our own Christian lives, contradictions for which we are not totally responsible but which we have to live with and face constantly. We have to work with them and resist the temptation to scapegoat others" (*Springs*, 157).[4]

---

[4] Jacques Ellul's *The Technological Society*, which Merton was reading at the end of 1964, gave him further grounding for his comments here. His journal entries on Ellul's book demonstrate the similarities he saw between Ellul's and Marcuse's ideas: "I am going on with Ellul's prophetic and I think very sound diagnosis of the Technological Society. How few people

A prophetic community, then, according to Merton, must learn to acquire a high tolerance for ambiguity and learn patience when sifting through the murky waters of uncertainty. In his view, all too many Christians lacked the fortitude for such prophetic endeavors. The easy way out was too quickly to point the finger in one direction or the other instead of remaining with the discomfort of ambiguity. The Old Testament prophets, many of whom did not want to be prophets at all, attested for Merton to the type of fidelity required of the true prophet: "we're in the same boat. God lays on us the burden of feeling the contradictions in our world and church and exposing them, insofar as we are honestly able to do that" (*Springs*, 157–58).

A key concept in Merton's prophetic methodology is seen here in the phrase "insofar as we are honestly able to do that." As Merton showed throughout his writing, he had little tolerance for a rogue "prophetism" with little regard for humility and personal integrity. In his view, the true prophet must be formed in the ways of selfless concern, free from egocentric interests and ideological preservation, before being able to minister prophetically in an authentic Christian spirit. For him, true prophetic activity was completely dependent on purity of heart.

---

really face the problem! It is the most portentous and apocalyptical thing of all, that we are caught in an automatic self-determining system in which man's choices have largely ceased to count." See *Dancing in the Water of Life*, ed. Robert E. Daggy, The Journals of Thomas Merton, vol. 5 (New York: HarperCollins, 1997), 161. Yet Merton was restrained in his response to Ellul's prognosis: "I think Ellul is perhaps too pessimistic. Not *unreasonably* so—but one must still have hope. Perhaps the self-determining course of technology is not as inexorably headed for the end he imagines. And yet certainly it is logical. But more is involved, thank heaven, than logic. All will be brought into line to 'serve the universal effort' (of continual technological development and expansion). There will be no place for the solitary! No man will be able to disengage himself from society!" (*Dancing*, 163). Noting both the irony and ambiguity of his relationship with technology, Merton remarked, "Should I complain of technology with this hissing, bright green light with its comforts and dangers? Or with the powerful flashlight I got at Sears that sends a bright hard pole of light probing deep into the forest?" (*Dancing*, 163).

As was discussed above, Merton's answer to the problem of language and the challenge of the contradictions of society was silence: "What does a contemplative do about this? The mere fact of living in silence, a kind of silence that might be called electric with this sense of contradiction, is important. Our silence can't be just nice and cozy, narcissistic and sweet. It's a silence in which there is pain, where we know we *should* say something but haven't got anything to say. People should be able to sense that our silence comes from deep reflection and honest suffering about the contradictions in the world and in ourselves" (*Springs*, 158).

Yet, he lamented, what often happens is quite the opposite: "Instead, they often see us living a silence that is reassuring and pleasing to our benefactors, in which the world's all right, after all" (*Springs*, 158). In such a scenario, he thought, silence becomes a way of evading one's prophetic responsibility. Instead of escaping behind the façade of silence, contemplative communities are challenged with discovering creative ways to communicate effectively in a society where they function with a closed language where meanings of words move on shifting sand.

In a later session, Merton initiated a discussion on the "feminine mystique" (*Springs*, 161).[5] Patrick O'Connell has commented, "Perhaps the most significant (and, in its own way, the most prophetic) conference is one that deals with a topic not discussed elsewhere by Merton in any detail: the role of women in the church and in society."[6] Merton began speaking about this sensitive topic by first acknowledging the struggle that many women faced in finding their place in the church. The struggle, for Merton, pivoted around what he called the "feminine mystique," which he described as "an idealization of supposed special feminine qualities which are put on a pedestal and made much of" (*Springs*, 161). A deeper problem facing the women religious he was addressing was what he called "a

[5] Although Merton makes no reference to Betty Friedan's *The Feminine Mystique* (New York: W. W. Norton, 1963), he seems to borrow the phrase from her title, as well as the general idea put forth in her book—that women had grown dissatisfied with and frustrated by prescribed roles.

[6] O'Connell, "Springs," 452.

cloistered, contemplative mystique" (*Springs*, 161). By this he meant that the contemplative nun was stereotyped as being essentially "passive" and "mysterious." The problem with such a caricature, as with any stereotype, he felt, was that it limited the personal value of a given individual or group. Cloistered women were certainly not the only group who could be considered "passive" and "mysterious." As he remarked, "But *everybody* is mysterious and sometimes passive" (*Springs*, 161). What added to the confusion, he said, was that many women favored the stereotype and found security in playing a particular role. Of course, the problem with role playing, for Merton, was obvious: it limited authenticity.

Merton was bold in his assessment as well as his remedy. He told his audience, "We have to face the fact that the cloistered contemplative nun has been 'officially' appointed to live out this feminine mystique. I think you have an absolute duty to rebel, for the good of the Church itself" (*Springs*, 162). The options, in Merton's view, were twofold: either perpetuate the "image of the mysterious, veiled, hidden woman who is an 'enclosed garden'" (*Springs*, 162) or assert the truth, that contemplative nuns were simply "*people* loving God" (*Springs*, 163).

As Merton saw it, the feminine mystique arose at a time when social structures were built exclusively by men, with women being forced to assume a special role in society and thereby beginning to be treated more as a commodity than a value—more as a thing than a person. The feminine mystique, he argued, initially offered religious women an opportunity to find their way into a form of life that provided them with the communal protection to grow beyond such dehumanizing social structures. The cloister became about the only place possible for a woman to find liberation and become an authentic person. What was once a tool for freedom and authentication had become, in his view, a tool for control and domination by an all-male hierarchy insensitive to the needs, aspirations, and unique gifts of female contemplative communities.

Merton's humanistic values surfaced in this session as the most significant component for authentic renewal for women religious. As he stated, "Being a *person* is what has to be emphasized" (*Springs*, 172). And what was true of women contemplative communities, he held, is ultimately true for all contemplative communities. He pointed out that the same struggles faced by women religious were a part of his own monastery. All contemplative communities must therefore work together and "fight against this" (*Springs*, 172). He suggested the need for a new theological anthropology that could offer new insight into what a human being is—both as man and as woman. This perspective once again showed that, for Merton, the prophetic stance against the dehumanizing tendencies of social and ecclesial structures ought to be approached with the full faculties available to the human person and not simply as an emotional reaction or rebellion due to pent-up frustration over an unfulfilled ideological agenda.

Concluding Remarks

Merton's decision to lead two retreats with contemplative nuns demonstrated both his pastoral concern for a group within the church that he thought needed special attention in the wake of the sweeping changes occurring within religious life after the Second Vatican Council and his methodological approach to such renewal. At the heart of his particular method was dialogue and creative interchange—sharing struggles and discerning the movement of the Spirit in a gathered contemplative community. As in other forms of religious life, his central test for genuine renewal here was authenticity of life, where the nun would be able to free herself from outdated sanctimonious accretions and develop a mature spiritual relationship in the spontaneity of a lively faith. Women should embrace only practices that fostered such human and spiritual development, he held, while resisting practices that threatened such development.

Merton located the root of the prophetic vocation in the quiet listening and discernment of this authentic way of being in the world. In the context of this sort of charismatic community, where the Word of God is revered and obeyed above all else and where the community has given itself in full availability to the Word, the prophetic vocation becomes a vital form of life within both individuals and the community as a whole. Merton therefore encouraged nuns to remain true to a contemplative posture of silence and humility toward the Word of God that promotes spiritual inspiration and purity of heart and protects from egocentric illusions that easily corrupt the prophetic endeavor. He affirmed that their vocation to be prophetic contemplatives was crucial for the well-being of the church and was one of the ways through which the church was led along the way of truth.

The contemplative posture toward the Word of God that Merton promoted was grounded in an ascesis of patient trust that provided space for the difficult and often messy process of discernment. As the Word of God emerges within the life of a contemplative community, the community learns the demanding lessons of selflessness and fidelity. Merton insisted that the prophetic vocation could only properly function within such an atmosphere.

The Word of God will inevitably lead the prophetic community to the margins of society—and, to a certain degree, to the margins of the church. It is a life that defies preconceived ideas and so is often misunderstood and is thus often persecuted. Yet, while marginal, it remains part of both society and church. Its prophetic credibility depends on the maintenance of this (however loosely) binding relationship.

Prophetic communities provide a vital ministry to the church's growth and development through unequivocal yet charitable critique and persuasive dialogue. It is significant to note that Merton is always careful to caution against what he calls "prophetism"—the tendency toward revolution built on obstinate ideological notions. He offers proper patterns of prophetic living, on the other hand, in the examples of Che Guevara, Malcolm X, and Martin Luther King, Jr., who demonstrated selfless concern over unjust social structures and inspired others by their willingness to be fully committed to what they believed to be the cause of justice.

Perhaps the most original insight Merton offered in his conferences pertains to the impotence of then-current prophetic movements. Because dissent had become an accepted reality in society, he noted, it had little power to transform. He found the answer to this predicament in the prophetic literature of the Old Testament. Like the Hebrew prophets, one must break free from society's predetermining conditions and create forms of life that foster authentic freedom. In this way one's relationship with the world becomes a sign of contradiction that demonstrates one's own enslavement to an illusory existence. Contemplative communities must provide a way of life that is multidimensional—free from the addictive patterns of promise and empty fulfillment characteristic of one-dimensional societies.

A major problem in regard to such unidimensionality emerges from the corruption of language. Words, Merton thought, had become too equivocal, with meaning being largely communicated through distorted ideas. He thus held that prophetic communities must pierce through this distortion and learn creative ways of communicating unequivocally—a tedious task requiring great patience and intuitive discernment. Silence once again surfaces as his answer to society's problems, with silence the cure of an unhealthy language. Contemplative silence, Merton pointed out, communicates compassion and presence to the contradictions embedded in a confused and chaotic society.

Merton revealed his own prophetic insights most sensitively and forthrightly as he drew attention to the problem of "the feminine mystique." In doing so, he exposed the dehumanizing tendencies of many in the church toward both female religious and contemplatives. Through the use of stereotypes, he thought, contemplative nuns had largely been controlled and contained. Such containment had an effect of limiting growth and contributing to artificial forms of life that denied the primary role of the Spirit in the life of a community. Merton encouraged the nuns to rebel against such tendencies, urging them to assert their unique personhood and spirit in order to carry their form of life into the future. Yet, he insisted, such assertiveness had to be as rational as emotional. Only then would such a prophetic revolt bear the traction for lasting change.

Conclusion

He did not say anything utterly strange,
At any rate to a thoughtful person.
Why then do we honor him, and call him prophet?

Because he said what we had always understood
When we were alone, when we were thoughtful.
We honor him because he made us remember,

Why, that we ourselves were serious once,
That we were children, and loved peace.
He gave us again the quietness of our minds.

The only strange thing was, his wild look.
But of course it was terrible to be where he had been:
To have dug those utterly simple sentences out of the soul's grave.[1]

—Mark Van Doren

That Thomas Merton possessed a prophetic spirit is little contested and has now become more obvious. Although not immediately evident in the early years of his monastic life, his prophetic spirit was germinating, awaiting release at the opportune moment. For him, that moment came on March 18, 1958. With his experience

---

[1] "Prophet," in *The Selected Letters of Mark Van Doren*, ed. George Hendrick (Baton Rouge, LA: Louisiana State University Press, 1987), 235. This poem, dated February 4, 1962, was addressed to Merton. Following the typed poem, Van Doren wrote, "Your last two pieces, on Christian Action and Father Metzger, came just as I was about to type this poem, which (believe it or not) it has taken me years to finish. I send it to you because I know now whom it fits. You. [P.S.] Whom, I mean, among the living. Live forever."

on the corner of Fourth and Walnut in Louisville, Merton's spiritual need to express himself prophetically was justified and blessed. It was a mystical insight that reconciled his early passion for justice with his equally passionate desire for solitude. It redefined his monastic identity, enlivening it with a goal far beyond Gethsemani's cloister. Because of that experience, the ten years that followed would be marked by an alternative spiritual trajectory. This paradigm shift in Merton's life and writings, while controversial at the time, was, as he would argue, in full accord with monasticism's *raison d'être*. Merton's efforts at monastic renewal were thus primarily an *aggiornamento* of monasticism's prophetic dimension.

The final ten years of Merton's monastic life were thereby characterized by a distinctively prophetic quality. This study has sought to demonstrate the foundational components of this prophetic quality by examining a number of the figures whom Merton described as prophetic and ascertaining his reasons, with the hope of bringing into a clearer focus a significant dimension of Merton's spirituality that has been previously little explored.

Merton's prophetic spirituality may be recognized as containing four major components: a certain way of seeing, his recognition of the values of simplicity and authenticity of life, a rooting in the charismatic dimension of the spiritual life, and—at the foundation of the other three—fidelity to God. Because of these four components, Merton's basic approach to the prophetic dimension of the spiritual life remains relevant today.

Merton's prophetic spirituality was conditioned by a certain way of seeing—what may be called *prophetic vision*. From childhood, Merton was exposed through the poetry of William Blake to an alternative vision of reality, stimulating his highly sensitized imagination. Over the course of Merton's life, his admiration of Blake's prophetic imagination increased. Blake helped Merton realize that this prophetic imagination was an integral component for diagnosing humankind's sicknesses as well as formulating creative remedies to heal them. The prophetic imagination also strengthened one's fidelity to the basic values of human life—values like simplicity, authenticity, and love—in the midst of modernity's efforts to disparage such values. Merton also responded powerfully to the way this prophetic imagination allowed Blake to assert himself as a courageous witness in the face of the ridicule that resulted from his critique of the modern mind.

Merton also recognized this creative, prophetic vision in contemporary Latin American poets and novelists such as Boris Pasternak, Albert Camus, and William Faulkner. Merton believed that poets were able to cut creatively through the distortion of language that modernity perpetrated on human communication, so providing a way of reaching into humankind's soul with potent symbols and imagery that were able to transform both mind and heart. Further, he thought that a creative intuition not bound and enclosed within the confines of the consciousness of the status quo enabled the poetic way of communicating prophetic insight. Creative intuition, he argued, derives from a contemplative mysticism that fosters the immediate experience of the divine in silent prayer as well as an experience, mediated mainly through the liturgy and nature. For Merton, attentiveness to God awakens one's prophetic sensibilities and inspires prophetic action.

Merton's prophetic spirituality was characterized by the premodern values of simplicity and authenticity of life. Through solitude, he argued, one's true self emerges and is liberated from the mechanizing tendencies of a technological society. Living authentically in one's true self exposes the dehumanizing effects of a one-dimensional society's addictive lifestyle and unmasks the illusions that trap people. Merton's reading of the leaders of the existentialist movement gave him a paradigm for understanding authenticity as a type of catalyst in the transformation of the self and of the world around him. It also showed him the need to promote a healthy understanding of Christian humanism, which gave sufficient priority and value to the formation of the human conscience and the person's individuality. This position appears in practical terms in Merton's advice to women's contemplative communities to break free from the "feminine mystique," which limited their own authentic, individual expression as human beings.

Most significant, Merton rooted his prophetic spirituality firmly in the charismatic dimension of the spiritual life, giving a remarkable priority to charismatic spirituality in the last ten years of his life. As a result, his spirituality of those years is correctly labeled *charismatic* rather than *contemplative*.[2] For him, the contemplative dimension of the spiritual life was to be fully intertwined with the prophetic dimension. His insistence on this vital relationship helped to highlight the fact that the essential ground of each is a dimension deeper than either in itself. This deeper dimension is a spirituality that enables one to live in openness and availability to the spontaneous movements of the Spirit of God—an openness that he called "charismatic." The charismatic dimension of the spiritual life was therefore a designation that for Merton encompassed realities both contemplative (living in the Spirit toward God) and prophetic (living in the Spirit toward the world).

As charismatic spirituality insists on personal experience as a crucial component in the spiritual quest, in Merton's view it seeks to foster a prophetic ear—a way of listening to and discerning God's voice and will. This activity is done both individually for one's self and collectively for one's community. By developing a prophetic ear one is able to discern and access the truths hidden in reality and is better able to manifest them to the world.

Charismatic spirituality also freely incorporates affect into one's experience with the divine. Merton depicts the passion of the prophets as a catalyst that moves others away from apathetic subjectivism and toward the ethical imperative of living justly with God and in the world.

Merton's efforts in the renewal of monasticism largely revolved around the need to restore this charismatic dimension to monasticism and indeed to the church. For Merton, overdependence on the institutional component of monasticism or the church to the detriment of the charismatic was the source of the diminishment

---

[2] This designation is legitimate only if the term *charismatic* is understood as Merton used it—as the experiential dimension of the spiritual life, encompassing the whole person and leading toward total availability to the spontaneous movements of the Spirit—and not understood in reference to meanings associated with the Roman Catholic *charismatic renewal* of the second half of the twentieth century, with its focus on the exercise of the spiritual gifts as articulated by Saint Paul in 1 Corinthians 12.

of spiritual vitality in both religious and ecclesial life. Therefore, he thought, the institutional aspect of religious and ecclesial life should always be the servant of the charismatic. At times, especially in his journals and letters, where he could be most candid, he expressed much frustration and disillusionment toward authority figures whom he believed to be incompetent. Yet even then he demonstrated fidelity and obedience. In the course of his life, his understanding of obedience, mainly through the help of Gabriel Marcel, developed to the point that it simultaneously allowed his own spiritual maturation and his fidelity to institutional authority.

Finally, fidelity to God was the foundational component of Merton's prophetic spirituality—its very essence. Living prophetically, Merton insisted, is completely dependent on faithfulness to the Word of God. In fact, one should not be concerned at all with playing the prophet but rather focus on being true to God in all of life's circumstances. Merton saw great danger in assuming the role of the prophet for the sake of championing one's ideological agenda, a revolutionary impulse that he called *prophetism*. To safeguard oneself from being consumed by this revolutionary spirit, he insisted on the need for humility and selfless concern—for purity of heart—in the prophetic endeavor. Nevertheless, he pointed out, fidelity to God often leads to a marginal existence in which one becomes a sign of contradiction to the values of the world and the misplaced values that may be present in the church.

Through these four components of prophetic spirituality Merton aimed at the reconciliation of humankind, indeed the whole cosmos, with the God who loved it all into existence. The prophet's job, he said, was to help make heaven and earth one. Through life in the Spirit, the prophet's spirit becomes a type of magnetic force making the future reality of the eschatological kingdom approach earth's moment in time a little more quickly.

Many of the elements of Merton's prophetic spirituality have been echoed in the teachings of the late Pope John Paul II, Pope Emeritus Benedict XVI, and Pope Francis. John Paul II's first encyclical, *Redemptor Hominis*, about the church's responsibility for the truth, emphasized the role of fidelity and simplicity in the church's prophetic ministry:

In the light of the sacred teaching of the Second Vatican Council, the Church thus appears before us as the social subject of responsibility for divine truth. With deep emotion we hear Christ himself saying: "The word which you hear is not mine but the Father's who sent me." In this affirmation by our Master do we not notice responsibility for the revealed truth, which is the "property" of God himself, since even he, "the only Son," who lives "in the bosom of the Father," when transmitting that truth as a prophet and teacher, feels the need to stress that he is acting in full fidelity to its divine source? The same fidelity must be a constitutive quality of the Church's faith. . . .

Consequently, we have become sharers in this mission of the prophet Christ, and in virtue of that mission we together with him are serving divine truth in the Church. Being responsible for that truth also means loving it and seeking the most exact understanding of it, in order to bring it closer to ourselves and others in all its saving power, its splendor and its profundity joined with simplicity.[3]

In his foreword to Niels Christian Hvidt's *Christian Prophecy: The Post-Biblical Tradition*, Benedict XVI (then Joseph Cardinal Ratzinger) made the following descriptive statements about the nature of prophecy:

The prophet is someone who tells the truth on the strength of his contact with God—the truth for today, which also, naturally, sheds light on the future. It is not a question of foretelling the future in detail, but of rendering the truth of God present at this moment in time and of pointing us in the right direction. . . . Essentially, he does not describe the ultimate realities but helps us to understand and live the faith as hope.

---

[3] John Paul II, "Redemptor Hominis," in *The Encyclicals of John Paul II*, ed. J. Michael Miller (Huntington, IN: Our Sunday Visitor, 1996), 46–96, here 81–82.

Even if, at a moment in time, the prophet must proclaim
the Word of God as if it were a sharp sword, he is not
necessarily criticizing organized worship and institutions.
His mandate is to counter misunderstanding and abuse of
the Word within the institution by rendering God's vital
claim ever present.[4]

A little later he continued:

I tend to see the root of the prophetic element in that "face
to face" with God, in "talking with Him as with a friend."
Only by virtue of this direct encounter with God may the
prophet speak in moments of time. (*Christian Prophecy*, viii)

And again,

It seems clear to me that—considering the entire life of
the Church, which is the time when Christ comes to us in
Spirit and which is determined by this very pneumato-
logical Christology—the prophetic element, as element of
hope and appeal, cannot naturally be lacking or allowed
to fade away. Through charisms, God reserves for himself
the right to intervene directly in the Church to awaken
it, warn it, promote it and sanctify it. I believe that this
prophetic-charismatic history traverses the whole time of
the Church. It is always there especially at the most critical
times of transition. (*Christian Prophecy*, viii)

Pope Francis, most strikingly of all, has embodied the spirit of
prophecy as Merton conceived it. From his imaginative reconcep-
tualization of the papacy, focused on simplicity and mercy to the
marginalized, to his cogent criticisms of flawed economic systems
that oppress the poor and of an ecclesiology more interested in
self-preservation than service, Pope Francis is currently demonstrating the persuasive power of a prophetic spirituality. His teach-

---

[4] Joseph Ratzinger, foreword to *Christian Prophecy: The Post-Biblical
Tradition*, by Niels Christian Hvidt (New York: Oxford University Press,
2007), vii–ix, here vii.

ing supports his action. In the highly publicized interview with Antonio Spadaro, editor-in-chief of *La Civiltà Cattolica*, the Italian Jesuit journal, Francis remarks:

> Religious men and women are prophets. . . . They are those who have chosen a following of Jesus that imitates his life in obedience to the Father, poverty, community life and chastity. In this sense, the vows cannot end up being caricatures; otherwise, for example, community life becomes hell, and chastity becomes a way of life for unfruitful bachelors. The vow of chastity must be a vow of fruitfulness. In the church, the religious are called to be prophets in particular by demonstrating how Jesus lived on this earth, and to proclaim how the kingdom of God will be in its perfection. A religious must never give up prophecy. This does not mean opposing the hierarchical part of the church, although the prophetic function and the hierarchical structure do not coincide. I am talking about a proposal that is always positive, but it should not cause timidity. . . . Being prophets may sometimes imply making waves. . . . Prophecy makes noise, uproar, some say "a mess." But in reality, the charism of religious people is like yeast: prophecy announces the spirit of the Gospel.[5]

In a homily given in the Vatican's Casa Santa Marta on December 16, 2013, Pope Francis pointed specifically to the task of the true prophet:

> a prophet is someone who listens to the words of God, who reads the spirit of the times, and who knows how to move forward towards the future. True prophets hold within themselves three different moments: past, present, and future. They keep the promise of God alive, they see the suffering of their people, and they bring us the strength to look ahead. God looks after his people by giving them prophets in the hardest times, in the midst of their worst suffering. But

[5] Antonio Spadaro, "A Big Heart Open to God," *America* (September 30, 2013): 14–38, here 26–27.

when there is no spirit of prophecy amongst the people of God, we fall into the trap of clericalism.[6]

Thus all three of these popes have emphasized themes important in Merton's writing on prophetic Christianity. While John Paul II mentioned fidelity to the truth and a conjoined simplicity of life, Benedict XVI focused on another aspect of Merton's understanding of the role of the prophetic ministry in the life of the church: in the person of the prophet is the convergence of past, present, and future. The prophet must simultaneously call God's people back to covenant faithfulness and forward to eschatological fulfillment, both of which are made concrete in the present moment. Benedict also admitted to the possible "abuse of the Word within the institution," which the prophet is to remedy—another marked concern of Merton. Benedict also brought out the contemplative and charismatic elements of prophetic Christianity. Francis's prophetic concerns combine his predecessors' ideas and reveal, particularly in his own witness of these prophetic values, the reality of what Merton envisioned the church could be by embracing its charismatic dimension.

[6] Official Vatican Network, "Pope Francis: Without Prophecy, only Clericalism," News. VA, http://www.news.va/en/news/pope-francis -without-prophecy-only-clericalism.

Bibliography
Works by Thomas Merton

Books

Cassian and the Fathers: Initiation into the Monastic Tradition. Edited by Patrick F. O'Connell. MW 1. Kalamazoo, MI: Cistercian Publications, 2005.

The Climate of Monastic Prayer. CS 1. Kalamazoo, MI: Cistercian Publications, 1969.

The Collected Poems of Thomas Merton. New York: New Directions, 1977.

Conjectures of a Guilty Bystander. 1966; New York: Image Books, 1989.

Contemplation in a World of Action. Notre Dame, IN: University of Notre Dame Press, 1998.

Contemplative Prayer. Garden City, NY: Image Books, 1971.

Disputed Questions. New York: Harcourt Brace Jovanovich, 1960.

Emblems of a Season of Fury. New York: New Directions, 1963.

Faith and Violence: Christian Teaching and Christian Practice. Notre Dame, IN: University of Notre Dame Press, 1968.

Gandhi on Non-Violence. New York: New Directions, 1964.

Honorable Reader: Reflections on My Works. Edited by Robert E. Daggy. New York: Crossroad, 1989.

The Last of the Fathers: Saint Bernard of Clairvaux and the Encyclical Letter Doctor Mellifluus. New York: Harcourt, Brace and Company, 1954.

The Literary Essays of Thomas Merton. Edited by Patrick Hart. New York: New Directions, 1981.

Mystics and Zen Masters. New York: Farrar, Straus and Giroux, 1967.

The New Man. New York: Farrar, Straus and Giroux, 1961.

The Nonviolent Alternative. Edited by Gordon Zahn. New York: Farrar, Straus and Giroux, 1980.

Opening the Bible. Collegeville, MN: Liturgical Press, 1970.

Peace in the Post-Christian Era. Maryknoll, NY: Orbis Books, 2004.

Pre-Benedictine Monasticism: Initiation into the Monastic Tradition, 2. Edited by Patrick F. O'Connell. MW 9. Kalamazoo, MI: Cistercian Publications, 2006.

Raids on the Unspeakable. New York: New Directions, 1966.

Seeds of Destruction. New York: Farrar, Straus and Giroux, 1964.

The Seven Storey Mountain. New York: Harcourt Brace, 1948.

The Sign of Jonas. New York: Harcourt, Brace and Company, 1953.

The Springs of Contemplation: A Retreat at the Abbey of Gethsemani. Edited by Jane Marie Richardson. New York: Farrar, Straus and Giroux, 1992.

Thomas Merton on Saint Bernard. CS 9. Kalamazoo, MI: Cistercian Publications, 1980.

A Thomas Merton Reader. Edited by Thomas P. McDonnell. Garden City: Image Books, 1974.

Thomas Merton: Spiritual Master. Edited by Lawrence S. Cunningham. New York: Paulist Press, 1992.

The Wisdom of the Desert: Sayings from the Desert Fathers of the Fourth Century. Translated by Thomas Merton. New York: New Directions, 1960.

Journals

The Asian Journal of Thomas Merton. New York: New Directions, 1968.

Dancing in the Water of Life: Seeking Peace in the Hermitage. Edited by Robert E. Daggy. The Journals of Thomas Merton, vol. 5. New York: HarperCollins, 1997.

Entering the Silence: Becoming a Monk and a Writer. Edited by Jonathan Montaldo. The Journals of Thomas Merton, vol. 2. New York: HarperCollins, 1996.

Learning to Love: Exploring Solitude and Freedom. Edited by Christine M. Bochen. The Journals of Thomas Merton, vol. 6. New York: HarperCollins, 1997.

The Other Side of the Mountain: The End of the Journey. Edited by Patrick Hart. The Journals of Thomas Merton, vol. 7. New York: HarperCollins, 1998.

Run to the Mountain: The Story of a Vocation. Edited by Patrick Hart. The Journals of Thomas Merton, vol. 1. New York: HarperCollins, 1995.

A Search for Solitude: Pursuing the Monk's True Life. Edited by Lawrence S. Cunningham. The Journals of Thomas Merton, vol. 3. New York: HarperCollins, 1996.

Turning Toward the World: The Pivotal Years. Edited by Victor A. Kramer. The Journals of Thomas Merton, vol. 4. New York: HarperCollins, 1996.

Letters

The Courage for Truth: The Letters of Thomas Merton to Writers. Edited by Christine M. Bochen. New York: Farrar, Straus and Giroux, 1993.

The Hidden Ground of Love: The Letters of Thomas Merton on Religious Experience and Social Concerns. Edited by William H. Shannon. New York: Farrar, Straus and Giroux, 1985.

The Road to Joy: The Letters of Thomas Merton to New and Old Friends. Edited by Robert E. Daggy. New York: Farrar, Straus and Giroux, 1989.

The School of Charity: The Letters of Thomas Merton on Religious Renewal and Spiritual Direction. Edited by Patrick Hart. New York: Farrar, Straus and Giroux, 1990.

Six Letters: Boris Pasternak and Thomas Merton. Foreword by Naomi Burton Stone. Introduction by Lydia Pasternak Slater. Lexington, KY: The King Library Press, 1973.

Survival or Prophecy? The Correspondence of Jean Leclercq and Thomas Merton. Edited by Patrick Hart. Foreword by Rembert Weakland. Afterword by Michael Casey. MW 17. Collegeville, MN: Cistercian Publications, 2008.

Thomas Merton and James Laughlin: Selected Letters. Edited by David D. Cooper. New York: W. W. Norton, 1997.

Witness to Freedom: The Letters of Thomas Merton in Times of Crisis. Edited by William H. Shannon. Thomas Merton Letters, vol. 5. New York: Farrar, Straus and Giroux, 1994.

Short Writing

"Alfonso Cortes." In *The Literary Essays of Thomas Merton*, edited by Patrick Hart. New York: New Directions, 1981. 311–12.

"Ascesis of Sacrifice: Pasternak's Letters to Georgian Friends." *The New Lazarus Review* 1 (1978): 55–62.

"Author's Note." In *Seeds of Destruction.* New York: Farrar, Straus and Giroux, 1964. xiii–xvi.

"'Baptism in the Forest': Wisdom and Initiation in William Faulkner." Introduction to *Mansions of the Spirit* by George A. Panichas. New York: Hawthorn, 1967. Repr. in *The Literary Essays of Thomas Merton*, edited by Patrick Hart. New York: New Directions, 1981. 92–116.

"Blake and the New Theology." *Sewanee Review* 76, no. 4 (1968): 673–82. Repr. in *The Literary Essays of Thomas Merton*, edited by Patrick Hart. New York: New Directions, 1981. 3–11.

"Camus and the Church." In *The Literary Essays of Thomas Merton*, edited by Patrick Hart. New York: New Directions, 1981. 261–74.

"Camus: Journals of the Plague Years." In *The Literary Essays of Thomas Merton*, edited by Patrick Hart. New York: New Directions, 1981. 218–31.

"The Death of God and the End of History." *Theoria to Theory* 2, no. 1 (1967): 3–16. Repr. in *Faith and Violence: Christian Teaching and Christian Practice.* Notre Dame, IN: University of Notre Dame Press, 1968. 239–58.

"Faulkner and His Critics." *The Critic* 25 (1967): 76–80.

"Faulkner Meditations: *The Wild Palms.*" In *The Literary Essays of Thomas Merton*, edited by Patrick Hart. New York: New Directions, 1981. 515–36.

Foreword to *Bernard of Clairvaux.* By Henri Daniel-Rops. Translated by Elisabeth Abbott. New York: Hawthorn Books, Inc., 1964. v–vii.

"Herakleitos the Obscure." In *A Thomas Merton Reader*, edited by Thomas P. McDonnell. Garden City, NY: Image Books, 1974. 258–71.

Introduction to *The Monastic Theology of Aelred of Rievaulx: An Experiential Theology*, by Amédée Hallier, translated by Columban Heaney. CS 2. Shannon: Irish University Press, 1969. vii–xiii.

Introduction to *Religion in Wood: A Book of Shaker Furniture*, by Edward Deming Andrews and Faith Andrews. Bloomington, IN: Indiana University Press, 1966. vii–xv.

"Louis Zukofsky—The Paradise Ear." In *The Literary Essays of Thomas Merton*, edited by Patrick Hart. New York: New Directions, 1981. 128–33.

"A Message to Poets." In *The Literary Essays of Thomas Merton*, edited by Patrick Hart. New York: New Directions, 1981. Repr. in Thomas Merton, *Raids on the Unspeakable.* New York: New Directions, 1966. 371–74.

"Nature and Art in William Blake: An Essay in Interpretation." MA thesis, Columbia University, 1939.

"Pablo Antonio Cuadra." In *The Literary Essays of Thomas Merton*, edited by Patrick Hart. New York: New Directions, 1981. 321–22.

"Pasternak's Letters to Georgian Friends." In *The Literary Essays of Thomas Merton*, edited by Patrick Hart. New York: New Directions, 1981. 81–91.

"The Plague of Camus: A Commentary and Introduction." In *The Literary Essays of Thomas Merton*, edited by Patrick Hart. New York: New Directions, 1981. 181–217.

"Preface to the Argentine Edition of *The Complete Works of Thomas Merton.*" In Thomas Merton, *Honorable Reader: Reflections on My Works*, edited by Robert E. Daggy. New York: Crossroad, 1989. 35–44.

Preface to *A Thomas Merton Reader*, edited by Thomas P. McDonnell. Garden City, NY: Image Books, 1974. 13–18.

"Prophetic Ambiguities: Milton and Camus." In *The Literary Essays of Thomas Merton*, edited by Patrick Hart. New York: New Directions, 1981. 252–60.

"Rubén Darío." In *The Literary Essays of Thomas Merton*, edited by Patrick Hart. New York: New Directions, 1981. 305–306.

"Saint Aelred of Rievaulx and the Cistercians." *Cistercian Studies* 20 (1985): 212–23.

"The Stranger: Poverty of an Antihero." In *The Literary Essays of Thomas Merton*, edited by Patrick Hart. New York: New Directions, 1981. 292–301.

"Terror and the Absurd: Violence and Nonviolence in Albert Camus." In *The Literary Essays of Thomas Merton*, edited by Patrick Hart. New York: New Directions, 1981. 232–51.

"Three Saviors in Camus: Lucidity and the Absurd." In *The Literary Essays of Thomas Merton*, edited by Patrick Hart. New York: New Directions, 1981. 275–91.

"Why Alienation Is for Everybody." In *The Literary Essays of Thomas Merton*, edited by Patrick Hart. New York: New Directions, 1981. 381–84.

Tapes

Life and Contemplation. Audiocassette. Electronic Paperbacks. Chappaqua, NY, 1972.

Life and Prophecy. TM9. Audiocassette. Credence Cassettes. Kansas City, MO, n.d.

The Meaning of Monastic Spirituality. AA2085. Audiocassette. Credence Cassettes. Kansas City, MO, n.d.

The Prophets. Vols. A4520–A4521. Audiocassette. Credence Cassettes. Kansas City, MO, July 1962.

True Freedom. AA2803. Audiocassette. Credence Cassettes. Kansas City, MO, n.d.

Secondary Sources

Adam, Karl. *Two Essays by Karl Adam: Christ and the Western Mind; Love and Belief.* Translated by Edward Bullough. New York: Macmillan, 1930.

Altizer, Thomas J. J. *The New Apocalypse: The Radical Christian Vision of William Blake.* East Lansing, MI: Michigan State University Press, 1967.

Andrews, Edward Deming, and Faith Andrews. *Religion in Wood: A Book of Shaker Furniture.* Bloomington, IN: Indiana University Press, 1982.

Bamberger, John Eudes. *Thomas Merton: Prophet of Renewal.* MW 4. Kalamazoo, MI: Cistercian Publications, 2005.

Beer, John. *William Blake: A Literary Life.* New York: Palgrave Macmillan, 2005.

Belcastro, David Joseph. "Merton and Camus on Christian Dialogue with a Postmodern World." *The Merton Annual* 10 (1997): 223–33.

Blackham, H. J. *Six Existentialist Thinkers.* New York: Harper & Row, 1959.

Bochen, Christine M. "The 'Fourth and Walnut' Experience." In *The Thomas Merton Encyclopedia*, edited by William H. Shannon, Christine M. Bochen, and Patrick F. O'Connell. Maryknoll, NY: Orbis Books, 2002. 158–60.

Brueggemann, Walter. *The Prophetic Imagination.* Minneapolis, MN: Fortress Press, 1978.

Bultmann, Rudolf, and James C. G. Greig. *Essays: Philosophical and Theological.* New York: Macmillan, 1955.

Camus, Albert. "Albert Camus—Banquet Speech." *Nobelprize.org.*, http:// www.nobelprize.org/nobel_prizes/literature/laureates/1957/camus -speech.html.

———. *The Fall.* Translated by Justin O'Brien. New York: Knopf, 1966.

———. *The Myth of Sisyphus, and other Essays.* Translated by Justin O'Brien. New York: Knopf, 1955.

———. "Neither Victims nor Executioners." In *The Pacifist Conscience*, edited by Peter Mayer. New York: Holt, Rinehart and Winston, 1966. 423–39.

Casey, Michael. Afterword to *Survival or Prophecy? The Correspondence of Jean Leclercq and Thomas Merton*, edited by Patrick Hart. Foreword by Rembert Weakland. MW 17. Collegeville, MN: Cistercian Publications, 2008. ix–xv.

Chiaromonte, Nicola. "Pasternak's Message." *Partisan Review* 25 (1958): 127–34.

Coomaraswamy, Ananda. "On Being in One's Right Mind." *Review of Religion* 7 (1942): 32–40.

Cooper, David D. "From Prophecy to Parody: Thomas Merton's *Cables to the Ace*." In *The Merton Annual: Studies in Thomas Merton, Religion, Culture, Literature and Social Concerns*, vol. 1, edited by Patrick Hart. New York: AMS Press, 1988. 215–33.

Cruickshank, John. *Albert Camus and the Literature of Revolt.* New York: Oxford University Press, 1960.

Cunningham, Lawrence S. *Thomas Merton and the Monastic Vision.* Grand Rapids, MI: Eerdmans Publishing Company, 1999.

Daggy, Robert E. "'A Man of the Whole Hemisphere': Thomas Merton and Latin America." *The American Benedictine Review* 42, no. 2 (1991): 122–39.

Daniel-Rops, Henri. *Bernard of Clairvaux.* New York: Hawthorn Books, Inc., 1964.

Del Prete, Thomas. "The Geography of Nowhere: Living Beyond Boundaries." *Merton Seasonal* 24, no. 3 (1999): 3–8.

Erdman, David V. *Blake, Prophet Against Empire: A Poet's Interpretation of the History of His Own Times.* Princeton: Princeton University Press, 1969.

Fry, Timothy, ed. *The Rule of St. Benedict.* Collegeville, MN: Liturgical Press, 1981.

Hallier, Amedee. *The Monastic Theology of Aelred of Rievaulx.* Translated by Columban Heaney. Shannon: Irish University Press, 1969.

Hart, Patrick. Introduction to *The Literary Essays of Thomas Merton,* edited by Patrick Hart. New York: New Directions, 1981. xi–xvi.

———. Preface to *Run to the Mountain: The Story of a Vocation,* edited by Patrick Hart. The Journals of Thomas Merton, vol. 1. New York: Harper-Collins Publishers, 1995.

Hart, Patrick, ed. *Survival or Prophecy? The Letters of Thomas Merton and Jean Leclercq.* New York: Farrar, Straus and Giroux, 2002.

Heschel, Abraham J. *The Prophets.* New York: Harper & Row, 1962.

Higgins, Michael W. *Heretic Blood: The Spiritual Geography of Thomas Merton.* Toronto: Stoddart Publishing, 1998.

———. "Merton and the Real Poets: Paradise Re-Bugged." In *Merton Annual: Studies in Culture, Spirituality and Social Concerns,* vol. 3, edited by E. E. Daggy and Robert Daggy. New York: AMS Press, 1991. 175–86.

———. "Monasticism as Rebellion: Blakean Roots of Merton's Thought." *The American Benedictine Review* 39, no. 2 (1988): 177–188.

———. "A Study of the Influence of William Blake on Thomas Merton." *The American Benedictine Review* 25, no. 3 (1974): 377–88.

Hunt, John W. *William Faulkner: Art in Theological Tension.* Syracuse, NY: Syracuse University Press, 1965.

Jaspers, Karl. *Man in the Modern Age.* Translated by Eden and Cedar Paul. London: Routledge & Kegan Paul, 1966.

John Paul II. "Redemptor Hominis." In *The Encyclicals of John Paul II,* edited by J. Michael Miller. Huntington, IN: Our Sunday Visitor, 1996. 46–96.

Joyce, James. *A Portrait of the Artist as a Young Man.* 1916; New York: Washington Square Press, 1998.

Kaplan, Edward K. "Abraham Heschel and Thomas Merton: Prophetic Personalities, Prophetic Friendship." *The Merton Annual* 23 (2010): 106–15.

Kierkegaard, Søren. *Journals and Papers.* Translated and edited by Howard V. Hong and Edna H. Hong. Vol. 5. Bloomington, IN: Indiana University Press, 1978.

———. *The Present Age.* Translated by Alexander Dru. New York: Harper and Row, 1962.

Kilcourse, George. *Ace of Freedoms: Thomas Merton's Christ.* Notre Dame, IN: University of Notre Dame Press, 1993.

———. "Spirituality and Imagination: Thomas Merton's Sapiential Thinking." In *Toward an Integrated Humanity: Thomas Merton's Journey*, edited by M. Basil Pennington. CS 103. Kalamazoo, MI: Cistercian Publications, 1988. 114–31.

Kramer, Victor A. "Thomas Merton Global Prophet." *Cross Currents* 58, no. 4 (2008): 518–20.

Labrie, Ross. "Thomas Merton on Art and Religion in William Faulkner." *Religion and the Arts* 14 (2010): 401–17.

Leclercq, Jean. "Merton and History." In *Thomas Merton: Prophet in the Belly of a Paradox*, edited by Gerald Twomey. New York: Paulist Press, 1978. 213–31.

Lévi-Strauss, Claude. *Tristes Tropiques.* Translated by John and Doreen Weightman. New York: Penguin Books, 1974.

Luppé, Robert de. *Albert Camus.* Translated by John Cumming and J. Hargreaves. New York: Funk & Wagnalls, 1968.

Marcel, Gabriel. *Homo Viator: Introduction to the Metaphysic of Hope.* Translated by Emma Craufurd. New York: Harper & Row, 1962.

———. *Man Against Mass Society.* Chicago: Henry Regnery Company, 1952.

Marcuse, Herbert. *One-Dimensional Man: Studies in the Ideology of Advanced Industrial Society.* Boston: Beacon Press, 1964.

McInerny, Dennis Q. *Thomas Merton: The Man and His Work.* CS 27. Washington, DC: Consortium Press, 1974.

Merton, Thomas, and James Laughlin. *Thomas Merton and James Laughlin: Selected Letters.* Edited by David D. Cooper. New York: W. W. Norton, 1997.

Merton, Thomas, and Boris Pasternak. *Six Letters: Boris Pasternak and Thomas Merton.* Lexington, KY: The King Library Press, 1973.

Miłosz, Czesław. *The Captive Mind.* New York: Vintage Books, 1953.

Mott, Michael. *The Seven Mountains of Thomas Merton.* New York: Harcourt Brace, 1984.

Nouwen, Henri. *Thomas Merton: Contemplative Critic.* Ligouri, MO: Ligouri/Triumph, 1991.

O'Connell, Patrick. "The Literary Essays of Thomas Merton." In *The Thomas Merton Encyclopedia*, edited by William H. Shannon, et al. Maryknoll, NY: Orbis Books, 2002. 260–63.

———. "Prophecy." In *The Thomas Merton Encyclopedia*, edited by William H. Shannon, Christine M. Bochen, and Patrick F. O'Connell. Maryknoll, NY: Orbis Books, 2002. 372–74.

———. "The Springs of Contemplation: A Retreat at the Abbey of Gethsemani." In *The Thomas Merton Encyclopedia*, edited by William H.

Shannon, Christine M. Bochen, and Patrick F. O'Connell. Maryknoll, NY: Orbis Books, 2002. 451–52.

———. "The Strange Islands." In *The Thomas Merton Encyclopedia*, edited by William H. Shannon, Christine M. Bochen, and Patrick F. O'Connell. Maryknoll, NY: Orbis Books, 2002. 453–56.

———. "Theory of Poetry." In *The Thomas Merton Encyclopedia*, edited by William H. Shannon, Christine M. Bochen, and Patrick F. O'Connell. Maryknoll, NY: Orbis Books, 2002. 360–63.

———. "Wisdom and Prophecy: The Two Poles of Thomas Merton's Mature Spirituality." *The American Benedictine Review* 60, no. 3 (2009): 276–98.

Official Vatican Network. "Pope Francis: Without Prophecy, only Clericalism." News. VA. http://www.news.va/en/news/pope-francis-without -prophecy-only-clericalism.

Panichas, George A. "Pasternak's Protest and Affirmation." In *The Reverent Discipline: Essays in Literary Criticism and Culture*. Knoxville, TN: The University of Tennessee Press, 1974.

Pasternak, Boris. *Doctor Zhivago*. London: Pantheon Books, 1958.

Peifer, Claude. "The Rule of St. Benedict." In *The Rule of St. Benedict*, edited by Timothy Fry. Collegeville, MN: Liturgical Press, 1981. 65–112.

Pennington, M. Basil. *Thomas Merton, Brother Monk: The Quest for True Freedom*. New York: Continuum, 1998.

———. *Thomas Merton, My Brother: His Journey to Freedom, Compassion, and Final Integration*. Hyde Park, NY: New City Press, 1996.

Pennington, M. Basil, ed. *Toward an Integrated Humanity: Thomas Merton's Journey*. CS 103. Kalamazoo, MI: Cistercian Publications, 1988.

Poks, Małgorzata. *Thomas Merton and Latin America: A Consonance of Voices*. Saarbrücken (Ger): Lambert Academic Publishing, 2011.

Ratzinger, Joseph. Foreword to *Christian Prophecy: The Post-Biblical Tradition*, by Neils Christian Hvidt. New York: Oxford University Press, 2007. vii–ix.

The Rule of Saint Albert. http://carmelnet.org/chas/rule.htm.

Shannon, William H. "Letters." In *The Thomas Merton Encyclopedia*, edited by William H. Shannon, Christine M. Bochen, and Patrick F. O'Connell. Maryknoll, NY: Orbis Books, 2002. 255–56.

———. Preface to *The Hidden Ground of Love: The Letters of Thomas Merton on Religious Experience and Social Concerns*. By Thomas Merton. New York: Farrar, Straus and Giroux, 1985.

———. *"Something of a Rebel": Thomas Merton, His Life and Works: An Introduction*. Cincinnati, OH: St. Anthony Messenger Press, 1997.

Shannon, William H., Christine M. Bochen, and Patrick F. O'Connell, eds. *The Thomas Merton Encyclopedia.* Maryknoll, NY: Orbis Books, 2002.

Soloviev, Vladimir. *The Meaning of Love.* London: Centenary, 1945.

Spadaro, Antonio. "A Big Heart Open to God." *America*, September 30, 2013:14–38.

Twomey, Gerald, ed. *Thomas Merton: Prophet in the Belly of a Paradox.* New York: Paulist Press, 1978.

Van Doren, Mark. "Prophet." In *The Selected Letters of Mark Van Doren*, edited by George Hendrick. Baton Rouge, LA: Louisiana State University Press, 1987. 235.

Vatican Council II. *Gaudium et Spes* (Pastoral Constitution for the Church in the Modern World). http://www.vatican.va/archive/hist_councils /ii_vatican_council/documents/vat-ii_const_19651207_gaudium -et-spes_en.html.

Weakland, Rembert. Foreword to *Survival or Prophecy? The Correspondence of Jean Leclercq and Thomas Merton*, edited by Patrick Hart. Afterword by Michael Casey. MW 17. Collegeville, MN: Cistercian Publications, 2008. ix–xv.

Wieman, Henry Nelson. *The Source of Human Good.* Carbondale, IL: Southern Illinois University Press, 1946.

Woodcock, George. *Thomas Merton: Monk and Poet.* Vancouver: Douglas & McIntyre, 1978.